WORSHIP

The Christian's
Highest Occupation

WORSHIP

The Christian's Highest Occupation

By

ALFRED P. GIBBS

With an appendix on
"DIRECT ADDRESS TO THE LORD JESUS"

With a foreword by
GEORGE M. LANDIS

P. O. Box 2216 Kansas City, Kansas 66110

CONTENTS

OUTLINE OF THE SUBJECT

Chapter Twelve

Chapter Thirteen

Chapter Fourteen

Chapter Fifteen

Chapter Sixteen

Chapter Seventeen

FOREWORD

It has been our privilege to read *"Worship, The Christian's Highest Occupation"* in manuscript. We acknowledge a great debt of gratitude to the author for being the first to bring to our attention, over thirty years ago, many of the precious truths contained in this book; and the acceptance of which radically changed the course and character of our ministry.

Here is a book with which we thoroughly agree and which we can heartily endorse without reservation.

The title is challenging and the treatment convincing. The author's assertion that "worship is associated with spiritual maturity," is equally true of this book. Even a casual reader would soon detect that it is not the vaporizings of a novice ambitious to become an author; but rather the product of firm convictions based upon a careful searching of the Scriptures, and matured by meditation and by years of deep experience in the Christian path, and strengthened by keen observations. Alfred P. Gibbs believes and therefore writes.

In his own inimitable way, the author proceeds in an orderly and cumulative fashion. His homiletic gift is evident and most helpful to the reader. The book is marked by clarity of thought and expression, made more forceful by vivid figures of speech and graphic illustrations.

The reader is soon aware of the fact that worship is not a subject which can be developed and dismissed with a paragraph, but, instead, is impressed with the vastness and importance of the theme. Basic facts on the subject are drawn from both the Old and New Testaments. Practical applications and responsibilities are made clear and inescapable.

The truth concerning worship is faithfully presented and false theories and practices are mercilessly exposed, frequently by the apt use of sanctified irony. Clouds which confuse many on the subject are dispelled as a number of distinctions of truth are drawn. We cite several. The contrast between the ritualistic worship of Judaism and the spiritual worship of Christianity and the superiority of the latter, is worth the reading of the book. The difference between worship and ministry is clearly drawn and is most helpful in these days when Christendom seems to know little about, and values less, the privilege of worship, and emphasizes service almost to the exclusion of worship. The place of worship, within the veil, is clearly distinguished from the place of meeting; something which most religious systems utterly fail to see.

The chapters which deal with the worshipper, his privileges and perils, the things to be sought and the things to avoid, the preparation of heart and mind for true worship, are most searching.

The description of the worship of the wise men is a spiritual classic, and might well be printed in pamphlet form for wider distribution.

Certain adult Bible classes would find this volume suitable for a text book for a series of studies on worship. Elder brethren would render a great service by circulating copies among those young in the faith.

We hope and pray that the book may have the wide reading which it merits, and that it may be used of God in leading many into an appreciation and practice of "the highest occupation of the Christian."

GEO. M. LANDIS.

11

INTRODUCTION

If the title of this book is correct, as we believe it is, then the importance of the subject will be obvious to every child of God. A great deal of confusion exists in Christendom as to just what constitutes worship. It is often confounded with listening to a sermon; with service for the Lord on behalf of others; with testimony to Christ's saving and satisfying grace; with the preaching of the gospel; with ministry of the Word to believers, and with prayer.

Many Christians put the emphasis of their lives on service for God, to the exclusion of the worship of God. Others swing to the other extreme, and so stress the importance of worship, that service for the Lord is viewed as being of little or no consequence. We must beware of lopsidedness, or of seeking to push one truth of Scripture to an extreme the Bible does not warrant. The believer must seek to maintain the truth of God in its proper perspective and correct balance. The words of our Lord Jesus Christ give the proper order of precedence. In His reply to Satan's temptation, He said: "Thou shalt *worship* the Lord thy God, and Him only shalt thou *serve*" (Matt. 4:10). That quality of worship which does not result in service, and that service which does not flow from worship, both come short of the Divine ideal.

The order in which the heroes of faith are mentioned, in Hebrews chapter 11, is not without significance. The first name is that of Abel, who, by faith, "offered unto God a more excellent sacrifice than Cain" (v. 4). This surely speaks of *worship*. The next is Enoch, whose life was characterized by a *walk* of fellowship with God which delighted His heart. The third is Noah, who, in response to God's revelation, built an ark to the saving of his house. This certainly illustrates the *work* of faith. Thus the order of Divine precedence is here suggested: the *worship, walk* and *work* of faith.

To a great number of people the word, *"worship,"* only connotes the respectful and formal recognition of God, at a distance, on certain stated occasions, in accordance with an ecclesiastically prepared ritual, usually in buildings particularly designed for the purpose, and generally through the mediation of specially selected, theologically educated, and humanly ordained clergymen.

One sometimes sees signs outside a church building inviting all and sundry to: "Come and worship with us." On entering such a place, all one would hear would be a preaching service, with a sermon which might, or might not, lead the hearer ultimately to worship; but the mere fact of listening to a sermon, even though it may be on the *subject* of worship, is not worship.

The distinction between ministry and worship can be simply stated as follows: Ministry is that which *comes down* to us, from the Father, through the Son, in the power of the Holy Spirit, and through the human instrument whom God has gifted for this purpose. Worship is that which *goes up,* from the believer, by the Holy Spirit's power, through the Son, to the Father. Thus ministry is that which *descends* from God *to* us; while worship is that which *ascends* from us *to* God.

We shall consider the subject of worship under the following ten headings:

1. Its meaning, or definition.
2. Its importance.
3. Its authority.
4. Its object.
5. Its ground.
6. Its power.
7. Its manner.
8. Its hindrances.
9. Its place.
10. Its results.

13

Grateful appreciation is due to my very good friend and brother in Christ, George M. Landis, of Fayetteville, Pennsylvania, for his kindness in reading the manuscript, and writing a foreword to this book.

A detailed outline of the subject will be found at the beginning of the book. This brief analysis will enable the reader to grasp the argument as a whole, and also facilitate quick reference to any particular part in which he is interested.

May it be ours, as we study this important subject, not only to gain an intellectual apprehension of what the Bible teaches regarding worship; but to so adjust our lives to this knowledge that we shall be found amongst those who "worship God in spirit and in truth." By this we shall not only be enabled to bring glory to His name, but also delight to His heart.

PREFACE TO SECOND EDITION

It is with gratitude to God that a second edition of this book has become necessary. It is sent forth thoroughly revised, and with an addition in the form of an appendix which is devoted to the subject of, "Direct Address to the Lord Jesus."

May God be pleased to continue His good hand on the message of this book, and use it to lead many more believers to a greater appreciation of their privileges as "a kingdom of priests unto God," and a more faithful discharge of their responsibilities to God in this important matter of their worship.

A. P. G.

I. The Meaning of Worship.

Under this heading we shall consider seven things, namely: 1. Some good definitions; 2. The word translated, "Worship" in the New Testament; 3. Its first mention in the Bible; 4. Some distinctions between prayer, praise and worship; 5. Worship is giving to God; 6. The holy perfume; 7. The meaning of the word in the Old Testament.

1. Some good definitions.

The term, "Worship," like many other great words, such as "grace" and "love," defies adequate definition. The meaning of these words, like the exquisite perfume of a rose, or the delightful flavor of honey, is more easily *experienced* than *described.*

Many have attempted to define the meaning of worship, and though unsuccessful in their attempts, yet their definitions have value. The following helpful quotations have been culled from various writers. One describes it as: "The overflow of a grateful heart, under a sense of Divine favor." Here the writer has emphasized the fact that worship is a spontaneous thing. It is not something which has to be laboriously pumped up, but that which springs up, and overflows from a heart filled with a sense of the greatness and goodness of God. David spoke of this in Psalm 45:1, when he sang: "My heart is inditing a good matter." The marginal rendering is: "My heart boileth, or bubbleth up." As he meditated on the glory and majesty of God, as revealed, both in creation and His word, his heart began to warm within him, until it boiled over, and there ascended to God the fragrance of his

worship. He speaks of this experience again in that well
known twenty-third Psalm, and sang: "Thou anointest
my head with oil, my cup runneth over"! (Ps. 23:5).

Another has defined worship as: "The outpouring of
a soul at rest in the presence of God." Here the accent
is on the spiritual condition of the one who worships.
The believer is at rest. That is to say, he is in the full
consciousness and enjoyment of his assurance of perfect
acceptance before God, through the person of Christ.
He has been brought to realize that, in Christ, he is seen
by God as sanctified, redeemed, regenerated, justified,
and blessed with all the spiritual blessings in the heavenlies. As he thus basks in the sunshine of Divine favor,
his heart goes out in adoration to the One who made it all
so blessedly and gloriously actual in his experience. With
the writer of the Canticles he exclaims: "I sat down under His shadow with great delight, and His fruit was
sweet unto my taste. He brought me to the banqueting
house, and His banner over me was love" (S. of S. 2:3-4).

Another has put it thus: "Worship is the occupation of
the heart, not with its needs, or even with its blessings,
but with God Himself." Here the writer has sensed the
subtle distinction that exists between prayer, praise and
worship, which we shall discuss more fully later on.
David knew what this meant, for we are told that when
Nathan was commissioned by the Lord to tell him that
the throne of his kingdom should be established for ever,
David's heart was so full that he went in and sat before
the Lord. As he did so he was soon lost in wonder and
praise, and exclaimed: "Wherefore Thou art great, O
Lord God, for there is none like Thee, neither is there
any God beside Thee, according to all that we have heard
with our ears" (II Sam. 7:18-22).

Still another has expressed himself as follows: "Worship is the upspring of a heart that has known the Father

as a Giver, the Son as Savior, and the Holy Spirit as the indwelling Guest." In this definition, the essential prerequisite of the worshipper is indicated. Thus it is only the regenerated believer that can spiritually and intelligently worship the Father and the Son, through the power of the indwelling Holy Spirit. An unsaved person, though perfectly able to recognize God as supreme, and Creator of the universe, has not been brought into living relationship with Him as Father, and consequently is unable to really appreciate what only the Holy Spirit can reveal. We are told that "the natural man receiveth not the things of the Spirit of God: for they are foolishness unto him: neither can he know them, because they are spiritually discerned" (I Cor. 2:14-15).

Christ used the analogy of "living water" to describe the spiritual life which He came to make possible to all who believe (John 4:13-14). This "living water" *comes in* to the believer at the new birth (John 3:5). It *springs up,* within him, in worship (John 4:14). It then *flows out,* from him, in service (John 7:37-39). Thus worship really consists of this "living water" returning to its source. Long ago Solomon made the discovery that though all the rivers ran into the sea, yet the sea did not become any fuller thereby. He correctly assigned the reason as follows: "Unto the place from whence the rivers come, thither they return" (Eccles. 1:7). Thus the spiritual life which flows from God *to* us, returns to Him in worship *from* us, and thus the Divine cycle is complete.

Worship could well be pronounced, "worthship," for it consists of the ascription of worth to One who is worthy. A striking example of this can be seen in the last book of the Bible. In chapter four, the living creatures and the elders are described as falling down and worshipping the One who occupies the throne, and saying: "Thou art worthy, O Lord, to receive honor and glory and power,

for Thou hast created all things, and for Thy pleasure
they are and were created." In chapter five, the number-
less hosts, who surround the Lamb, join in a glorious
chorus and sing: "Worthy is the Lamb that was slain to
receive power, and riches, and wisdom, and strength, and
honor, and glory, and blessing!" It will be seen in these
two instances, that not a single petition occurs. It is worship in its purest form, for it is the ascription of worth
to One who alone is worthy, or in other words, worthship.

2. The word most commonly translated "worship" in the New Testament

is "Proskuneo." It means to do reverence, or homage, by
prostration; to pay Divine homage, to worship, and adore.
A few instances will suffice. In Matt. 2:2, 11, the wise
men are recorded as saying: "Where is He that is born
King of the Jews? . . . We are come to worship Him . . .
And when they saw the young child, they fell down and
worshipped Him." The same word is used in describing
Christ's reply to Satan's temptation: "Thou shalt worship
the Lord thy God, and Him only shalt thou serve" (Matt.
4:10). Again it is used in John 4:24, where our Lord
declares: "God is a Spirit, and they that worship Him
must worship Him in Spirit and in truth." The word
"latreus," which is seldom used, refers largely to the
worship of the sanctuary, and is so used in Phil. 3:3, and
Heb. 10:2.

3. The first mention of the word in the Bible.

One of the many rules determining the real meaning
of a word in holy Scripture, has been aptly termed: "The
law of first mention." This rule affirms that the first
mention of a word, or doctrine, in the Bible, determines
its meaning throughout the whole range of the Scriptures.
If this be true, then the first mention of the word "worship," is full of deep spiritual significance for us.

In Genesis 22: 5, Abraham is described as saying to the young men who accompanied him and Isaac to the mountains of Moriah: "Abide ye here with the ass, and I and the lad will go yonder and worship, and come again to you." In this first recorded mention of the word, many things concerning worship are clearly indicated.

We learn, first, that *worship is based on a revelation from God.* See v. 1-2. *"And God said."* It was in response to a word from God that Abraham acted. It was not something he thought up himself, but was his response to a Divine revelation. *Faith always presupposes a previous revelation.* We are told that: "Faith cometh by hearing, and hearing by *the word* of God" (Rom. 10: 17). For one to act without Divine authority is presumption in the worst degree. Take faith away from Abraham's act in offering up Isaac, and it becomes murder! The *worship* of the Lord, as also the *work* of the Lord, must be guided by the *word* of the Lord. The believer's authority in worship is not the traditions of men, however hoary with antiquity, nor the subtle reasonings of human wisdom, however plausible; but the *clear revelation of God's word.*

Secondly, we discover that *worship is conditioned by faith in, and obedience to that Divine revelation* (v. 3). Abraham's response was unquestioning, prompt and full. Unhesitatingly, he obeyed God's command. He arose early in the morning, saddled the ass, cut the wood for the burnt offering, secured the services of two young men, took Isaac his son, and made his way in the direction God had indicated. The inspired writer puts it thus: "By faith Abraham, when he was tried, offered up Isaac" (Heb. 11: 17). In other words, Abraham *did* something in response to God's word. Thus prompt, unquestioning obedience to the known will of God, as revealed in His word, is essential to true worship. It is one thing to know what God has revealed concerning worship; and another to turn from all humanly conceived views and act, promptly and fully, on that Divine revelation. This is faith.

Thirdly, we gather that *worship involves a costly presentation to God* (v. 2). In Abraham's case, it meant the offering up of his only and well beloved son, the darling of his heart, his dearest possession, and the one in whom all his hopes of future posterity were centered. God was careful to emphasize this phase of his worship, for He said: "Take now thy son, thine *only son,* Isaac, *whom thou lovest* . . . and offer *him* for a burnt offering." (v. 2). Worship is not a cheap thing, to be offered thoughtlessly or carelessly, with no sense of the self-sacrifice involved.

David realized this aspect of worship and declared: "Neither will I offer burnt sacrifices unto the Lord my God of that which dost cost me nothing" (II Sam. 24:24). Thus when Abraham spoke of "worship," he understood it to mean that it involved the greatest sacrifice he had ever been called upon to make. His heart was wrapped up in his son, yet he evidenced his willingness to give to God his heart's best treasure.

We need ever to keep this in mind in our estimation of worship. It is spoken of as a "sacrifice of praise" (Heb. 13:15). Sacrifice connotes cost, and true worship will soon be discovered to be a costly thing. It is very much easier to let someone else do our worshipping for us. Many seem content to lean back on their chairs and allow some clergyman to perform this act for them, and thus lose both the ability and joy of worship. Many a believer has had to seal his testimony with his own life's blood, in order to maintain a good conscience before God in this matter of worship. "The noble army of martyrs" give eloquent witness to this fact. Worship will involve considerable *cost* to the believer, in the outlay of time for spiritual preparation; in the effort of Bible study; in the

loss of the prestige of one's social, business and ecclesiastical circle, and in the outlay of money. All this entails
cost, but the energy expended in offering true worship,
brings both pleasure and glory to God.

Fourthly, we learn that *worship necessitates a deliberate separation unto God.* (v. 5). Notice Abraham's
words to the two young men: "Abide ye here with the ass,
and I and the lad will go *yonder* and worship." The two
young men could answer to the things which would combine to hinder the believer from entering by "the new and
living way" into the holiest, to pour out his heart in adoring worship. Like Abraham, each Christian must resolutely say to all his home cares, business affairs and
hobbies, etc.: "Abide ye here, while I go yonder and
worship." We are all conscious, more or less, of intruding
thoughts which often seek, even in our holiest moments,
to divert our minds from occupation with God to the exclusion of all else.

Many a meal has been imaginatively planned, cooked
and served in a meeting which was convened particularly
to enable the people of God to worship. Many a business
deal has been thought out, when the believer was sup-
posedly deep in meditation, and others imagined his heart
was overflowing with worship! These unlawful and distracting thoughts must be dealt with in the same uncom-
promising manner as Abraham dealt with these two
young men. They must be made, by a definite decision
of the will, to abide outside of our meditations, lest they
rob God of the worship due to His name. This calls for
real concentration of thought, and the repudiation of all
self interests. This is by no means pleasing to the flesh,
which loves to wander, unrebuked, into the forbidden
fields of fancy.

God's exhortation to the believer connotes both privilege and responsibility: "Having an high Priest over the

house of God; let us draw near with a true heart, in full assurance of faith" (Heb. 10:22). Here is our privilege: "having an high Priest." Here is our responsibility: "Let us draw near." Worship therefore calls for spiritual activity, or *the energy of faith,* by which the Christian is enabled to go from "here" to "yonder," and thus worship undistractedly in the presence of God.

It is significant that, in Abraham's case, after he had parted from the young man, he *ascended* the mountain, until he reached the summit, where his act of worship was consummated. In like manner the believer, having left the sordid things of earth behind, ascends the heights, until he experiences the reality of being, "Shut in with God, far, far above the restless world that wars below." Here his soul basks in the full enjoyment of the presence of the One Whom he worships.

Fifthly, we perceive that *worship predicates the absolute renunciation of self, in all its varied forms.* When Abraham said he was going to "worship," he knew that it meant the offering up of his son, and this involved utter self-abnegation. Needless to say, this denial of self is entirely contrary to the flesh with its desire for self-will, self-esteem and self-expression. There must be no intrusion of the flesh in true spiritual worship. Just as Abraham, by this act of offering up his son, resolutely denied the appeal of the flesh for self-expression; so each believer must recognize that the true worshipper is he who "worships God in the Spirit, rejoices in Christ Jesus, and has no confidence in the flesh" (Phil. 3:3).

As Abraham approached God, *with his son,* to worship; so the believer must learn that, as a worshipper, he must not only come to God *in* Christ, and *through* Christ, but also *with* Christ. God is infinitely delighted with His Son, for He testified, again and again: "This is My beloved Son, in whom I am well pleased." Only as the believer concentrates his mind's *attention* and his heart's *affection* upon the Father's well beloved Son, will he learn to appreciate the glories and excellencies that are resident in Christ. As he comes into the Father's presence with his mind and heart full of Christ, and mentions these excellencies which he has found in His Son, then the fragrance of his worship will rise as incense, and be well pleasing to the One who has so completely revealed Himself in the Son of His love.

W. B. Dick, has beautifully expressed this thought in the following words:

> "We would, O God, present before Thy face
> The fragrant name of Thy beloved Son;
> By faith we view Him in that holy place
> Which, by His dying, He for us has won.
>
> We share Thy joy in Him who sitteth there,
> Our hearts delight in Thy delight in Him;
> Chiefest of thousands, fairer than the fair,
> His glory naught can tarnish, naught can dim."

Sixthly, we are impressed with the fact that *worship glorifies God.* (vs. 16-18). This act of worship on the part of Abraham delighted God's heart, and brought from Him an expression of His appreciation. David, by the Spirit, was made to realize this truth, for God said through him: "Whoso offereth praise glorifieth Me, and to him that ordereth his conversation aright, will I show the salvation of God" (Ps. 50:23). Worship gives to God the place of absolute pre-eminence and thus glorifies Him, to the exclusion of all others. We shall discuss this more fully, later on in our study.

Lastly, we discern that *worship results in blessing to the worshipper.* "Because thou hast done this thing, and hast not withheld thy son, thine only son: that in blessing I will bless thee, and in multiplying I will multiply thy seed as the stars of heaven, and as the sand which is upon

the sea shore, and thy seed shall possess the gate of his
enemies; and in thy seed shall all the nations of the earth
be blessed; because thou hast obeyed My voice" (v. 16-
18). In the first place, God gave him back his son.
Though Abraham may have ascended the mount with a
heavy *burden,* he certainly descended it with a happy
song on his lips, and a holy joy in his heart. God will be
no man's debtor. All who honor Him shall be honored,
by Him, in return. He will pour multiplied blessings into
the heart of the one who, with a single eye, obeys Him
fully, and gives Him the glory due to His name.

Then again, think of Abraham's greater appreciation
of Isaac, as he witnessed his willing obedience unto death.
Isaac might easily have run away when his father con-
fided to him that he was to be the sacrifice. He might
have resisted as his father bound him and laid him on
the altar, but he did nothing of the kind. As God restored Isaac to Abraham, it was with a deeper sense of
his preciousness to him.

This is what God does for each true worshipper. He
gives back, to the believer, His beloved Son, in all the
glory of His blessed Person, and grants to him a far
greater appreciation of all those Divine attributes, so perfectly revealed in Him, and expressed by Him. God not
only gave His Son *for* us, on the cross, for our *salvation;*
but He now gives His Son *to* us, on the throne, for our
satisfaction.

It is a significant thing that we are not specifically
told that Isaac came down from the mount with Abraham.
Of course we know that he did, but this fact is not mentioned. The next time Isaac's name is introduced, it is in
connection with a bride that is to be wooed and won for
him. This delightful "courtship by proxy," so full of typical significance, is recorded in Chapter 24. This beautiful romance in consumated when Isaac receives Rebecca

to be his bride. For the sake of him, "whom, having not seen, she loved," she made the long journey across the desert sands to be united to him as his chosen bride. The last sight the world had of Christ was on the altar of Calvary. The next sight it shall have of Him is when He is manifested in glory with His blood-bought Bride. No wonder the Divine revelation concludes: "Even so, come Lord Jesus, Amen!"

CHAPTER TWO

The Meaning of Worship

(Continued)

Having considered the first mention of the word "worship," and gleaned something of what is involved in its use, let us now glance at:

4. Some distinctions between prayer, praise and worship.

Broadly speaking, prayer is the occupation of the soul with its *needs*. Praise is the occupation of the soul with its *blessings*. Worship is the occupation of the soul with *God Himself*. Prayer and praise may be mingled in worship, and included in the general thought; but properly speaking, each, in itself, does not constitute worship. "Lord, save my soul," is *prayer*. "Thank you, Lord, for saving my soul," is *praise*. "Thank you, Lord, for what Thou art," is *worship*.

Perhaps an illustration may help to make this somewhat subtle distinction a little clearer. Let us suppose a person who cannot swim falls into a river. As he vainly struggles to save himself, and realizes how hopeless his case is, he cries from the depths of his heart: "Help! Help! Save me! Save me!" This is *prayer*. No convicted sinner needs to be taught to pray. An old Puritan's terse commentary on Psalm 107, where sinners, in their extremity are described as crying to God for deliverance, was: "Misery wonderfully indoctrinates a person in the art of prayer!"

In response to this drowning person's cries for help, a well dressed gentleman suddenly appears. Without a moment's hesitation he plunges into the river and, at the risk of his own life, brings him safely to shore. The response of the saved person is immediate. He overwhelms his rescuer with *praise* and exclaims: "How can I ever express my gratitude to you for your brave act in saving my life! Thank you, ten thousand times!" Surely this illustrates what takes place when a sinner is brought to realize that Christ, the Son of God, by His substitutionary work on Calvary, has made possible his salvation from sin's penalty. Upon his acceptance of Christ as his own personal Savior, he is assured, from God's own word, that he is now saved. This fills his soul with joy, and his lips with songs of praise to the One who has saved him.

But now the rescuer, after seeing the one whom he has saved safely home, turns to him and hands him his card saying: "Here is my name and address. Would you please do me the honor of coming to my home tomorrow evening at 6: 30 and dining with me. In this way, we can become better acquainted with each other." Accordingly, the following evening the rescued man goes to the address on the card. To his astonishment, he finds himself in the wealthiest part of the town. Furthermore, he discovers that his rescuer's house is the grandest of all the palatial mansions in that district. He rings the bell and the butler appears. After giving his name, he is ushered into the drawing room. The host then appears and immediately, like the perfect gentleman he is, puts his guest at ease. Dinner is announced and, during the course of the very excellent meal, the host skillfully steers the conversation so as best to entertain his guest. When the meal is over, the guest has been charmed beyond measure at the nobility of his host's character. He has been impressed with his kindliness, intellect, hospitality, wisdom, graciousness, tact and humility of spirit. In other words, he now appreciates the moral excellence, and the intrinsic worth of his host's *character, entirely apart from what he has done for him as his savior.* While he does not forget, for one

moment, that his host was his rescuer, yet his gratitude
for what he did for him is now exceeded by his admiration
and appreciation because of *what he is, in himself*. Moreover, the more he gets to know his host by visiting him,
talking and walking with him, the greater this sense of
appreciation grows.

This will serve to illustrate that fine distinction which
exists between praise and worship. The believer can
never forget that the Lord Jesus Christ is his Savior, and
that He has redeemed him at the infinite cost of his most
precious blood. Yet, as he comes to know the Lord more
intimately, his gratitude to Him as Savior, merges with
and is superceded by an ever-increasing appreciation of
the preciousness of His glorious Person, as the displayed
excellencies of His perfect character are revealed, by the
Spirit, through the word of God. The Christian, by communion with his Lord, is made to realize and exclaim
with another: "My Beloved is . . . the chiefest among ten
thousand . . . Yea, He is altogether lovely!" (S. of S. 5:10,
16).

> "Chiefest of ten thousand!
>   Fairest of the fair!
> Altogether lovely,
>   Beyond all compare!
> Lord of all creation;
>   Man of Calvary!
> Son of God who loved and
>   Gave Himself for me!"

Now let us use another illustration, this time based
on an actual incident. A tenement building was ablaze
in London. On the top story, a young woman was seen
standing at a window crying for help, for she was trapped
by the flames beneath. Her case looked hopeless until a
young fireman, seeing her peril, mounted a ladder and,
at the risk of his own life, brought her safely down to the
ground. In the excitement of the moment, the girl neg-

lected to thank her rescuer for his brave deed, so the following day she called at his home to thank him for what
he had done. He, in turn, reciprocated the call, and the
acquaintance thus formed developed into friendship. This
eventually ripened into love, and they became engaged.
One day they both stood before a marriage officer, plighted
their troth to each other and became man and wife.

Now this woman never allowed herself to forget that
this fireman was her savior and that, but for him, she
might have been burned to death; but he was now much
more to her than a savior: he was her husband, her lover,
her companion through all life's vicissitudes and her all
in all. So it is with all Christians. The One who went to
Calvary to make their salvation possible, has now united
them to Himself in a bond that neither time nor eternity
shall sever. He is not only the Savior, but the Lover,
Friend, Counsellor, Guardian and Guide to all who know
Him. The words of God through Isaiah are peculiarly appropriate in this connection: "Thy Maker is thy Husband" (Isa. 54:5).

5. Worship is giving to God.

Salvation is something received *by us,* as a free gift
from God (Rom. 6:23). Worship is something presented
by us *to* God, as a willing acknowledgment of our deep
appreciation of what He is and all He has done.

We shall consider three instances of this aspect of
worship which are recorded for us in the word of God.
They should combine to make this abundantly clear to
every believer.

A. *The first instance we shall look at is the Israelite*
described in Deut. 26:1-11. Let each believer read this
portion carefully for himself. Here is God's own picture
of what is involved in the phrase: "And thou shalt . . .

worship before the Lord thy God" (v. 10). Let us briefly
examine this chapter, so full of spiritual significance, and
notice seven things regarding this worshipper.

(1) The worshipper is one who has experienced what it means to be redeemed by blood and by power.

(vs. 5-8).

He was a redeemed man, who had been sheltered by
the blood of the Passover lamb. (Exod. 12:12-13). God
instructed him to recall the fact that he had once been a
slave under the bitter bondage of the Egyptians; but the
Lord had looked upon his "affliction, labor and oppres-
sion," and had brought him out of this dreadful condition
by His "mighty hand, and with an outstretched arm, and
with great terribleness, and with signs and wonders."

Surely we have, in these words, a graphic illustration
of that far greater work that God has done for every believer. Though once, by nature, lost in sin and under its
dread condemnation; yet because of the redeeming work
accomplished by His beloved Son on Calvary, a full, free
and eternal salvation has been provided for every sinner
who will own his need, trust Christ as his Savior and own
Him as the Lord of his life. Happy indeed is that person
who can take the words of this Israelite upon his lips and
truthfully testify: "And the Lord brought me forth . . .
with an outstretched arm, out of my sin, my need and my
bondage, into the glorious liberty of the children of God!"

Properly speaking, it is only one who has thus experienced God's saving power in his own life, that can
approach God as an intelligent and consistent worshipper.
Peter reminded those Christians, to whom he wrote, that
they had "not been redeemed with corruptible things, as
silver and gold . . . but with the precious blood of Christ."
As redeemed ones, they could now offer up "spiritual

sacrifices, acceptable to God by Jesus Christ" (I Pet. 1: 18-19; 2: 5).

(2) The worshipper is viewed as having an inheritance in the land. (v. 1).

"When thou art come in unto the land which the Lord thy God giveth thee for an inheritance." This person had been the subject of Divine guidance, for he had been led by the cloud by day and the pillar of fire by night. He had been the object of God's providing care, for he had eaten of the manna from heaven, and had drunk of the waters that flowed from the smitten rock. Now, by God's grace, he is viewed as having been brought through the Jordan, and actually living in the land that God had promised.

The typical significance of this should be obvious to each believer. The Christian is viewed in Scripture as being already "seated in the heavenlies in Christ Jesus" (Eph. 2: 6). He is assured, by God Himself, that "in Christ" he has "obtained an inheritance, being predestinated according to the purpose of Him who worketh all things after the counsel of His own will" (Eph. 1: 11). With the blessed consciousness that all this is now his, the believer can come boldly to the throne of grace and offer his grateful worship.

(3) The worshipper was one whom God had blessed. (v. 2).

He was instructed to take of the first fruits of the harvest, with which God had blessed him, and present it to the Lord as an act of worship. God's promises of blessing to Israel were largely *temporal* and *material,* and were conditioned upon their obedience to His commandments. "It shall come to pass if thou wilt hearken diligently unto the voice of the Lord thy God, to observe to

do all His commandments which I command thee this
day, that the Lord thy God will set thee on high above all
the nations of the earth: and all these blessings shall come
upon thee and overtake thee, if thou shalt hearken unto
the voice of the Lord thy God. Blessed shalt thou be in
the city, and blessed shalt thou be in the field. Blessed
shall be the fruit of thy body, and the fruit of thy ground,
and the fruit of thy cattle, the increase of thy kine and
the flocks of thy sheep. Blessed shall be thy basket and
thy store. Blessed shalt thou be when thou comest in, and
blessed shalt thou be when thou goest out" (Deut. 28:1-
6).

In contrast to the earthly blessings of Israel, the
blessings of the believer are *eternal* and *spiritual.* How
wonderfully the epistle to the Ephesians opens! "Blessed
be the God and Father of our Lord Jesus Christ, who hath
blessed us with all spiritual blessings, in the heavenlies,
in Christ Jesus" (Eph. 1:3). He then proceeds to enumerate some of these blessings, such as the Christian being chosen, predestinated, redeemed, etc. Paul then points
out the far reaching consequences of the bestowal of
all those blessings. They shall redound, first to the praise
of the glory of the grace of the Father who planned it;
secondly, to the glory of the grace of the Son, who provided it; thirdly, to the glory of the grace of the Holy
Spirit, who empowered it and made it actual in the believer's experience. (See Eph. 1:6, 12, 14).

Thus both in the Old Testament, and in the New Testament, the worshipper does not come *to be blessed;* but because he has already *been* blessed. Perhaps a good definition of a Christian is: "one whom God has blessed."
Each believer can therefore truthfully testify: "The blessing of the Lord, it maketh rich, and He addeth no sorrow
with it" (Prov. 10:22).

(4) The worshipper is seen to be a grateful person.
(vs. 2, 3).

He is described as first *gathering* this gift of the first fruits, then *placing* it in a basket, and finally *bringing* it before the Lord. There was to be nothing of a haphazard character in this offering. His act of worship consisted in picking the fruit with care, in arranging it in orderly fashion in the basket, and then making the effort to travel to the place God had selected. This, at least, suggests his appreciation of all that God was and had done for him. By this act he joined the great company of those who, through the ages, have sung: "God hath done great things for us, whereof we are glad" (Ps. 126:3).

God wants an appreciative people, who are not satisfied to be always receiving from Him, but who also desire to give to Him. God wants us to be like the Samaritan whom the Lord healed of his leprosy. While his nine companions went their way, he returned to the Savior, fell at His feet and gave Him thanks. Christ's comment on this act is significant: "There are not found that returned to give glory to God save this stranger" (Luke 17:12-19).

Altogether too many Christians suffer from what has been well termed, "the gimme's." Every time they come into God's presence it is to ask Him to "give them" something. "Give me this;" "Give me that;" "Give me the other;" is their constant and monotonous cry. They are like some little children who only come to their parents to get something from them, and never think of giving anything to their parents in return. There is a story of a little girl who brought great joy to her mother. One day she came in from her play, sat down on a chair, and watched her mother as she ironed. Her mother inquired: "What do you want, dear?" The child replied: "I don't want anything, mother. I just want to sit here and look at you and love you!"

Our Lord clearly indicated that God, the Father, was seeking for worship from His children. "The true worshippers shall worship the Father in spirit and in truth: for the Father seeketh such to worship Him" (John 4: 23). God greatly desires that those whom He has so abundantly blessed, will respond to His desire for worship and, as they wait in His presence, will pour out their love for Him in worship and adoration. We are told that the words, "think" and "thank," were originally the same. Whether this be true or not, one thing is certain: a *"thinkful"* Christian is certain to become a *"thankful"* Christian, for he has only to *remember*, to *rejoice*.

God's word to Israel was: "None shall appear before Me *empty"* (Exod. 23:15). It is pathetic indeed, at a meeting convened particularly for worship, to see so many who apparently have neither taken the time nor made the effort to put anything in their basket of gratitude. The long periods of silence in many worship meetings are often, not the silences of worshipful adoration, but the silences of *spiritual poverty*. It will be noted that in Deut. 26, it is *individual* worship that is in view. It goes without saying, that the *quality* of our *collective* worship, will be conditioned by the *spirituality* of *each believer* present at the meeting convened for that purpose.

The obvious teaching of this passage in Deut. 26 is that each believer should be spiritually exercised during the week, and personally select and arrange his basket of first fruits. He should then bring with him, to the assembly of God's people, a heart filled with his own individual appreciation of all that God is, as revealed in His beloved Son. As each Christian does this, the spiritual tone of the worship meeting will be lifted to a high plane, and God

THE MEANING OF WORSHIP

will receive that which He seeks—the worship of His beloved, blood-bought and Spirit-born children. May we not disappoint Him in this!

(5) The worshipper is anticipated as being obedient to God's word. (v. 2).

He was told to go "unto the place which the Lord thy God shall choose to place His name there." This place was afterwards designated. At first it was at Shiloh, where "the whole congregation of the children of Israel gathered together," and the tabernacle was pitched. See Josh. 18:1. Later on, this place was transferred to Jerusalem, where the temple was built. See I Kings 8:29. It is important to note that God did not leave the choice of the place of worship to the caprice of the worshipper. He selected one specific place, where He placed His name and made this place known to His people. The worshipper was instructed to come to this place and offer his gift of the first fruits, if he was to be well pleasing to God. It is conceivable that an Israelite, when in the land, might have argued: "I don't think it makes any difference *where* one takes his offering. Personally, I very much prefer Jericho to Jerusalem; for Jericho is much closer to where I live. Besides, the way to Jerusalem is uphill, and this calls for more effort than I care to make. In view of this, I shall worship God at the place of *my* choice."

All this sounds very much like the present day attitude of many Christians. In fact, it is quite common to hear a young convert advised to "join the Church of his choice." On many decision forms, a space is left for the person who professes to be saved to indicate, on the dotted line, his "Church preference." Has God left the believer no directions as to this matter of his Church fellowship? Is each Christian left to follow his own inclinations in this important matter? Of course not. The same God, who indicated to the Israelite in the Old Testament just when, how, and where to worship; has left us, in the New Testament, clear directions as to this matter. The well known words of the Lord Jesus should come home to every Christian's heart: "Where two or three are gathered together in My name, there am I in the midst of them" (Matt. 18:20).

Each believer would do well to examine his position in regard to his church, or assembly fellowship. He should make sure that he has the support of the general teaching of the New Testament scriptures, both as to his *warrant* for meeting with believers, and also the *conduct* of such assembly gatherings. These Divine principles of church fellowship have been clearly laid down, and should be whole-heartedly obeyed, cost what it may. *

(6) The worshipper is seen to be a humble person.
(vs. 5-9).

No provision was made for either pride of race, place, face, or grace. His confession was: "A Syrian ready to perish was my father." He gave himself no "airs," evidenced no superiority complex, and assumed no patronizing manner as he came into the presence of God. There was to be no self-glorification, or display of that obnoxious thing, the flesh, which Christ declared "profiteth nothing" (John 6:63). There was to be no place for snobbery, for all Israel had a common ancestry—"a Syrian ready to perish." (A snob has been well defined as a person halfway up the ladder of fame, who spends all his time *licking* the feet of those above and *kicking* the ones below!) Of all snobbery, none is quite so nauseous as the religious brand, personified in the Pharisee, whose uplift was confined exclusively to his nose, and who prayed thus with

* See "An Introduction to a Study of Church Truth," and "Scriptural Principles of Gathering," by the same author.

himself: "God, I thank Thee I am not as other men are," etc. (Luke 18:11-12).

Each believer would do well to lay this to heart as he approaches God's holy throne. God hates pride in any shape or form. Through Isaiah, He has declared: "Thus saith the high and lofty One that inhabiteth eternity, Whose name is holy. I dwell in the high and holy place, with him also that is of a contrite and humble spirit" (Isa. 57:15). Again we read: "God resisteth the proud, but giveth grace to the humble" (James 4:6). Pride ill becomes one who is "only a sinner, saved by grace," and who, but for the grace of God, might even now be in hell. Humility of spirit is therefore an essential accompaniment of worship.

(7) The worshipper is described as giving to God.
(vs. 10-11).

"Thou shalt set it (the gift) before the Lord thy God, and worship before the Lord thy God." It will be noted in this chapter that the worshipper *does not ask God for a single thing*. He does not come to God with a *petition* on his lips, but with a *present* in his hand. Though it is quite true that he only brought to God what God had previously given to him, yet God was delighted with the gift and credited it to his account! (v. 10). A little girl once climbed into her daddy's lap and asked him for a quarter. When the father asked her what the money was for, she artlessly replied: "Why, it's your birthday to-morrow and I want to buy you a present." Accordingly, her father gave her the quarter and, sure enough, on the morrow he was the recipient of a little present from his daughter, for which he himself had paid! It is hardly necessary to add how much her father appreciated this token of his child's remembrance and affection.

David clearly realized this fact, for he said to God: "But who am I, and what is my people, that we should be able to offer so willingly after this sort? For all things come of Thee, and of Thine own have we given Thee!" (I Chron. 29:14). God freely and unstintingly pours His multiplied blessings upon His people. Is it too much for Him to expect that they shall bring Him the first fruits of their appreciation of what He is and all He has done? Alas, how little worship God receives from His children! How often so-called "worship meetings" degenerate into mere glorified prayer meetings! One brother rises and prays: "O Lord, help us to worship." Another pleads: "O Lord, grant that we may truly worship Thee," etc., etc. The person described in Deut. 26 did not say: "Lord, help me to bring my basket of first fruits." He *brought it,* and said: "And now, behold, *I have brought the first fruits,*" etc., (v. 10). The worship meeting does not exist for the purpose of enabling us to pray that we *might* worship God, but for the actual presentation of our worship to Him. The logical conclusion is, if there was more prayer offered *before* the worship meeting, there would be no need to pray at the worship meeting.

CHAPTER THREE

The Meaning of Worship

(Continued)

B. Our next instance of worship as giving to God is that of the wise men (Matt. 2:1-12).

Of the purpose of their long journey from the east, there is no doubt, for they inquired: "Where is He that is born King of the Jews? for we have seen His star in the east, and are *come to worship Him*" (v. 2). As we concentrate our attention on these men whose mission was the worship of the Son of God, several things impress us:

(1) That worship is an act of those who are wise.

As to the *number* of these men, we do not know, for Scripture does not inform us; but as to their *description*, we are left in no doubt. They were "wise" men. Though the worldly-wise may sneer and dub the Christian a fool, yet God views him as being wise in Christ. It has been well said that "nine-tenths of wisdom consists of being wise in time!" God's complaint regarding Israel was: "O that they were wise, that they understood this, that they would consider their latter end!" (Deut. 32:29). The first glimmerings of spiritual sanity are seen in a person when he is made to realize his true condition as a lost and guilty sinner, and turns to the Lord in true repentance and faith. This is what is implied by being "made wise unto salvation" (II Tim. 3:15).

Modern education makes no provision for the acquisition of *spiritual* wisdom. In most of the institutions devoted to so-called "higher learning," the fact of God's reality and His revelation through His word is scarcely ever mentioned, except perhaps in ridicule. In this respect they have filled the description of those mentioned in Romans 1:22: "Professing themselves to be *wise*, they became *fools*." No man is truly wise, however great his stock of worldly wisdom may be, or however many his degrees of learning; until he has put God first in his consciousness, made the word of God the supreme authority of his life, and come to know Christ as his own personal Savior and Lord. Only then, like these wise men, will he be in the position and condition to worship.

God's estimation of the wisdom of this world, divorced from a knowledge of Himself, has been thoroughly gone into, and should be carefully and prayerfully pondered by every child of God. Read I Cor. 1:18-31.

(2) That worship calls for Divine guidance.

These men were led by a star in the heavens, until they were brought into the presence of the Son of God, to present their gifts in worship. The application of this to the present day is surely obvious. If we would worship God as we should, then we must not only be "made wise unto salvation;" but we must have a heavenly, authoritative and infallible guide in the matter of our worship. Needless to say, this guide is the Bible, the Divinely inspired word of God. It is this book which the indwelling Holy Spirit uses to lead the believer into a knowledge and appreciation of all truth. See John 16:13-15.

Wise indeed is that believer who, like the magi of old, is not content to be guided by the traditions of his fathers, however hoary with antiquity; or even "the dictates of his own conscience;" but who rests not until he has a "thus saith the Lord," for both the assurance of his salvation and the manner of his worship.

(3) That worship necessitates both separation and renunciation.

These men, at God's call to worship, and led by the star, left their country, homes and loved ones and became strangers and pilgrims. Between them and the place to which God was leading them were many weary miles of desert travel. For the sake of the One whom they wished to worship, they turned their backs on the comforts of civilization. They counted the price well worth while when, at long last, they were ushered into the presence of Deity clothed with humanity and prostrated themselves in adoration before Him.

Likewise, he who would worship God in accordance with those principles laid down in His word, must be prepared to suffer for his whole-hearted obedience to Divine guidance. He may, and probably will, find himself opposed, at every turn, by his nearest friends and relatives. Some have had to face the prejudiced opposition and even persecution of highly organized religious systems; while others have had to cut across the long established customs of their particular society circle. The path of whole-hearted obedience to God's word has never been cheap, or easy to the flesh; but the compensating joy of obedience more than makes up for the sacrifice involved.

(4) That worship calls for both concentration of mind and determination of will.

These wise men, after their long and ardous journey, finally arrived in Jerusalem, "the city of the great King." Instead of finding themselves in the congenial atmosphere of glad expectation of their coming Messiah and King, they discovered, to their astonishment and chagrin, that the very people whose King they had come to worship were not only unaware of His arrival, but manifested

the twin evils of apathy and antipathy to their mission!
(Ps. 48:2). Blank stares greeted their query: "Where is
He that is born King of the Jews?" Apparently the star,
which had attracted and led these wise men, possessed no
significance to the leaders of Israel. We are told that
both Herod the King and "all Jerusalem with him," were
"troubled" at this question.

What should have been "the Hope of Israel," became
an annoyance, for it disturbed their smug complacency.
These religious leaders of Israel could turn to the holy
Scriptures at Herod's command, and quote the prophecy
of Micah regarding the place of Christ's birth; *but we do
not hear of one of them accompanying the wise men to
Bethlehem,* or joining with them in their worship of the
Messiah! Such was the apathy of the nation which God
had selected for this very purpose! (Rom. 9:4-5).

Not only were the magi faced by indifference but, in
the case of Herod, by opposition veiled by hypocrisy.
This arch fiend, well named "the bloody," plotted the de-
struction of this Child, whom he feared would occupy the
throne he had gained by usurpation. How good it is to
note that neither the apathy of Israel nor the antipathy of
Herod affected these wise men. They had *concentrated
their minds* on their mission of finding and worshipping
Christ. This, coupled with their *determination of will* to
allow nothing to hinder them, finally resulted in the
realization of their quest.

The believer, who seeks to worship God in a manner
well pleasing to Him, will also discover his need of these
two virtues. This *concentration of mind* is not easy, but
it must be rigidly practiced, lest distracting, wayward
and unlawful thoughts are allowed to rob God of the
worship due to His name. *Determination of will* is also
essential if the opposition of that triumvirate of evil: the
Devil, the world and the flesh, is to be overcome. The

Devil, with his host of wicked spirits, will do his best to hinder. The world, with its pleasures, riches and cares, will combine to stifle the heaven-born desire to worship. The flesh, with its love of ease, self-esteem and self-indulgence, will seek to erect a barrier that will hinder the believer from "entering into the holiest" to pour out his heart in worship to God.

(5) That worship is accompanied by joy.

We are told that after they had been sent on their way to Bethlehem, the star again became their guide until it "stood over the place where the young Child was." This further token of Divine leading and approval caused them to "rejoice with exceeding great joy" (v. 10). From this we may surely learn that occupation with the Son of God not only leads to worship, but fills the worshipper with a holy, indescribable joy, that almost amounts to rapture. David sensed this long ago and said: "In Thy presence is fulness of joy, and at Thy right hand are pleasures for evermore" (Ps. 16:11). In Psalm 43:4 he says: "I will go unto the altar of God, unto God, my exceeding joy: yea upon the harp will I praise Thee, O God my God." When the Lord appeared to His disciples, after His resurrection, we are informed, in a triumph of understatement: "Then were the disciples glad when they saw the Lord" (John 20:20).

The humanly-conceived religious systems of earth are characterized largely by the element of *fear* and dread of the false deity, whom its devotees seek to propitiate by their prayers, works and offerings. Christianity, on the contrary, is characterized by *joy*. The believer, assured of his eternal blessedness and "acceptance in the Beloved," is enabled to "joy in God through the Lord Jesus Christ" (Romans 5:11). This "joy of the Lord, which is our strength," must not be confused with that hilarity of spirit

which the careless and Godless worldling exhibits on those
occasions when he is able to banish God from his thoughts,
and shut his eyes to the fact of his sinfulness and the
dread consequences of dying in that condition.

(6) That worship is conditioned upon seeing the
Son of God.

It was when they saw the Lord Jesus that they fell
down in adoration before Him. It is only when, by faith,
the believer sees and is occupied with the One, through
Whom the Father has been pleased to reveal Himself in
all the glory of His Divine attributes, that he is enabled to
worship as he should. It was said of Christ: "No man
hath seen God at any time; the only begotten Son, which
is in the bosom of the Father, He hath declared Him"
(literally, "told Him out") (John 1:18). All that can be
seen of the Father is through His Son, and all that can be
experienced of the Father is through the Holy Spirit.
Thus the glorious triunity of the eternal Godhead: Father,
Son and Holy Spirit, is revealed before the wondering and
worshipping hearts of His redeemed people.

It is sadly possible for the Christian to have his spiritual vision beclouded, either through carelessness of walk,
worldliness of life, or unjudged and unconfessed sin. In
such a case, no worship ascends from the altar of his soul.
Spurgeon had this in mind when he wrote his beautiful
communion hymn:

> "If now, with eyes defiled and dim,
>   We see the signs, but see not Him;
> O may His love the scales displace,
>   And bid us see Him face to face!"

How often, like the two doubtful and discouraged disciples on their way to Emmaus, the eyes of our hearts
are veiled, so that we do not realize the presenec of the
Lord (Luke 24:16). Paul prayed for the believers in

Ephesus that: "the eyes of their understanding might be enlightened" (Eph. 1:18). As the presence of Christ is sensed, and His beauties and glories apprehended by the soul, it will not be long before the believer is lost in wonder and worship. The writer of the epistle to the Hebrews speaks of this glorious sight, and says: "But we see Jesus, who was made a little lower than the angels for the suffering of death, crowned with glory and honor" (Heb. 2: 9). Miss Thompson's beautiful hymn summarizes this thought:

> "Gazing on the Lord in glory,
> While our hearts in worship bow;
> There we read the wondrous story
> Of the cross, its shame and woe.
>
> Gazing on it we adore Thee,
> Blessed, precious, holy Lord!
> Thou, the Lamb, alone are worthy—
> This be earth's and heaven's accord!"

(7) That worship is a presentation of our gifts to God.

We read that these wise men "presented unto Him gifts, gold, frankincense and myrrh." The typical significance of these gifts is beautiful. Gold speaks of *Deity*, as a study of the Tabernacle makes plain. Frankincense gives forth its *perfume* only as it is brought into contact with fire. Myrrh speaks of *suffering*, and is associated with the death and burial of our Lord. Thus these wise men, by the gifts they presented to Him, typically expressed first, their faith in His essential and eternal Deity; second, their appreciation of the fragrance of His sinless life which should ascend, as a sweet perfume, to His Father; and third, their estimation of the virtue and value of His vicarious sufferings, by which the redemption of humanity should be accomplished.

Every believer may well profit by their example as he comes to God in worship. Nothing delights the Father more than to receive, from His people, the gifts of their appreciation of His Son as they muse upon Him. They may think of Him in the aspect of His *official glories,* as possessing full Deity, equal and eternal with the Father, and the Holy Spirit. They may meditate on His *moral glories,* as the perfect Man on earth, who fully and perfectly translated all the will of His Father into the terms of actual life, thus glorifying Him on earth. They may be occupied with His *redemptive glories,* which He acquired by the substitutionary sacrifice of Himself upon the cross, and concerning which God has signified His full acceptance, by raising Him from the dead, and glorifying Him at His own right hand. In whatever aspect Christ is contemplated, it always results in worship to God.

May it be ours to follow the example of these wise men in their quest, and allow nothing and no one to turn us aside, until, led by the Spirit of God through the Word, we are brought consciously into the presence of the Son of God and present the gift of our worship to the Son and to the Father, who "seeketh worshippers to worship Him in Spirit and in truth" (John 4:23-24).

CHAPTER FOUR

The Meaning of Worship

(Continued)

C. The third instance that illustrates the meaning of worship, as giving to God, is the case of *Mary of Bethany*. The story is recorded in John 12:1-11, and is perhaps one of the most striking and beautiful instances of worship in the whole range of Scripture. The outline that follows is not original. It is a good example of that scriptural ability to really "distinguish between things that differ."

Let us examine this incident *negatively,* and seek to discover what Mary did *not* come to do on this memorable occasion. From this *negative* approach, we can learn much of the *positive* character of true worship.

(1) Mary did not come to hear a sermon,

even though the greatest Teacher the world has ever known was there, and of Whom it was said: "Never man spake like this Man." It had been her privilege, in times past, to sit at His feet and hear His word. The lessons she had learned had not been forgotten; but *this* was not her purpose as she came into the presence of the One she loved above all others.

We have before pointed out that the Lord's supper, instituted by Christ on the eve of His betrayal and death, exists for the purpose of enabling believers to remember Him, and thus give to Him and the Father the worship of their hearts. Therefore the primary purpose of such a gathering is not to hear an exposition of the word of God by some able teacher, good though this may be on some other occasion; but to spend the time in occupation with the One whose supper it is, and Who said: "This do for a remembrance of Me" (I Cor. 11:24).

(2) Mary did not come to make a request

of Him, as she had done before (John 11:32). Her purpose was not to pour out her soul in earnest supplication before Him who had omnipotence at His command, and could have granted any request she might make. Though she fully realized the value of prayer, yet this was not the motive that actuated her as she came to Him. She came not to *get,* but to *give.*

Likewise the Lord's supper does not exist for the purpose of enabling believers to supplicate the throne of grace, invaluable though prayer is. This gathering of believers is for worship which, as we have seen, is distinct from prayer.

(3) Mary did not come to meet her fellow believers.

There were many there, and she loved them all dearly, for they loved her Lord; but it was not to be occupied with the Lord's people, or to enjoy fellowship with them that was her uppermost thought. She desired to be occupied with the Lord Himself, to the exclusion of every other person and every other thing on earth.

Surely this should be the purpose that should animate the breast of every Christian as, responsive to the word of his Lord, he seeks to gather with his fellow believers for the purpose of remembrance and worship. Fellowship with Christians is good and necessary, but it is not the greatest thing. The good is often allowed to become the enemy of the best. It is possible for our fellow believers to loom so large in our consciousness that the Lord Himself is relegated to a secondary place. Fellowship primarily is "with the Father and with His Son," and fel-

lowship with each other naturally flows from this union
and communion with Him.

(4) Mary did not come to be refreshed by Him,

though this might well have been her motive. After the
humdrum round of domestic or business duties, she might
have argued that she needed the spiritual relaxation and
refreshment that only He could impart, but this was not
her motive in coming.

There is surely nothing more refreshing to the believer, weary with his battle with the world, the flesh and
the Devil, than to come and sit quietly in the presence of
the Lord, there to have his cares dissipated, and the calm
of heaven enter his soul. Mary's act teaches us that this
is not the greatest thing in life. She came, not to be refreshed herself, but to *refresh the Lord* and fill His soul
with joy! We are all fundamentally selfish in our outlook
on things. We think very largely in terms of what this,
or that, will bring in pleasure or satisfaction to us.

By this act Mary anticipated the cross and its sufferings, and saw to it that her Lord was refreshed on the
eve of His redemptive work. Thus, on this occasion, she
did for her Lord what David's men once did for him. At
his express desire for a drink of the water from Bethlehem's well, three of his mighty men broke through the
surrounding host of the Philistines to gratify their king's
request, and satisfy his desire. (II Sam. 23:15-17). Mary's
beautiful deed surely teaches us that worship is not intended to produce *self-satisfaction* in the believer, but to
give satisfaction to the Savior.

(5) Mary did not come to meet the host,

nor even her own relatives in the flesh. We are not told
who the host was on this occasion, but Mary had no
eyes for him, her eyes were upon Another. She viewed

the Lord as the host and came to do Him honor. Christendom, with its special caste of clergy, has very largely eliminated from people's minds the fact that, at the Lord's supper, Christ is the host at His own table, and all the gathered believers are but guests at His invitation. Scripture knows nothing of an "officiating clergyman," apart from whose presence the Lord's supper cannot be celebrated! How often the "minister" is allowed to become "the host," or the focal center of attraction; and people consequently are more occupied with his appearance, personality and eloquence than they are with the Lord Himself. Thus, perhaps quite unconsciously, man is allowed to usurp the place that Christ has reserved for Himself, as the Host at His own supper. As the hymn puts it:

> "The Host art Thou, O blessed Lord,
>   Thy honored guests are we;
> With grateful and adoring hearts,
>   We would remember Thee.
>
> Lord Jesus Whom, unseen, we love,
>   As thus we muse on Thee;
> We none would see, save Thee alone,
>   Thou Man of Calvary!"

May it be ours to give the Lord His rightful place as the divine Host at His own supper, and refuse to allow any man, however pleasing his personality, however dynamic his leadership, or however gifted his ministry, to rob Christ of His rightful place of absolute pre-eminence.

(6) Mary did not come to Him because it was the popular thing to do.

On the contrary, it was at a time when the pent up hatred of both the religious and political world was about

to break upon the Son of God. Save for a few incon-
spicuous disciples, mostly of the common class, He was
the "despised and rejected of men." The period of His
popularity had waned, and the eve of His betrayal and
crucifixion was at hand. It was "six days before the
Passover," when the world should stain its hands with the
blood of the Christ of God, that Mary came with her love
gift to pour on the feet of the Savior. By this act she
proclaimed louder than any words could say, her sincere
love and devoted loyalty to the One whom the world
would not acknowledge. Thus she took her stand for
Him and shared in His rejection.

The believer must also be prepared, in loyalty to his
Lord and to His word, to brave the contempt of the political world, and even the persecution of false religious systems and political organizations, in order to worship God
in a manner pleasing to Him. The path of wholehearted
discipleship has never been crowded, or popular. The
Christian, who seeks to carry out those scriptural principles of gathering, which are laid down in the Bible, will
find plenty of opposition, even from those who claim to be
fundamental in their doctrinal beliefs. If however, like
Mary, he has a single eye to the glory of Christ, he will
"count all things but loss for the excellency of the knowledge of Christ Jesus, his Lord" (Phil. 3:8).

He must be prepared, as a worshipper, to experience
something of what Paul calls "the fellowship of His sufferings" (Phil. 3:10). He can rest assured that, as in the
case of Mary, his faithfulness to the Lord and to His word
shall not pass unnoticed, nor remain unrewarded by Him
in "that day," when all His own shall appear before the
judgment seat of Christ (Rom. 14:10).

(7) Mary did not come to withhold her best, but poured it all out fully, freely and joyously at the feet of her Lord.

Let us note several things in connection with this gift she made, and which so beautifully illustrates true worship:

(a) *Her gift was a very costly one* (v. 3). To secure it she had denied herself many things that would have been perfectly legitimate for her to purchase for her own use. Inasmuch as the laborer of that period received but a penny a day for his services, her gift represented a *whole year's salary.* Thus it was no inconsiderable gift that she brought. Mary's heart had been so completely won to the Savior that she did not count the cost of expressing her appreciation of him.

Love is ever measured by the sacrifice it makes on behalf of its object. Our Lord "loved the Church, and *gave Himself* for it" (Eph. 5:25). Can we do any less for Him? That worship which costs nothing in the way of time, energy, thought and money is not worthy of the name. Like Mary, each believer must be prepared to pay for the privilege of worship, however great the cost may be. David could say: "I will not give sleep to mine eyes, or slumber to mine eyelids, until I find out a place for the Lord, an habitation for the mighty God of Jacob" (Psa. 132:4-5).

(b) *Her gift had been reserved for this special purpose* (v. 7). She had treasured in her heart the words that fell from His lips as she had sat at His feet. Consequently, she knew He was to be betrayed, crucified, buried and rise again. Thus, in spiritual discernment, she far surpassed the disciples. They never seemed to really grasp the full significance of His words, even though He used the plainest of language in describing these mo-

mentous events which were to take place, and become the
"Center of two eternities, which look, with rapt, adoring
eyes, onward, and back to Thee!" (See Matt. 16:21; Mark
10:32; etc.). Mary thus had the signal honor of being *the
only one who anointed the Lord for His burial;* the other
women came too late! (See Mark 16:1-6; Luke 23:55-56).
Mary of Bethany had no need to go to the tomb, for she
knew that the One, whose word had called Lazarus from
death to life, would take up the life He had laid down
for her redemption (John 10:17-18).

How good it is when believers come, first as individuals to Him, with their treasured store of the costly spik-
enard of their appreciation of Him; and then, collectively
with their fellow saints, pour out the perfume of their
adoration in His presence. Such an offering not only
honors the Son, but delights the heart of the Father also.

(c) *Her gift was all brought to the feet of Christ*
(v. 3). Those feet which had walked the dusty and rug-
ged roads of Palestine, and had carried blessings everywhere they went, were indeed "beautiful" to her (Rom.
10:15). She knew those feet were soon to carry Him
willingly to Calvary, there to be pierced for her transgressions and wounded for her iniquities. She knew also
that, as her Messiah, He should one day occupy a throne
and, in resurrection glory, should reign until God made
His enemies to become the footstool of His feet (Psa. 110:
1-2).

Doubtless she had all this in mind as she approached
Him with her precious gift, which she now unreservedly
poured out, in its *entirety,* at His feet. She kept back
nothing for her own use, but yielded her all to Him. There
were no mental reservations with her gift. She desired
no half measures by which to express her devotion to her
Lord. Unlike Ananias and Sapphira who, to make "a

fair show in the flesh," "kept back part of the price," she willingly and gladly gave her all to Him (Acts 5:2).

The believer can surely profit by her noble example which, in turn, received Christ's unstinted commendation. Worship must be whole-hearted if it is to be pleasing to Him. Lukewarm devotion, half-hearted praise, and divided affections, are alike nauseating to Him. (See Rev. 3:14-18). He rightly demands, deserves and should receive the place of absolute pre-eminence in every department of the believer's life. May it be ours, like Mary, not to disappoint Him in this respect, but delight His heart with our whole-souled devotion and worship.

(d) *Her gift was accompanied by an attitude of utter self-abnegation.* We are told that after she had anointed His feet with the perfume, she wiped them with her hair. The Scripture informs us that a "woman's glory is her hair." Thus by this act she literally brought her glory to His feet in lowly, yet sublime adoration. (I Cor. 11:15).

What a beautiful picture this is of that necessary attitude of heart humility which should characterize the worship of God's people! God has distinctly declared that "no flesh should glory in His presence" (I Cor. 1:29). The flesh, whatever form it may assume, should have no place in worship. All the natural glories, or excellencies that man may possess must be brought into the dust in the presence of the God of the universe. Here, brilliant intellect, physical strength and skill, capable leadership, persuasive eloquence, magnetic personality, artistic genius, nobility of birth, the possession of vast wealth, political prominence, or profound learning has no place whatever. There can be no reason or room for pride in the presence of Deity. We do well to sing Isaac Watt's beautiful hymn:

> "When I survey the wondrous cross,
>   On which the Lord of glory died;
> My richest gain I count but loss,
>   And pour contempt on all my pride.

> Forbid it, Lord, that I should boast,
>   Save in the cross of Christ, my God;
> All the vain things that charm me most,
>   I sacrifice them to His blood."

(e) *Her gift resulted in the whole house being filled*
with the exquisite fragrance of the perfume she had so
lavishly poured on His feet. All the occupants of the
house shared in the benefits of her munificent gift. The
Lord Himself was given His rightful place as supreme.
She herself would long bear the fragrance of the spike-
nard everywhere she went. Each member of that company, as he left that place, would carry on his person,
some traces of that sweet perfume. True there were
those who criticized the act, and referred to it as "waste";
but the Lord's commendation more than compensated her
for the adverse criticism she received.

We have seen that Scripture views worship as both an
individual and collective act. It is only as each believer
in an assembly gathering brings to the feet of his Lord
the treasured gift of the perfume of his appreciation and
worship, that the whole gathered company of Christians
will be affected by it. The sweet fragrance of such a
volume of worship will linger pleasantly in the memory
of those present. Furthermore, some of its savor will be
carried by them to others, who will thus take note that
they have "been with Jesus" (Acts 4:13). It was when
the whole congregation "were as one, to make one sound
to be heard in praising and thanking the Lord . . . that
then the house was filled with a cloud . . . for the glory of
the Lord had filled the house of God" (II Chron. 5:13-14).

These three illustrations from Scripture should surely
suffice to drive home the truth, which was stated at the
beginning of this particular heading, that worship is
giving to God.

Chapter Five

The Meaning of Worship

(Continued)

As we further think of the definition of worship, let us now consider:

6. The Holy Perfume. (Exod. 30:34-38).

This beautiful picture of worship is given to us as part of God's revelation to Moses in regard to the Tabernacle, concerning which He had said: "Make me a sanctuary, that I may dwell among them" (Exod. 25:8). Minute instructions were given regarding the details of its furnishings, and we find God repeatedly saying to Moses: "And look that thou make them after their pattern, which was showed thee in the mount" (Exod. 25:9; 40:26:30:27:8, cp. Heb. 8:5).

Three things impress themselves on the mind as one reads this passage regarding the holy perfume.

(1) The exclusive use of it.
(vs. 37-38).

It was reserved solely for use in the worship of God in the sanctuary. God expressly forbade its manufacture for any other purpose. The obvious inference from this is that worship belongs to God alone, and that He will share this honor with none. David, "the sweet Psalmist of Israel," by the Spirit's inspiration wrote: "He is thy Lord, worship thou Him" . . . "Exalt ye the Lord our God, and worship at his footstool, for He is holy" . . . "O come, let us worship and bow down: Let us kneel before the Lord, our Maker" (Psa. 45:11; 99:5; 95:6). It will be recalled that the first demand of the law was: "Thou shalt have no other gods before Me . . . for I, the Lord thy God, am a jealous God" (Ex. 20: 3-5).

There is no substitute for spiritual worship. It is the unique right, the sole property, and the exclusive privilege of God Himself and He will not tolerate any rival. Idolatry, in its essence, is simply that by which man seeks to displace God, or which attempts to relegate Him to a position of secondary importance. An idol is anything that a man worships in his heart, to the exclusion of God. It was because of the idolatrous apostasy of Israel that God set them aside nationally, allowed them to go into captivity, and scattered them to the four corners of the earth. (See II Kings 17: 7-18; II Chron. 36: 14-17). We do well to pay good heed to the Divine dictum: "I am Jehovah, that is My name, and My glory will I not give to another" (Isa. 42: 8). He alone claims the title of, "Holy and Reverend" (Ps. 111: 9).

There is always the subtle danger of becoming more occupied with the visible, than the invisible; with the temporal, than the eternal; with an outward and formal ceremony, than an inward and spiritual reality. There can therefore by no substitute for spiritual worship, however ornate may be the ritual, or gorgeous the vestments, or beautiful the building, or well phrased the prayers, or smoothly conducted the service. Undoubtedly all this has an appeal to the esthetic senses, and is well pleasing to the flesh, for man is naturally religious; but it is not spiritual, and consequently cannot please God.

(2) The ingredients that formed it.
(vs. 34-36).

Four ingredients, compounded in equal proportions, composed this perfume, and each part was necessary to the whole. These ingredients were stacte, onycha, galbanum and frankincense. Each of these four things has a

typical significance which we shall not dwell on now.
Let us think of them as four elements which, when compounded together in the heart of the believer, as he sits
in the presence of God, causes the perfume of his worship
to ascend to the Father and the Son.

(a) *The first ingredient is remembrance.* It is good
for the believer to use his memory to recall what he used
to be by nature, and what he now is, by God's matchless
grace. The words of Paul to the saints at Ephesus are
pertinent to this: "Wherefore remember that ye being in
time past Gentiles in the flesh . . . but now, in Christ
Jesus . . . are made nigh" (Eph. 2:11, 13). Let each
Christian call to mind his black past, when he was without God, without Christ, without life and without hope.
Then let him contrast this with his present acceptance in
the Beloved, together with all the spiritual blessings that
are now his present and eternal possession. Surely the
result of such remembrance will cause him to lift his heart
in adoration to the One who made this so blessedly actual
in his experience.

His memory should also be focussed on the Person and
work of the Lord Jesus Himself. The purpose of the
Lord's supper, as indicated by the Lord Himself is: "This
do for a remembrance of *Me.*" In view of this, worship
will become an essential feature of such a meeting, for
worship is kindled upon the fires of remembrance. As
David puts it: "While I was musing, the fire burned; then
spake I with my tongue" (Ps. 39:3). It is memory that
enables us to recall the record of His matchless life, as
given in the holy Scriptures.

The Christian should therefore concentrate upon
Christ's wondrous words, His mighty deeds, His perfect
and holy character, His absolute obedience to the Father's
will, His infinite grace in going to the cross, His completed

work of redemption accomplished by the sacrifice of Himself, His victorious resurrection, His glorious ascension, and His present ministry as the great high Priest of His people. As he does so, the believer's heart will warm within him, and his worship shall rise to God as a fragrant perfume.

(b) *The second ingredient is gratitude.* As memory recalls all that God is and has done, the heart responds, even as the strings of a harp break forth into song beneath the skilful hands of a master musician. We have before noted that the gratitude of the believer delights the heart of the Father. Socrates, the great Grecian philosopher, declared that gratitude was the greatest of all the virtues, and ingratitude the basest of all the vices. A study of the great worship hymns indicate how great a part gratitude plays in their composition. Hannah Burlingham beautifully expresses it thus:

> "The knowing this, that us He loves,
>   Hath made our cup run o'er;
> Jesus, Thy name our spirit moves,
>   Today and evermore."

The "Ter Stegen" hymns are amongst the finest we have. One of them, by Ernst C. Homburg, written nearly 300 years ago, is redolent with gratitude:

> "O Lord, from my heart I do thank Thee
>   For all Thou hast borne in my room,
> Thine agony, dying unsolaced,
>   Alone in the darkness of doom,
> That I, in the glory of heaven,
>   For ever and ever might be—
> A thousand, a thousand thanksgivings
>   I bring, blessed Savior, to Thee!"

(c) *The third ingredient is reverence.* This is produced as the soul apprehends, in some measure at least, the greatness of God, the majesty of His Divine character, and the glory of His unique attributes, as displayed in His omniscience, omnipotence, omnipresence and immutability. We are living in an age characterized largely by cynicism, flippancy and lightness regarding Divine things. The modern trend is to humanize Deity and deify humanity, and that has not aided in man's concept of God. One has only to read the Scriptures to discover that whenever a person was brought consciously into the presence of God, it filled him with a holy awe, humbled him in the dust and produced a deep reverence for God.

Moses, the great leader of Israel, was taught this lesson many times. At God's first revelation to him at the burning bush, the voice of Jehovah said: "Draw not nigh hither; put thy shoes from off thy feet, for the place whereon thou standest is holy ground" (Ex. 3:5). At God's revelation to him on the mount, in response to his request to see God's glory, God gave him a vision of Himself. At this august spectacle we read: "Moses made haste, and bowed his head towards the earth, and worshipped" (Ex. 34:8).

Isaiah, whose magnificent concept of Deity has thrilled the hearts of the people of God for twenty-five centuries, had to lay to heart this essential requirement. In chapter six of his prophecy, he describes the vision he had of the glory of God which completely revolutionized his life. This sight not only filled him with a sense of his own littleness, uncleanness and insufficiency, but indelibly impressed upon him God's greatness, holiness and power.

Daniel, "the man of desires," tells us that when he saw the majestic vision of God: "There remained no strength in me, for my comeliness was turned in me into corruption and I retained no strength" (Dan. 10:5-11).

We could add others to this list, but these will suffice to indicate how necessary it is that godly reverence accompany all our dealings with Divine things. This reverence must always be present if our worship is to be acceptable to the One who is described as "The high and lofty One, who inhabiteth eternity," and who hath declared: "Let all the earth fear the Lord: Let all the inhabitants of the world stand in awe of Him" (Ps. 33:8).

Familiarity with God can never produce contempt, for those who know Him best, love and fear Him most. The more God impresses the soul with His Person, the greater that individual is filled with holy awe as he stands in the presence of Him, before Whose eyes "all things are open and naked" (Heb. 4:13). It should be obvious that humility of mind, sobriety of manner, and sincerity of spirit are essential to and fitting in the presence of the One who said: "Ye shall . . . reverence My sanctuary. I am Jehovah" (Lev. 19:30).

(d) *The fourth ingredient is amazement.* We have before indicated that worship has, as one of its basic requirements, the element of wonder. He who ceases to wonder, ceases to worship. The hymn writer has put it thus:

> "I stand all amazed in the presence
>   Of Jesus the Nazarene,
> And wonder how He could love me,
>   A sinner, condemned, unclean!
>
> O how wonderful! O how marvelous!
>   And my song shall ever be,
> O how wonderful! O how marvelous!
>   Is my Savior's love to me!"

One of the many titles of Deity is "Wonderful." Everything about the Almighty takes upon itself this character. As the believer thinks of the wonder of His Person, His creation, His word, His Son, His love, His salvation and of each Christian's blessedness, he is led to exclaim with another:

"That Thou shouldst love a wretch like me,
    And be the God Thou art,
Is darkness to my intellect,
    But sunshine to my heart!"

(3) The purpose of it.

It was for God's pleasure and for His glory. These ingredients, equally compounded together, combined to produce a perfume which ascended to God in a fragrant stream and brought great pleasure to Him. Likewise, when a believer sits in the presence of God, with an equal measure of remembrance, gratitude, reverence and amazement well compounded in his heart, there will undoubtedly rise, from the censer of his soul, a silver stream of humble, reverent, sincere and adoring worship to his God and Father, and to the Lord Jesus Christ. This, in turn, will delight God's heart, for it fulfils His desire for the worship of His people. This was expressed by His Son in these words: "The hour cometh, and now is, when the true worshippers shall worship the Father in Spirit and in truth; for the Father seeketh such to worship Him" (John 4:23).

Our last consideration, under the heading of the meaning of worship, is:

7. The root meaning of the word in the Old Testament.

Those competent to judge have affirmed that the root meaning of the Hebrew word carries the thought of "a dog to its master." As one approaches the town of Hartsdale from the city of New York, he will observe, to his left, an animal cemetery. It is perhaps the most ornate in the world. Beneath marble monuments, some costing hundreds of dollars, lie the remains of pet animals and even birds.

Many of these tombstones bear sentimental epitaphs, such as: "Momsie's only baby." Others are grotesque, as one over a dog which reads: "He cannot come to us, but we can go to him!" However, there is one epitaph that stands out from them all. It is of a dog whose master caused to be inscribed: "To the memory of Bruce, the devoted servant, faithful friend, warm admirer, and ardent worshipper of his master." Then follows the name of its owner. Does this not aptly describe what a dog is? Dogs have been described, and not without some cause, as "man's best friend." A cynic once remarked: "The more I know of human beings, the better I appreciate dogs!"

Let us use an illustration to clarify this point. We will suppose that a man, warmly clad, ventures forth on a blustery and bitterly cold night. The temperature is below zero, and the streets are practically deserted. Presently he sees a poor, neglected, shivering and half starved cur, sheltering behind a telephone pole from the biting wind. Some cruel boys have tied a can to its tail, and it has been kicked from pillar to post, until now it is almost at the end of its tether. It will never survive a night like this on the streets.

The man pauses and looks the dog over. What a pitiable sight it is: thin, miserable, frightened, homeless, hungry and on its last legs! His compassion is stirred and, yielding to the impulse of the moment, he stoops down, reaches out his hand and calls to the dog. Suspicious at first, for the dog has good reasons for distrusting mankind, it gradually approaches, until at length it comes under his hand. The man pats it on the head, strokes it, all the while speaking kindly words. Then, after removing the string and the can from its tail, he lifts it up, opens his overcoat, pops it in, and carries it back to his home. When he enters his home he says to his wife: "I've found a poor starving dog on the street, that will surely die tonight, unless it finds a home. Please put a sack in the corner of the kitchen and we'll take care of it for at least tonight." Accordingly, the dog is gently placed on the sack, and a delicious bowl of hot bread and milk is given it, followed by some scraps from the evening meal. For the first time in many days the dog wags its tail in gratitude for this unusual kindness.

The next morning it greets its benefactors with another friendly wag of its tail, and they decide to give it a permanent home. A month passes by, and what a wonderful change it produces in that dog! As a result of good food and proper care, one would scarcely recognize the fine looking animal as that miserable starving cur of four weeks ago.

One evening, as the man is sitting in an easy chair, with one hand hanging over the arm of the chair, he suddenly feels something warm and wet on his hand. Glancing down he sees the dog looking up at him with adoring eyes as, again and again, it licks the hand of the one to whom it owes everything. The dog had not come into the room to beg for a bone, or even to be petted. It wanted nothing from its owner but the privilege of sitting in his presence, so that it might look at him with rapt, adoring eyes and, every now and then, to enjoy the privilege of licking the hand of the one whom it loved above all others. This is *worship*.

Now apply this to the believer, who once was a lost, guilty and helpless sinner, deserving only the judgment of a holy God. Now, through the grace of the Lord Jesus Christ, and by faith in His substitutionary sacrifice and glorious resurrection, and acceptance of Him as Savior and Lord, he has been redeemed, saved and brought into a place of acceptance, provision and security. Surely it is not too much for the Lord to expect that His people, saved at such an infinite cost, will want, like that dog, to come into His presence in order to be occupied only with the One whom, "having not seen, they love" with all their hearts. May it be yours and mine to know something, by experience, of the real meaning and nature of worship, and thus fulfil His purpose in our salvation.

The words of Miss C. A. Wellesley will form a fitting conclusion to this section of our study:

> "Occupied with Thee, Lord Jesus, In Thy grace;
> All Thy ways and thoughts about me
> Only trace
> Deeper stories of the glories
> Of Thy grace.
>
> Taken up with Thee Lord Jesus I would be;
> Finding joy and satisfaction
> All in Thee;
> Thou the nearest and the dearest
> Unto me."

CHAPTER SIX

II. The Importance of Worship.

Having considered, in a somewhat lengthy manner, the meaning of worship, let us now discuss its importance, as seen in both the Old and New Testaments. Since worship is the Christian's highest occupation, it logically follows it must be of much importance. We shall consult the Scriptures and notice a sevenfold testimony to the fact of its importance.

1. It was the first commandment of the Law.
(Exod. 20:1-2)

The law is the revelation of the righteous requirements of a God of infinite holiness. Divine righteousness has been well defined as "God's consistency with His own character." Inasmuch as God is infinitely holy, therefore His demands must be consistent with Himself. This law consists of ten commandments, which together form one law and not ten laws, as some mistakenly imagine. A reading of these commandments will at once reveal the importance of worship. This, as we have already seen, gives to God the place of absolute pre-eminence. Here God says: "Thou shalt have no other gods before Me." (v. 3). Not only does God claim the first place, but He goes on to reveal His hatred and intolerance of everything that would deprive Him of this position. Later on in this same book He says: "Thou shalt *worship no other god*: for the Lord, whose name is Jealous, is a jealous God" (Exod. 34:14).

Many things may arise in the life of a believer which will tend to draw away his heart from God as the supreme Object of his affection. The example of a backsliding

Israel is quoted by the Spirit as a warning of this peril.
(Read I Cor. 10:1-12). It is dreadfully possible for self,
in its many and varied forms, to ascend the throne of the
heart and displace God in the believer's life, so that little
or no worship ascends to Him. Among the many idols
that have been known to turn a Christian's heart from
God are business, wealth, home, family, possessions, tal-
ents, popularity, power and pleasure. Later on, we shall
look at some of these in detail. The concluding words of
John's first epistle should be soberly pondered by every
believer: "Little children, keep yourselves from idols"
(I John 5:21).

2. It is seen in the prominence it receives in the gatherings of God's people, at the various feasts He ordained.

(Lev. 23).

God gave instructions that His people should periodically assemble themselves together. This was done in
order to give them the double opportunity of acknowledg-
ing Him as the Giver of every good and perfect gift, and
of worshipping before Him. In Deut. 12:5-7, both the
place and the purpose of such feasts is indicated: "Unto
the place which the Lord your God shall choose out of all
your tribes to put His name there, even unto His habitation shall ye seek, and thither shalt thou come. And
thither ye shall bring your burnt offerings, and your
sacrifices, and your tithes, and heave offerings of your
hand, and your vows and your freewill offerings, and the
firstlings of your herds, and of your flocks. And there ye
shall eat before the Lord your God, and ye shall rejoice in
all that ye have put your hands unto, ye and your house-
holds, wherein the Lord thy God hath blessed thee."

The first *place* which God selected was Shiloh and
afterwards, Jerusalem; but the *purpose* for which these

gatherings were convened remained the same. In brief, the purpose was to worship Jehovah and rejoice before Him. This fact is seen in the opening verses of I Samuel. This book opens with a description of a man named Elkanah, of whom it is said: "And this man went up out of his city yearly to worship, and to sacrifice unto the Lord of Hosts in Shiloh" (I Sam. 1:3).

These feasts of Jehovah were seven in number, and are full of rich spiritual significance, as indeed are all the types. The reader will be well repaid by making a study of their typical character. The names of these feasts were the Passover, Unleavened Bread, Firstfruits, Pentecost, Trumpets, Atonement and Tabernacles.

When we turn to the New Testament, we discover that the Lord Jesus made a similar provision for His redeemed people by instituting the Lord's supper. The purpose of this ordinance is clearly indicated by the Lord's own words: "This do for a remembrance of Me" (I Cor. 11: 23-26). At this weekly feast of remembrance, worship becomes the predominant feature, as we have already seen. From Acts 20:7, it seems clear that it was the custom of the early Church to come together each Lord's day to break bread in remembrance of the Lord Jesus, and thus express their unity in Christ, and their fellowship together in the bonds of Christian love.

Besides the Lord's supper, other gatherings are mentioned in the Acts. The saints are described as gathering together for prayer, for the ministry of the word, and for a united testimony in the gospel. (See Acts 12:12; 11: 22-26; 2:6-12). Christ's well known words are surely appropriate in this connection: "Where two or three are gathered together in My name, there am I in the midst of them" (Matt. 18:20). At such gatherings of the Lord's people, every believer should seek to be present. He should lay to heart the exhortation: "Not forsaking the assembling of ourselves together, as the manner of some is . . . and so much the more, as ye see the day approaching" (Heb. 10:25).

3. The Typology of the Old Testament gives worship the prominent place.

Dr. Griffith Thomas once remarked that the Old Testament was characterized by three things. First, it was a book of unfulfilled prophecies; second, of unexplained ceremonies; third, of unsatisfied longings. As one turns to the New Testament, these unfulfilled prophecies, which speak of a coming Messiah, are meticulously and wonderfully fulfilled in Christ. The unexplained ceremonies become crystal clear, and scintillate with spiritual significance in the light of Christ's Person and work. The unsatisfied longings of the heart find their complete satisfaction in the One Who said: "Take My yoke upon you and learn of Me, for I am meek and lowly in heart and ye shall find rest unto your souls" (Matt. 11:29).

Two Scriptures will suffice to indicate the value of these types and shadows of the Old Testament. Concerning the incidents of Israel's history, we read: "Now all these things happened unto them for ensamples, (or types) and they are written for our admonition" (I Cor. 10:11). The other declares: "For whatsoever things were written aforetime, were written for our learning, that we, through patience and comfort of the Scriptures, might have hope" (Rom. 15:4). The epistle to the Hebrews is particularly rich in typical teaching.

In thinking of this typology of the Old Testament, which places the supreme emphasis on worship, we shall consider five instances:

(1) In the description of the Tabernacle.
(Exod. 25:10; 23; 31).

The purpose of its erection is not left unexplained. God said: "Make Me a sanctuary, that I may dwell among them" (Exod. 25:8). God gave the pattern, or building plan, of this tabernacle to Moses in the holy mount where he was closeted with Deity for forty days. The first article of furniture that God describes is the ark of the covenant, overlaid with the mercy seat. Why is this particular thing selected as the first to be described? The answer is obvious. It was of this ark of the covenant, overlaid with the mercy seat, that God said: "There will I meet with thee, and I will commune with thee from above the mercy seat" (Exod. 25:22). Thus the ark and the mercy seat constituted the *place of worship,* where God and man could meet together and enjoy sweet communion with each other.

Then follows the description of the other furniture of the tabernacle in the order named: The table of shewbread, the candlestick, the brazen altar, the altar of incense and the laver. It is important to notice that *this is quite different from the order of our spiritual apprehension* of the truths typified by these things. We begin, as sinners, at the brazen altar. It is here we learn the truth of the substitutionary sacrifice of the Lamb of God. From this, we proceed to learn the value of the other furnishings until, at last, we come to the realization of the spiritual significance of the mercy seat and of our highest occupation, the worship of God. It is not without the deepest significance that it requires seven chapters, containing 243 verses, to give the description of the tabernacle, whose primary purpose was the worship of Jehovah. The account of the creation of the heaven and the earth occupies but one chapter, containing only 31 verses.

(2) In the order of the camp of Israel.
(Numbers 1:52-53; 2:1-2).

We are told that "God is not the Author of confusion, but of order" (I Cor. 14:33). This fact is evidenced very clearly in God's instructions as to where each of the twelve tribes should be located, in relation to the tabernacle.

The center of the camp was occupied by the tabernacle which, of course, speaks typically of Christ in the midst of His people. Those camping nearest to the tabernacle were the priests, the sons of Aaron, whose responsibility it was to officiate in the nation's *worship*. A little farther off were the Levites, whose duties were associated with the *service* of the tabernacle. Still further off, and forming a circle around the tabernacle, were the other tribes, who constituted the *warriors* of Israel. Thus the order of precedence is given by Divine authority. First the *worshippers*, then the *workers* and finally, the *warriors*.

(3) In the threefold division of Israel.

We have before noted this division; the priests, the Levites and the tribes. It is interesting and instructive to notice the *ages* at which these men entered upon their various duties. The priests had to be *thirty years* of age before they were considered competent to engage in the worship of Jehovah. (Num. 4:3). The Levites must be *twenty-five years* of age before they could undertake their duties in connection with the service of the sanctuary. (Num. 8:24). The *warriors* from amongst the tribes could enter the army at the age of *twenty*. (Num. 1:3). Worship is thus seen to be associated with *spiritual maturity*. *Warfare* is the characteristic of youth and immaturity; *work*, of a little later in life; while *worship* comes still later. Worship therefore calls for greater spiritual knowledge, deeper discernment and richer experience than work, or warfare; though both these are necessary in the Christian life.

(4) In the description of the five principal offerings.
(Levit. Chapters 1-7)

These offerings, which combine to typically set forth the sacrifice of Christ, are given in a certain order. These, as in the case of the furnishings of the tabernacle, are not given in the order in which *we* spiritually apprehend their typical significance; but they appear in the order of *Divine* appreciation. These offerings combine to present the virtue and value of Christ's Person and His sacrificial work in five distinct aspects. Let us note them carefully.

(a) *The Burnt Offering,* or literally, the "ascending offering" (Lev. 1). This "sweet savor" offering was consumed, in its entirety, by fire upon the altar. In fact, this offering gives its title to the brazen altar, for it is called "the altar of the burnt offering" (Exod. 30:28; 40:10, etc.). The whole of this offering was exclusively for God's eye, estimation and pleasure. How eloquently this presents to us Christ's perfect dedication of Himself to His Father for His supreme delight and acceptance. From the stable of Bethlehem to the cross of Calvary, our Lord's path on earth was marked by His willing submission to His Father's will, His absolute obedience to His Father's word and His perfect fulfilment of His Father's righteous demands. His whole life is summed up in the words: "I delight to do Thy will, O My God; yea, Thy law is within My heart." (Ps. 40:7-8; Heb. 10:7-9). Thus Christ's sacrifice was primarily for God.

Just as the burnt offering was wholly devoted to God, so also is worship. It ascends from the heart of the believer, as did the burnt offering from the altar, to bring delight to God alone. Thus, first in the order of mention and of Divine preference is this burnt offering, which speaks of worship. Then follows the description of the other four offerings.

(b) *The Meal Offering*. (Lev. 2). This speaks of Christ's offering of Himself to God for the service of man. It consisted of fine flour, with oil poured over it, and frankincense placed upon it. This was then offered upon the altar as a sweet savor unto the Lord. This typifies Christ as the Bread of God, in Whom the Father found complete satisfaction.

(c) *The Peace Offering*. (Lev. 3). This indicates that aspect of Christ's sacrifice by which our peace with God was secured, and fellowship with God made possible, for both God and man shared in this offering. Thus a table was provided, at which God and man could sit, and each enjoy his portion of the offering. In this offering both God and man are seen finding their satisfaction in the Person and work of Christ.

(d) *The Sin Offering*. (Lev. 4). This illustrates the tremendous truth that Christ died because of what we *are* by nature—sinners. By His sacrifice, the believer's *sin*, that is, the root principle from which *sins* spring as the fruit, has been condemned, and put away from before the eye of God. (Read Heb. 9:27; Rom. 8:3; II Cor. 5:21).

(e) *The Trespass Offering*. (Lev. 5). This presents the work of Christ in relation to our *sins*, the evil things we have *done*, both in thought, word, deed and attitude. These sins have been borne in His own body, and the full penalty paid by His most precious blood. (I Pet. 2:24; Isa. 53:5-6).

It is good for the believer to realize that the sacrifice of Christ was of such tremendous importance that it required each of these five offerings in order to deal with all its implications. In the order of our *spiritual discernment* and appreciation of these offerings, we think first of ourselves and our sin and need, so we approach God by way of the *trespass* offering. Later on, we see that Christ not only died to put our sins away, but to put *sin* away; that He not only died for what we *did*, but for what we *were*. Thus we learn the value of the *sin offering*. Later still, we grasp something of what it means to have fellowship with God because of the peace Christ has made, and come to appreciate the *peace offering*. Still later, we apprehend the perfection of Christ's life on earth and His service to God on our behalf, and come to value the *meal offering*. Later still, the greater aspect of His sacrifice is made clear to us as we study the Word, and we are brought to a fuller estimate of the Godward aspect of Christ's sacrifice, and see how perfectly it delighted the heart of the Father and brought glory to His name. Thus we enter into the truth of the *burnt offering*.

(5) In the vision of Isaiah.
(Isa. 6:1-3).

The call and commission of this man of God was preceded by a vision which further illustrates the importance of worship. In his vision he saw the Lord; "Sitting upon a throne, high and lifted up, and His train filled the temple." Above the throne stood the seraphims, each having six wings. We are expressly told the purpose of these wings: "With twain he covered his face, with twain he covered his feet, and with twain he did fly." As they attended the Lord upon His throne, they cried one to another: "Holy, holy, holy, is the Lord of Hosts: the whole earth is full of His glory!"

Thus these angelic beings, which stood in the presence of the God of the universe, used *four* of their wings to indicate their attitude of reverence and worship, and only *two* to accomplish their service.

These five instances, selected from many others in the Scriptures, should surely serve to impress us with the supreme importance of worship, as seen in the high estimate that God places upon it.

CHAPTER SEVEN

The Importance of Worship

(Continued)

4. Moses learned the importance of worship.
(Exod. 33:11; 34:9).

Moses, the great leader of Israel, had many and varied experiences in God's dealings with him, but it is doubtful if any could compare with the one described in Exod. 33 and 34. Let us look at it for a little while and learn, still further, the importance of worship.

(1) Moses had been chosen by God.

It is perfectly true that Moses chose God of his own volition, for the Scripture plainly affirms: "By faith Moses, when he was come to years, (or maturity), refused to be called the son of Pharoah's daughter; choosing rather to suffer affliction with the people of God, than to enjoy the pleasures of sin for a season" (Heb. 11:24-25). Yet this choice of Moses was due to God's primary choice of him, even as is the case of every believer. We read that we were "chosen in Christ before the foundation of the world" (Eph. 1:4). The movement of a soul towards God, is but the effect of the movement of God towards that soul. From this we learn that the worshipper is one who has been chosen and called of God.

Isaac Watts beautifully expressed this in a hymn:

> "Why was I made to hear Thy voice
>   And enter while there's room,
> When thousands make a wretched choice
>   And rather starve than come?
>
> 'Twas the same love that spread the feast
>   That sweetly forced me in.
> Else I had still refused to taste,
>   And perished in my sin."

(2) Moses had been redeemed to God.

He had experienced the deliverance of the Passover, together with all who had availed themselves of this divine provision for their salvation and security. He had been commanded by God to proclaim to the people of Israel: "The blood shall be to you for a token . . . When I see the blood, I will pass over you." Thus he had learned the value of the sprinkled blood of the Lamb to give *safety,* and the spoken *word* of the Lord to give *certainty* to all who took advantage of God's provision in salvation.

(3) Moses enjoyed rare intimacy and communion with God.

We are told that "the Lord spake unto Moses face to face, as a man speaketh unto his friend" (Exod. 33:11). It was this holy intimacy with God that distinguished Moses from all his contemporaries. At his death he had the unique honor of having God as his grave Digger and chief Mourner. In fact, God not only buried Moses, but also buried his grave and the cemetery; for "no man knoweth of his sepulchre until this day" (Deut. 34:5-6). Over that lonely, unknown grave on Mount Nebo's lofty height, God wrote his epitaph: "There arose not a prophet since in Israel like unto Moses, whom the Lord knew face to face" (Deut. 34:10).

What holy intimacy is implied by these words! Moses was a man who enjoyed the hallowed privilege of communion with God, with nothing between to mar the fellowship. Communion is one of those words impossible to define, but which, thank God, each believer may experience. Blessed indeed is that person who enjoys such intimacy with God, and over whose tomb can be truthfully inscribed: "Here lies the body of a person, with whom God communed face to face, as a man speaketh to his friend."

(4) Moses aspired to a fuller revelation from God which should result in his greater appreciation of Deity.

The effect of communion with God is an ever-increasing desire for greater communion and an enlarged capacity for Him. Paul ever kept this before him as the supreme passion of his life. He expressed it thus: "That I may know Him, and the power of His resurrection, and the fellowship of His sufferings, being made conformable unto His death" (Phil. 3:10-11). Notice Moses' two-fold request for this greater knowledge of God.

(a) *He desired to know God's way.* "Shew me now Thy way that I may know Thee" (v. 13). By God's "way" is meant the revelation of the outgoings of Deity, as evidenced by His dealings with men. David prayed: "Cause Thy face to shine upon us . . . that Thy way may be known upon earth, Thy saving health among all nations" (Ps. 67:1-2). David, by the Spirit exclaimed: "Thy way, O God, is in the sanctuary: Who is so great a God as our God?" (Ps. 77:13). It is here that His infinite holiness, inscrutable wisdom and illimitable power is revealed.

Through God's "way," we are enabled to perceive Deity on the march. Paul spoke of God's ways and exclaimed: "O the depth of the riches, both of the wisdom and knowledge of God! How unsearchable are His judgments and His ways past finding out!" (Rom. 11:33). However, the full revelation of God's "way" awaited the coming of the incarnate Son of God, Who said simply: "I am the Way" (John 14:6). By this He said, as it were: "Would you see the outgoings of Deity, the revelation of God's character as seen in His holiness, wisdom, love and power? Then look at Me. I am Deity on the march. 'I am the Way, the Truth, and the Life; no man cometh unto the Father but by Me.'"

God's answer to Moses' bold request was the gracious promise: "My presence shall go with thee, and I will give thee rest." In other words, God Himself would be the Way, and His presence with Moses would give him perfect confidence and complete rest as to the wisdom of all His dealings with Israel. Thus Moses' supreme confidence should be based upon the assured presence of God in every circumstance of life and all the varied experiences of the journey that lay before him.

(b) *He desired to see God's glory* (v. 18). Moses now gets bolder still, and actually asks the God of the universe to show him His glory! Perhaps the best definition of glory is, "displayed excellence." It represents those unique prerogatives and excellencies that can be displayed by God alone. "I am Jehovah, that is My Name, and My glory will I not give to another" (Isa. 42:8). Moses here says, in effect, "O God, let me see the display of all Thy Divine attributes, the bursting forth of all Thy effulgent brightness, as Thou dost demonstrate the unique excellencies of Thy Person, which distinguishes Thee from all Thy creation!"

As God has revealed His "way" in His Son, so also God has displayed all His "glory" in Him. One Scripture, out of many, will suffice to prove this: "For God, who commanded the light to shine out of darkness, hath shined in our hearts to give the light of the knowledge of the glory of God in the face of Jesus Christ" (II Cor. 4:6). Thus all the intrinsic excellencies of Deity are fully seen, harmoniously blended and marvelously displayed, in all their absolute perfection, in the Person of the Son of God. Christ's own words to Martha should be pondered by every believer: "Said I not unto thee, that, if thou wouldst believe, thou shouldst see the glory of God?" (John 11:

40). To believe on Christ, to receive Him, and to observe Him, is to see the glory of God displayed through Him.

(5) Moses was granted a rich provision by God.
(vs. 19-23).

Note God's answer to this bold request. Moses would not be permitted to see His face, yet he was to be allowed to see His "back parts" (v. 23). This expression has been better translated as, "afterglow." Let us illustrate. We cannot steadfastly gaze into the dazzling splendor of the midday sun, but we can appreciate its glories by means of a magnificent sunset. Likewise, God's uncreated glory is so surpassingly brilliant that no human eye could bear the sight; but we can appreciate it by the "afterglow" which we were permitted to see as we study His holy word. Eternity will provide God with the opportunity of displaying to His redeemed people "the exceeding riches of His grace in His kindness towards us through Christ Jesus" (Eph. 2:7). As we are occupied with the Lord Jesus, there will be an ever increasing apprehension and appreciation of the glory of God on the part of every believer.

In order that Moses might be enabled to see this tremendous spectacle, it was necessary that a four-fold provision be made for him by God, apart from which he could not possibly witness this demonstration of His glory. This provides us with a beautiful picture of the still more wonderful provision God has made for each believer in Christ, by which he is enabled both to appreciate the glory of God and, as a direct consequence, become a worshipper of Him.

(a) *Moses was first given a place of acceptance before God.* "There is a place by Me" (v. 21). By this placing of Moses in a position of acceptance, nearness and dearness to God, he was thereby fitted for the sight he was soon to witness. The Bible clearly indicates that the sinner has no standing before God, or acceptance in God's presence. By nature he is at "enmity to God," and is consequently "not subject to the law of God." While in this condition, he "cannot please God" (Rom. 8:7-8). Thus, by nature, the sinner has no place before God, or right to stand in His presence.

When a sinner, in true repentance, puts his confidence in Christ and His finished work, and receives Him as his own Savior, he is immediately given a place of acceptance by God which fits him for the Divine presence. Paul, by the Spirit, puts it thus: "Having predestinated us unto the adoption of children by Jesus Christ to Himself, according to the good pleasure of His will, to the praise of the glory of His grace, wherein He hath *made us accepted* in the Beloved" (Eph. 1:5-6). Catesby Paget's well known lines are appropriate in this connection:

> By nature and by practice far,
>   How very far from God!
> Yet now, by grace, brought nigh to Him,
>   Through faith in Jesus' blood.
>
> So near, so very near to God,
>   I cannot nearer be;
> For in the Person of His Son,
>   I am as near as He!
>
> So dear, so very dear to God,
>   More dear I cannot be;
> The love wherewith He loves the Son,
>   Such is His love to me!

We can assuredly gather, from what we have read, that worship necessitates that the worshipper be in a state of acceptance with God, and that this acceptance is based on God's sovereign grace.

(b) *Moses was then given a good foundation on which to stand.* "Thou shalt stand upon a rock" (v. 21). God saw to it that beneath Moses' feet was a solid, substantial

and immovable rock. Though he might tremble as he
stood on the rock, he could be certain that the rock would
not tremble under him! Of the typical significance of the
rock, we are left in no doubt. David sang: "The Lord is
my Rock" (Ps. 18:2). Moses himself, in his grand fare-
well song, exclaimed: "I will publish the name of the
Lord: ascribe ye greatness unto our God. He is the Rock,
His work is perfect" (Deut. 32:3-4). Paul, in his letter to
the Corinthians says: "Other foundation can no man lay
than is laid, which is Jesus Christ" (I Cor. 3:11). Our
Lord's words to Peter, when he made his memorable
confession of Christ's essential and eternal Deity, were:
"On this Rock, I will build my Church" (Matt. 16:18).

Only as we stand on this Rock can we appreciate the
glory of God, and become worshippers of Him in Spirit
and in truth. The Christian, like Moses, has a Rock on
which to stand, which all the storms of earth can never
shake. He rests his all upon the Deity of Christ's Person,
on the eternal value of the precious blood He shed, and
on the Divine authority and assurance of His holy word
and sings:

> "On Christ, the solid Rock, I stand,
>   All other ground is sinking sand."

(c) *Moses was then given a position in the Rock.* "I
will put thee in a clift of the rock" (v. 22). This rock had
a clift in it, and Moses was now placed in the *midst* of the
rock. Thus he was not only *on* the rock, but *in* it! He
was surrounded by the rock and, in this way, partook of
all the strength and security of his refuge. Is not this a
graphic illustration of what God has done for the believer?
Not only does the Christian have Christ as his *foundation,*
but also as his *habitation,* for he is described as being "in
Christ." In fact, these words, "in Christ," form the key
phrase of the Epistle to the Ephesians which unfolds, as

no other portion of God's word, the eternal blessedness of the believer (See Eph. 1:1-14).

A striking picture of this is seen in Proverbs 30:26. We are told that the conies (rock rabbits) are a feeble folk, yet they make their houses in the rocks. The coney is a feeble creature, and no match whatever for the large beasts of prey but, the moment danger threatens, it runs into the shelter provided by God. The moment it enters the rock, it can laugh in the face of the pursuing foe, for it has learned that to be *in* the rock, is to *be as* the rock.

Perhaps David had this in mind when he said: "I flee unto Thee to hide me" (Ps. 143:9). Again he said: "Thou art my strong Refuge . . . Thou art my hiding place" (Ps. 71:7; 32:7).

The story of how Toplady came to write his best known hymn is in order at this point. Overtaken by a storm, as he walked on a lonely moor in England, Augustus Toplady, knowing the location of a great rock with a clift in it, ran there for shelter. As he entered the cleft, the storm broke in all its fury; the lightning flashed, the thunder rolled and the rain descended in torrents. In the midst of all this storm, Toplady, in his refuge, was untouched, for the storm exhausted itself on the rock in which he was sheltered. As the storm raged, a verse from Isaiah 26:4 came to his mind, which reads: "Trust ye in the Lord for ever, for in the Lord Jehovah is the Rock of ages." (Marg.). As he thought upon this Scripture, the first two lines of a hymn suggested themselves to him:

> "Rock of ages, cleft for me,
> Let me hide myself in Thee."

Later, he added the other lines, and thus this beautiful and well loved hymn came into existence.

Nineteen hundred years ago, a far greater storm burst, in unparalled fury, upon the sinless and unprotected head

of our Divine Substitute: Christ, the Rock of Ages. All
the concentrated judgment of a holy God, because of our
sins, fell on Him who bore them all "in His own body on
the tree." In that "lone, dark and mysterious hour," Christ
received the full force of God's righteous judgment against
sin, and thus was cleft for us. On Calvary He accomplished all the work necessary for our salvation. Now
risen and glorified at God's right hand, He ever lives to
save all who will hide themselves in Him. Each believer
can now, reverently and rejoicingly, sing:

> "The tempest's awful voice was heard,
>   O Christ, it broke on Thee!"
> Thy open bosom was my ward;
>   It braved the storm for me.
> Thy form was scarred, Thy visage marred;
>   Now cloudless peace for me."

(d) Lastly, *Moses was given a perfect protection while
in the rock.* God said: "I will cover thee with My hand
while I pass by" (v. 22). There was no possibility of
Moses falling out of the rock, for his security therein was
guaranteed by the omnipotent covering hand of Him who
later said: "My sheep hear My voice, and I know them,
and they follow Me, and I give unto them eternal life, and
they shall never perish, neither shall any man pluck them
out of My hand" (John 10:27-28). Thus Moses enjoyed
the perfect peace which comes from the assurance of absolute security. He had been given a place of acceptance;
under his feet was a solid immovable foundation; around
him was his God—provided refuge; and enclosing him was
God's covering hand. He could now worship, without
one disturbing thought that if he did not hold on tight
enough, he would slip out of the rock and be lost!

Many of God's dear people are so occupied with their
efforts to "hold on to Christ," that they have neither the
time nor the inclination to worship! How much better

it is for the believer to rest, in perfect peace, upon His blessed guarantee of eternal security. Thus with "a heart at leisure from itself," he is enabled to worship the One who "doeth all things well."

(6) Moses was given a marvellous revelation of God.

(Exod. 34:5-7).

God saw to it that Moses was now in a proper position to appreciate the awe-inspiring spectacle he was about to witness, and which should result in drawing forth his heart's worship and adoration. He had a *place* of acceptance before God to *satisfy* him; a good *foundation* to *steady* him; a strong *refuge* to *shelter* him; and an omnipotent *hand* to *secure* him. What more could any person want?

Before his wondering eyes God now displayed the glory he had asked to see. We are told that "The Lord descended in the cloud, and stood with him there and proclaimed the name of the Lord. And the Lord passed by before him and proclaimed: 'The Lord, the Lord God, merciful and gracious, long suffering and abundant in goodness and truth, keeping mercy for thousands, forgiving iniquity and sin, and that will by no means clear the guilty, visiting the iniquity of the fathers upon the children, and upon the children's children, unto the third and to the fourth generation'" (Exod. 34:6-7). Moses had asked God to show him His glory, and God's response had been: "I will make all My *goodness* pass before thee, and I will proclaim the *name* of Jehovah before thee" (Exod. 33:19). Thus God's glory is His goodness, as revealed in His name, for God's names, in Scripture, predicate His character. God has said: "I am Jehovah, that is My name, and My glory will I not give to another" (Isa. 42:8).

Surely, in so far as the Old Testament is concerned, this was the most majestic display ever seen by mortal eyes. Compared with this, the most gorgeous spectacle staged by man sinks into utter insignificance. Here was a demonstration of the One who is described as being: "The King, eternal, immortal, invisible, the only wise God," to Whom be "honor and glory for ever and ever" (I Tim. 1:17). People have travelled thousands of miles, and put themselves to great expense and trouble to watch the coronation procession of some king, or the inauguration of some president; but Moses was the solitary witness of the incomparable spectacle of Deity in procession!

Yet, wonderful though this sight must have been, a greater was witnessed nineteen hundred years ago, when God came down to earth in the Person of the Lord Jesus Christ. Before the eyes of a wondering, yet unbelieving world, Deity was displayed in terms of a perfect human life. John, the beloved disciple, says of Him: "And the Word was made flesh, and dwelt among us, and we beheld His glory, the glory as of the only begotten of the Father, full of grace and truth" (John 1:14). The Son of God completely satisfied all His Father's desire and glorified His name, as never before. The writer of the epistle to the Hebrews thus describes His Person and work: "Who, being the brightness of His glory, and the express image of His Person, and upholding all things by the word of His power, when He had by Himself purged our sins, sat down on the right hand of the majesty on high" (Heb. 1: 3).

Moses was not permitted to see the face of God, but John, the beloved apostle, speaks of Christ as the One: "Which we have seen with our eyes, which we have looked upon, and our hands have handled, of the Word of life" (I John 1:1). Thus all the glory of God has been concentrated in the face of Him whom this world despised and crucified, but whom the Christian loves and honors above all others.

(7) Moses gave to God the humble, reverent, and sincere worship of his heart.

(Exod. 34:8).

We are told that the effect of this majestic display of God's glory was that "Moses made haste, and bowed his head towards the earth and worshipped." There was nothing else left for him to do under such circumstances. This majestic revelation put him where it will put every true believer, low at the feet of the One Who alone is worthy and to Whom worship rightly belongs.

Thus Moses learned, upon the holy mount, the significance of God's glory, as revealed in the display of His Divine attributes, and the importance and necessity for true spiritual worship in the presence of such an august Being. From this demonstration of God's glory and its resultant worship he returned, forty days later, to the camp of Israel a changed man. We are told that the glory upon which he had gazed so long was reflected in his face, for we read: "It came to pass . . . when he came down from the mount, that Moses wist not that the skin of his face shone."

From this we can surely gather that God will be no man's Debtor. When a believer gives to God the worship due to His name, he will unconsciously reflect that fact as he comes into contact with his fellow men. There will be something about him which will distinguish him from others, though he himself will be unaware of it. Occupation with Christ is the secret of the shining face and the satisfied heart. As the Scripture puts it: "We all, with open face beholding as in a glass the glory of the Lord, are changed into the same image, from glory to glory, even as by the Spirit of the Lord" (II Cor. 3:18).

5. David sensed the tremendous importance of worship.

We shall look at several of his statements in this connection. In Ps. 69:30-31, he declares: "I will praise the name of God with a song, and will magnify Him with thanksgiving. This also shall please the Lord better than an ox, or bullock, that hath horns and hoofs." In these words, David boldly affirms that praise and thanksgiving is of greater value to God than the offering of the most valuable of animal sacrifices. The horns speak of power and the hoofs of separation. Thus he affirms that even a life of power and separation is excelled by the greater value of worship.

In I Chron. 16, is described David's removal of the ark, this time in a scriptural manner, from the house of Obed-Edom to the tent he had prepared for it in Jerusalem. To celebrate this event, David, by the Spirit's inspiration, wrote a beautiful Psalm which was sung for the occasion. Let us glance at a few extracts from this magnificent hymn: "Glory and honor are in His presence; strength and gladness are in His place. Give unto the Lord, ye kindreds of the people, give unto the Lord glory and strength. Give unto the Lord the glory due to His name. Bring an offering, and come before Him: worship the Lord in the beauty of holiness . . . Blessed be the Lord God of Israel for ever and ever" (v. 26-29).

Again, in one of his beautiful Messianic Psalms, he writes of the "King's daughter," who is a type of the believer, and says: "Hearken, O daughter, and consider, and incline thine ear; forget also thine own people, and thy father's house; so shall the King greatly desire thy beauty: for He is thy Lord, and worship thou Him" (Ps. 45:10-11).

Notice the progression of thought. First there is an appeal for *concentration* of mind: "Hearken and consider, and incline thine ear." This is followed by a call to *re-nunciation*: "Forget also thy people and thy father's house." The result of this is *attraction* on the part of the King: "So shall the King greatly desire thy beauty." The effect of this is the *adoration* of the one who has thus been brought into Divine favor: "He is thy Lord and worship thou Him." Thus the close link is emphasized between the acknowledged Lordship of Christ and the believer's worship of Him. To own Him as Lord is to fall at His feet and render to Him the homage that is His due.

One more quotation will suffice to show how David realized the importance of worship. In Psalm 95, where the greatness of God is described, we read: "For the Lord is a great God, and a great King above all gods . . . The sea is His, and He made the dry land. O come, let us worship and bow down: let us kneel before the Lord our Maker. For He is our God, and we are the people of His pasture, and the sheep of His hand" (vs. 3-7). In this way the Holy Spirit, through the lips of "the sweet psalm-ist of Israel," calls upon all, who are "the sheep of His pasture," to bow in worship before their mighty Creator, Savior and Shepherd. The Christian does so, with the added knowledge that the same One who brought all things into being by the word of His mouth, became the Redeemer of His people, and bought them with his own most precious blood.

CHAPTER EIGHT

The Importance of Worship

(Continued)

6. The Revelation of the Son of God.
(John 4:20-24)

Our Lord's own teaching on the subject of worship, which is recorded in John 4:20-24, is of momentous importance to every believer. It seems strange that this great subject of worship was discussed with a fallen woman by a wayside well; while the subject of the new birth was propounded to a religious, moral and sincere Pharisee. We would have reversed the order of procedure, but not so our Lord. In His infinite wisdom He, "Who doeth all things well," revealed these wondrous truths to a poor sinner who needed Him. In His conversation with the woman at the well, Christ, in view of His sufferings and the glory that should follow, introduced at least seven great changes regarding worship, as it had previously been revealed in the Old Testament Scriptures.

(1) As to the place of worship. (v. 20).

This woman, though anything but chaste, was not unwilling to discuss religion and said to the Lord: "Our fathers worshipped in this mountain, (Gerizim) and ye say that in Jerusalem is the place where men ought to worship." Note carefully Christ's answer: "Woman, believe Me, the hour cometh, when ye shall neither in this mountain, nor yet at Jerusalem worship the Father" (v. 21). In other words, worship was *no longer to be confined to any definite place on earth* and, least of all, to any building erected by man on earth, however great its historic interest, however beautiful its architectural design, or however ornate the pomp and circumstance of its ritual.

Though both the tabernacle in the wilderness, and the temple in Jerusalem, had been erected by Divine command, and their services inaugurated by a demonstration of God's approval in the descending cloud of glory; yet God has done away with both; for they were but "figures" and "shadows," that awaited the advent of the incarnate Son of God. (Exod. 40: 34; I Kings 8: 10-11; Heb. 9: 22-28). After the tabernacle had served its purpose as the "place" of worship for Israel, it was superceded by the temple, erected in Jerusalem, "the place where God had chosen to put His name."

When Christ became incarnate and dwelt (literally, "tabernacled") among us, He fulfilled the type of the tabernacle. (See John 1: 14). But Christ also fulfilled the type of the temple. One day, the Jews challenged Him: "What sign showest Thou unto us, seeing that Thou doest these things?" He replied: "Destroy this temple, and, in three days, I will raise it up." At this, the Jews, thinking in terms of Herod's temple, which then stood in Jerusalem cried: "Forty and six years was this temple in building, and wilt Thou rear it up in three days?" Now note the comment that follows: "But He spake of the temple of His body" (John 2: 18-21).

Still later, faced by the unjust criticism of the Pharisees, who charged Him with doing unlawful things on the Sabbath day, Christ quoted David's act of eating the shew bread, and of the priests doing service on the Sabbath, and then added these tremendously significant words: "But I say unto you that, in this place, is One greater than the temple" (Matt. 12: 1-8). All that the temple stood for, in its provision of a way of approach to God by a Divinely appointed and accepted substitute, was all perfectly fulfilled in Him. All that the priesthood stood for, in its provision of a representative to present their worship to God, was fulfilled in Him who, as our great High Priest, not only became the acceptable *Offering,* but the accepted *Offerer.*

When, on the cross, He had completed all the work needed for our salvation, God rent the veil of the temple from top to bottom, in the midst. By this act, He signified that both the temple and the Levitical priesthood had served its purpose, and was now *done away with in Christ.*

This is the argument of Hebrews, chapters 7 to 10. A persistent, careful and prayerful reading of these chapters should be sufficient to deliver any believer from the confusion that obtains in Christendom, with its so called "consecrated places of worship;" its "officiating clergyman," who "administers the sacraments," its man-made ritual and prescribed "order of service," with its "beautiful generalities." According to the New Testament revelation, no provision whatever is made, or place found for such things in this present dispensation.

Worship is no longer a matter of *"place,"* but of *spiritual condition.* The believer is just as much at liberty to worship God from the midst of the wilds of Borneo, as from the heart of a nation's metropolis. It matters not whether a Christian is in the kitchen, the barn, the bedroom, the busy mart, or the open air; he can worship God *anywhere,* providing, of course, he is in the spiritual condition to do so. He needs no human intercessor to act as mediator, for he has in heaven a great high Priest, and therefore can go directly to Him. The Scripture makes it so perfectly simple: "Having, therefore, brethren, boldness (marg. "liberty") to enter into the holiest by the blood of Jesus, by a new and living way . . . and having an high Priest over the house of God, let us draw near with a true heart, in full assurance of faith," etc. (Heb. 10:19-22).

God no longer dwells in buildings made by man, as He did of old in the tabernacle and the temple. Paul, in his speech on Mars Hill makes this crystal clear: "God that made the world and all things therein, seeing He is Lord of heaven and earth, dwelleth not in temples made with hands" (Acts 17:24).

"The house of God," today, is *His people*. He dwells in the midst of His gathered saints, wherever they may meet in the name of the Lord Jesus Christ (Matt. 18:20). We are told in Hebrews 3:6, that "Christ is a Son over His own house, *whose house are we*"; and by "we" is meant Christians. Whether it be an individual Christian, or a small company of two or three, or a large gathering of believers; each may meet *anywhere on earth* and worship the Father and the Son. The Christian's "place of worship" is where his great high Priest is—in heaven. He enters there by faith, as he lays hold upon the two-fold provision he has in Christ: first, His redemption work, and second, His present ministry at the right hand of God.

(2) As to the Object of worship.

"The true worshippers shall worship the *Father*" (v. 23).

Israel worshipped Jehovah, Whose demonstrated holiness, majesty, glory, power and justice at Sinai, filled them with awe and terror. As they stood, trembling and afar off from the fearful spectacle, they said to Moses: "Speak thou with us, and we will hear, but let not God speak with us, lest we die . . . and Moses drew near unto the thick darkness where God was" (Exod. 20:19-21). Thus Jehovah, at the giving of the law, which revealed the righteous requirements that His holiness demanded, is described as being at a *distance*, dwelling in *darkness* and producing *dread* within the hearts of the people of Israel.

Now compare this with Christ's revelation as to the Object of the Christian's worship. It is "the Father." He is the same Being as the God of Sinai, for God is unchangeable in His character. He is equally as holy, righteous and just as He always was, and ever shall be; but He is now revealed, by His beloved Son, in a *different aspect*, even as "Father." It is a word that connotes comforting nearness, exquisite intimacy, assuring dearness, warm affection, tender care, enduring love, understanding pity, infinite forbearance and illimitable grace.

God has come forth from the enfolding clouds of darkness and, through "the Son of His love," stands revealed as the "God and Father of our Lord Jesus Christ," and of every true Christian who has been born into His family through faith in Christ. Creation could but unfold to us God's *eternal power* and wisdom. (Rom. 1:20). The law could but reveal God's *holiness,* righteousness, justice and truth. (Exod. 20:1-17). But the Lord Jesus has exposed to us God's *heart,* a heart filled with infinite love towards those who are undeserving of the least of His mercies.

How good it is for the believer to be able to constantly remind himself that it is to his Father that he comes to present his worship, a Father who has been described as:

> "Absolutely tender, absolutely true,
>   Understanding all things, understanding you;
> Infinitely loving, exquisitely near,
>   This is God our Father—what have we to fear?"

(3) As to the relationship of the worshipper.

Since it is God, revealed as "the Father," whom we worship; it follows logically that only those who have been brought into living and vital relationship with Him, can call Him such and worship Him. In the Old Testament, it was the children of Aaron, by *natural generation,* that were alone fitted to minister as priests in the worship of Jehovah.

In the New Testament, it is the children of God, by *supernatural regeneration,* that are alone constituted "a kingdom of priests unto God." (I Peter 2:5; Rev. 1:5-6). This is why the new birth is such an essential thing. By the regenerating power of the Holy Spirit, the believer is made a "partaker of the Divine nature," is born into the family of God, and has the unspeakable privilege of calling God his Father. No wonder John breaks forth in praise and joyously exclaims: "Behold, what manner of love the Father hath bestowed upon us, that we should be called the sons of God!" (I John 3:1; II Peter 1:4).

We have before noted that the natural man is not only dead in his trespasses and sins, but he can neither understand the things of God, nor does he desire to worship Him. He may be naturally possessed of a religious turn of mind, and even evidence a fair amount of morality and respectability, as did Nicodemus of old; but he must learn that: "Except a man be born from above, he cannot see the kingdom of God" (John 3:3). It is no longer, as in the case of Israel, the *national* worship of an earthly people that is in view; but rather the *individual* worship of God's heaven-born children, made such "by faith in Christ Jesus" (Gal. 3:22).

James G. Deck, in his well known and greatly loved hymn, has beautifully stated this fact:

> "Abba, Father, we approach Thee
> In our Savior's precious name,
> We, Thy children, here assembling,
> Access to Thy presence claim.
> From our guilt His blood hath washed us,
> 'Tis through Him our souls draw nigh,
> And Thy Spirit, too, hath taught us,
> 'Abba, Father,' thus to cry."

(4) As to the character of the worship.

It must be "in Spirit and in truth" (v. 24). In other words, it must be spiritual and sincere. Israel's worship of Jehovah had been largely characterized by the *visible* and *material*. It consisted largely in the offering of animal sacrifices, through the medium of a human priest, who was subject to disease, decay and death. This has now given place to a *spiritual* worship, through the meditation of a Divine high Priest who, by the "offering of Himself to God," has "perfected forever them that are sanctified." Now risen and glorified, Christ lives "in the power of an endless life," and thus has an "unchangeable Priesthood." (See Heb. 7: 23-27).

It is significant that, at the mock trial of our Lord, a most dramatic incident occurred. The last high priest of an old and passing dispensation, which had been characterized by failure, looked into the eyes of the great high Priest of a new and coming new dispensation, which was to be unfailing and unfading, and inquired: "I adjure thee, by the living God, that thou tell us whether Thou be the Christ, the Son of God." Note Christ's answer and its effect. "Jesus saith unto him: "Thou hast said: nevertheless, I say unto you, hereafter shall ye see the Son of Man sitting on the right hand of power, and coming in the clouds of heaven!'" At this plain and definite declaration, by our Lord, of His essential and eternal Deity, the high Priest rent his clothes and cried: "He hath spoken blasphemy." (Matt. 26: 57-68). By the rending of his clothes, Caiaphas violated an express command of God. Though doubtless he knew it not, by this act he *disqualified himself* for the office he held! God had given a distinct commandment as to this: "And he that is the high priest among his brethren, upon whose head the anointing oil was poured, and that is consecrated to put on the garments shall not uncover his head, nor rend his clothes" (Lev. 21:10). See also Lev. 10:6; Exod. 39:23).

We have before noted that the Aaronic priesthood, with all its ornate ritual and its many sacrifices, *came to an end at the cross.* The rent veil bears eloquent testimony to this fact. That which had previously shut men out from the presence of God was done away through the sacrifice of Christ. We are told that "Once in the consummation of the ages He hath appeared to put away sin by the sacrifice of Himself" (Heb. 9:12). As Bonar has so beautifully put it:

> "No blood, no altar now,
>   The sacrifice is o'er!
> No flame, no smoke ascends on high,
>   The Lamb is slain no more.
> But richer blood has flowed from nobler veins,
>   To purge the soul from guilt,
> And cleanse the reddest stains."

No longer is worship a thing of the *hand,* but of the *heart.* It no longer consists of an endless procession of lambs, heifers and bullocks, to be slain upon the blood-baptized altars of Jewry. The Christian is now urged to "offer spiritual sacrifices, acceptable to God by Jesus Christ" (I Peter 2:5). No longer do we need the mediation of the sons of Aaron, or *the sons of anyone else!* Each believer is constituted a priest unto God, and Christ alone is the great high Priest. He it is Who presents the spiritual worship of His redeemed people to His Father, in all the virtue and value of His blessed Person and work.

Much of the so-called "public worship," in Christendom, is merely a form of Christianized Judaism, and, in some cases, thinly veiled Paganism. This fact may easily be verified. One has only to compare the sacerdotalism that obtains in Christendom with the ritual of Judaism to be struck with the deadly parallel that exists between the two. In Judaism there was a separate priestly caste who alone could conduct the worship of Israel. In Christendom a man-made priesthood, called "the clergy," is essential to its worship, in spite of the plain teaching of the New Testament that all believers are priests. These priests of Judaism wore a distinctive dress, as also does the clergy. Judaism emphasized an earthy sanctuary, or building. In like manner, Christendom makes much of its concecrated "places of worship," and miscalls the edifice "a church," and refers to it as "the house of God." Jewish priests had an altar on which were offered sacrifices to God. Christendom has erected "altars" in these ornate buildings, before which candles burn and incense is offered and, in many cases, on which a wafer is kept, which is looked upon as the body of Christ! It is hardly necessary to say that all this copying of Judaism is absolutely foreign to the teaching of the New Testament.

Thus Christendom has initiated its own specially educated and ordained priesthood, whose presence is indispensable to "administer the sacraments." These men, robed in gorgeous vestments, from within a roped off "sanctuary," stand before a bloodless "altar," with a background of burning candles, crosses and smoking incense, and "conduct the worship" for the laity. With the use of an elaborate prepared ritual, with stereotyped prayers, and responses from the audience, the whole service proceeds smoothly and with mechanical precision. It is a marvel of human invention and ingenuity, with an undoubted appeal to the esthetic; but a tragic and sorry substitute for the spiritual worship which our Lord declared that His Father sought from His redeemed children.

Many years ago Alexander Hislop wrote a book entitled: "The Two Babylons." In this he proves quite conclusively that much of the ornate ritual of Roman

Catholicism was borrowed from the idolatrous practices of ancient Babylon. This book is still obtainable for all who wish to be informed on this subject.

(5) As to the time of worship.

"The hour cometh, and *now is*, when the true worshippers shall worship the Father" (John 4:23). Israel's worship of God, as we have already seen in the feasts of Jehovah, was confined largely to stated occasions and places. Then again, the Sabbath day loomed large on the horizon of their worship. Our Lord here makes clear that worship is no longer a matter of "days, and months, and times, and years;" for these things belong to the past dispensation of the law. (Gal. 4:10).

The New Testament knows of no "holy" days, which call for more sanctity than other days. The Sabbath, or the seventh day, belongs to Israel, and was a sign of God's covenant with it as a nation. (Exod. 31:13). The Lord's day, or the first day of the week, belongs to the Christian dispensation. It is "the day which the Lord hath made," and which commemorates the time when God took the Stone "which the builders rejected, and made it the headstone of the corner." (See Psalm 118:22-24; c. p. Matt. 21:42; Mark 12:10).

Worship is no longer limited to any day of the week, or even to any time of the day. We discover from Acts 20:7 that it was the custom of the early Church to meet together for the breaking of bread on "the first day of the week;" but worship is not confined to this day or occasion. At *any time* of any day, or night, the Christian can lift his heart in worship to the Father and the Son, in the energy of the Holy Spirit, and know that his worship will be acceptable.

Christendom makes much of special "days" and "seasons;" but the New Testament knows nothing of them.

These belong to Israel, and have been done away in Christ. Paul's letter to the Galatians was written for the purpose of opposing the false teachers of his day who tried to judaize Crristianity, and mix law with grace, to the confusion of the believers. Every Christian should familiarize himself with this epistle, until it becomes part and parcel of his being. It is the best antidote against Seventh-Day Adventism, or any other attempt to judaize Christianity, as seen in Christendom. Every day should now be holy unto the Lord.

While the child of God is fortunate indeed to be able to gather with his fellow saints on the Lord's Day for the remembrance of the Lord Jesus and the worship of God; yet worship, most emphatically, is not *confined* to this day, or occasion, or to any season of the year.

(6) As to the energy, or power for worship.

"They that worship Him must worship Him in Spirit and in truth" (v. 24). We have already noted that true worship must be spiritual. It must be empowered by, and under the guidance and control of the third Person in the Godhead, the Holy Spirit. In the Old Testament He is described as coming *upon* certain individuals, on particular occasions, in order to accomplish, through them, some specific purpose. (See Exod. 31: 3; Num. 24: 2; I Sam. 10: 10; II Chron. 15:1; Num. 11:29, etc.).

In the New Testament, our Lord taught that the Holy Spirit, who had been *with* His disciples, would be sent to be *within* them. Speaking of the Spirit He said: "For He dwelleth *with* you, and shall be *in* you" (John 14:17). This promise was fulfilled at Pentecost. Since that time every sinner, the moment he trusts Christ as his Savior, is indwelt by the Holy Spirit. By this act of the Spirit's indwelling, each Christian is sealed, or marked out as

Christ's property, unto the day of redemption. (See Eph. 1:13; 4:30). Not only so, but the Spirit imparts to each believer a divine nature, in the power of which he can live a life pleasing to God.

The Holy Spirit now seeks, from the word of God, to teach the believer, and thus guide him into all truth. (John 16:13-15). As He is allowed to dwell ungrieved in the believer, the Spirit will so impress him with Christ, that the Lord will become increasingly precious to him. Moreover, He will empower the Christian to offer intelligent, reverent and sincere worship to the Father and the Son. Thus the only two essentials for worship are: the *word of God in our hands* and the *Spirit of God in our hearts.*

It is possible for an *individual* believer to *grieve* the Holy Spirit by his misconduct, and for an *assembly* of saints to *quench* the Spirit by limiting His activity through His people, or by an attitude of censorious criticism towards them. (Eph. 4:25-32; I Thess. 5:19-20). Consequently, there is the constant need for the believer to be "filled with the Spirit" for, in this way, he will be susceptible to His guidance and enabled to offer acceptable worship to God. (Eph. 5:18).

(7) As to the importance of worship.

This is indicated by the words: "The Father seeketh such to worship Him" (v. 23). In the Old Testament, it was the *worshipper* who sought Jehovah. In the present dispensation, it is God, as the *Father,* who seeks the worship of His children. The importance of salvation is seen in the fact that Christ declared His purpose in coming into the world, as the Son of Man, was to "seek and to save that which was lost" (Luke 19:10). This search led Him all the way to the cross. The importance of worship is sensed by the fact that the occupation of the Father is to seek for worshippers, who shall worship Him in Spirit and in truth. What a tremendous thought this is! "The high and lofty One, Who inhabits eternity," not only condescends to *notice* a humble believer, but actually *desires* his sincere worship and *seeks* for it from him! It would be incredible, but for the fact that His own beloved Son stated it in words that cannot possibly be misunderstood. This statement alone should be sufficient to prove to every believer the importance of worship.

How good it would be if each believer were to lay to heart the wonderful fact that he can give to God, his Father, to whom he owes everything, that which shall bring delight to His heart! How tragic it is to think that so many Christians, either through ignorance of, or disobedience to this revelation, are keeping from their Father that which He so ardently desires them to give Him! One of the concluding questions of the Old Testament is: "Will a man rob God?" and the answer, alas, is in the affirmative. (Mal. 3:8). As Israel robbed Him in tithes and offerings, so many of His own children, for one cause or another, are withholding from God the worship He seeks and has every right to expect.

Thus, in this wonderful conversation with the woman at the well, our Lord made these drastic changes in worship. May it be ours to give good heed to the words of Him who "spake as no man ever spake," and see to it that our worship conforms to the pattern He has given. Let us ever remember that "God is light," therefore we must be *true;* "God is love," therefore we must be *trustful;* "God is fire," therefore we must *beware;* "God is Spirit," therefore we must be *real* and sincere. (I John 1:5; 4:8; Hebrews 12:29; John 4:24).

7. Lastly, the importance of worship is seen in that it is the occupation of eternity. (Rev. 4:5).

In the last book of the Bible, which forms the consummation of Divine revelation, we are given a glimpse into the eternity to which we are all fast hastening. From this revelation we discover that the worship of God is the chief occupation of the eternal state. In chapter 4, John describes the wondrous vision he was given after the voice said: "Come up hither, and I will show thee things which must be hereafter" (v. 1). Immediately he sees before him a throne in heaven and One who sits upon it. After describing its Occupant, he tells us of the twenty-four elders who sit before the throne, and the four living creatures who continually cry: "Holy, holy, holy, Lord God almighty, which was, and is, and is to come!" As these living creatures give glory and honor to Him who sits upon the throne, the twenty-four elders fall down before God, and worship Him that liveth for ever and ever, saying: "Thou are worthy, O Lord, to receive glory and honor and power; for Thou hast created all things, and for Thy pleasure they are, and were created." Here is pure worship, unmingled with any petition whatsoever. It is the ascription of worth because of the intrinsic worthiness of the eternal Godhead.

In Chapter five, John goes on to further describe what he saw. A book is produced, sealed with seven seals, and an angel proclaims: "Who is worthy to open the book, and to loose the seals thereof?" No one, either in heaven or on earth, or under the earth, was able to respond to the challenge and this caused John to weep. At this, one of the elders said to him: "Weep not. Behold the Lion of the tribe of Judah, the Root of David, hath prevailed to open the book, and to loose the seals thereof." As John watched breathlessly he saw, in the midst of the throne, a Lamb as it had been slain, Who came forth and took the book. At this, the elders and the living creatures again fell down before the Lamb and, as they bowed, they sang this magnificent hymn of worship: "Thou art worthy to take the book, and to open the seals thereof, for Thou wast slain, and hast redeemed us to God, by Thy blood, out of every kindred and tongue and people and nation, and hast made us unto our God kings and priests, and we shall reign on the earth." Then, round about the throne, the voices of myriads of angels took up the refrain and sang: "Worthy is the Lamb that was slain, to receive power, and riches, and wisdom, and strength, and honor, and glory and blessing!"

Following this song of the angels, John now heard the united voices of every creature which is in heaven, and on the earth, and under the earth, and such as are in the sea, saying with harmonious accord: "Blessing and honor and glory and power be unto Him that sitteth upon the throne, and unto the Lamb, for ever and ever!" At this, the living creatures responded: "Amen," and the elders "fell down and worshipped Him that liveth for ever and ever."

Thus John, at the very threshold of his marvelous vision of things to come, had impressed upon his heart the vital place and the vast importance that worship has in eternity. What a glorious day that shall be, when all the redeemed of all the ages shall be gathered together in the presence of the One whose precious blood has brought them there! What a volume of worship shall rise to the eternal Godhead, unmingled by one discordant note to mar its majestic harmony and exquisite cadence, for the flesh will have been left behind forever! There will be no denominational distinctions then to keep the people of God separated from each other by various little folds of men's making. Our Lord's words shall be fulfilled in their entirety: "There shall be one flock, and one Shepherd" (John 10:16). The desire, which He expressed in His prayer in John 17, shall be wonderfully answered: "That they all may be one, as Thou Father art in Me, and I in Thee, that they also may be one in us."

J. G. Deck has beautifully expressed this thought in his hymn:

> "If here on earth the thought of Jesus' love
>   Lift our poor hearts this weary world above,
> If even here the taste of heavenly springs
>   So cheers the spirit, that the pilgrim sings;
> What will the sunshine of His glory prove?
>   What the unmingled fulness of His love?
> What hallelujahs shall His presence raise?
>   What, but one loud, eternal burst of praise!"

Thus the worship, which begins on earth, forms but the prelude to our eternal occupation. May it be ours to form a right estimate of its tremendous importance and, by God's grace, see to it that much of it rises from our hearts during our lifetime on earth! In this way, we shall not only bring delight to the eternal Godhead, but be in harmony with God's revealed purpose and heaven's occupation.

CHAPTER NINE

III. Our Authority For Worship.

Having discussed the meaning and importance of worship, let us now occupy ourselves with a consideration of our *authority* for it. By this we mean the source of our information on the subject. How are we to know whom, when, how, where and when to worship? The answer to all these questions is found in *the word of God.* Just as the way of salvation, together with all the other great doctrines of Christianity, must have their foundation, explanation and final authorization in the holy Scriptures, so also in this vital matter of the believers' worship.

It will surely be admitted that we are living in days of confusion regarding this subject of worship. Christendom has become a babel of conflicting voices. Various rival religious organizations, all claiming to be right, are seeking, with a great deal of zealous and costly propaganda, to gain adherents to their particular beliefs.

In view of this confused state of affairs, how is the believer to know what God's desire is for him in regard to worship? Isaiah's words, in view of a somewhat similar situation, should come with force to the soul of every true Christian: "To the law and to the testimony: if they speak not according to this word, it is because there is no light in them" (Isa. 8:19-20). The word of God, and *this alone,* must be the *sole court of appeal* on all matters regarding any doctrine. Only a "thus saith the Lord" should carry conviction with the believer.

We shall first consider some false *conceptions* of worship. Secondly, we shall then examine some wrong *estimates* of it. Finally, we shall seek to show the all sufficiency and authority of holy writ in regard to the matter of our worship.

1. Some false conceptions of worship.

The present confusion in Christendom can be traced to many causes. We shall name and examine four of these. (1) Human tradition. (2) Man-made expediency. (3) The voice of the Church. (4) The dictates of one's own conscience. Let us look at these in the order named.

(1) Human tradition.
(Matt. 15:6-9; Mark 7:9-13).

It is a well known fact that history has a habit of repeating itself. We have already looked into Israel's history and discovered that it is God's picture book for the instruction of each Christian, for we are told: "Whatsoever things were written aforetime, were written for our learning, that we, through patience and comfort of the Scriptures, might have hope" (Rom. 15:4). One of the purposes for which God chose Israel as a nation was that they might be both the recipients, guardians and witnesses of the Divinely-inspired revelation of His word, as found in the holy Scriptures.

At the time Christ came to earth the authority of the Scriptures, as the sole court of appeal, had been largely superceded by an imposing array of Jewish traditions. These, in some cases, were actually allowed to take precedence, as an authority, over the word of God. These humanly-devised traditions, compiled over a long period of years by their learned teachers, or Rabbis, were gathered together in a book called "The Talmud." This, in turn, was in two main sections, the "Mishna," or the "Oral Doctrine," and the "Gemara," or the "Matter that is learned." Little by little, as time went on, this collection of writings and interpretations increased both in size and prestige, until it came to be accepted by the Jews as being of equal authority with the Scriptures; and, in some cases was actually allowed to supercede them.

This was the situation Christ faced, and which He roundly condemned, in the plainest of terms, before the Jewish leaders of His day. An instance of this is found in Mark 7: 9-13. Christ, addressing the scribes and Pharisees said: "Full well ye reject the commandment of God, that ye may keep your own tradition. For Moses said: 'Honor thy father and mother, and whoso curseth father or mother, let him die the death.' But ye say: 'If a man shall say to his father or mother: It is corban (or a gift) . . . he shall be free.' And ye suffer him no more to do ought for his father and mother; making the word of God of none effect through your traditions, which ye have delivered: and many such like things ye do."

This instance was but one of many such. This is the situation. Here was a son whose parents were badly in need of his money for their support. The law of God commanded this son to honor his parents, and thus supply their need with a gift of money. In order to avoid his plain responsibility in this matter, this son took the money, which should have been used to provide for his parents, and designated it as "Corban," or a gift to the temple. The religious leaders of the Jews excused this deliberate violation of the direct command of God, because their tradition affirmed such an act was permissible. Christ's significant words in this connection demand our most serious consideration: "Howbeit in vain do they worship Me, teaching for doctrines the commandments of men" (Mark 7: 7; Matt. 15: 9).

The most scathing words of fiery denunciation that ever fell from the lips of the Son of God were directed against the religious leaders of Israel. In Matt. 23, He used the phrase: "Woe unto you," eight times and con-

cluded: "Ye serpents, ye generation of vipers, how shall
ye escape the damnation of hell?" Christ's appeal was
always to the Scriptures. When a lawyer asked him:
"Master, what shall I do to inherit eternal life?" Christ
answered him: "What is written in the law? How read-
est thou?" (Luke 10:25-26). He affirmed again that:
"the Scripture cannot be broken." (John 10:35). In His
sermon on the mount He said: "Think not that I am come
to destroy the law, or the prophets: I am not come to destroy, but to fulfil" (or fill full) (Matt. 5:17). Christ
"magnified the law" in His life and, by fulfilling it, "made
it honorable." (Isa. 42:21). He fulfilled, to the minutest
detail, all its prophecies regarding His first advent, was
obedient to all its precepts, quoted it constantly and loved
it with all His heart. He never allowed the traditions
of men any place whatever in His life.

Now let us see how history has repeated itself. As in
Christ's day, tradition had been allowed to supercede the
word of God as to the sole and final authority in Israel;
so today, in Christendom, the same thing, in large measure, has been allowed to take place. By Christendom we
mean the sum total of all those religious systems and organizations that name the name of Christ, whether they be
good, bad or indifferent. We must ever distinguish between Christendom and Christianity. The former centers
itself with a system of belief; the latter is centered in a
Person, the Son of God.

There is one great religious system that has practically
substituted the Breviary for the Bible, and its clergy
would gladly suppress, for obvious reasons, the publica-
tion, reading and study of the Bible by the so called
"laity." Even Protestantism has also been adversely affected by tradition. In some of its denominations the
prayer book, with its order of service, is more often seen
and used than the Bible. By some, the voluminous writ-

ings of the early fathers, who lived immediately after the
apostles, are given almost equal authority with the word
of God. It did not take long, in those post-apostolic days,
for a *mode of procedure* to develop into a *custom*. This,
in turn, became a *tradition* until, gradually, it was allowed
to supercede the word of God as the sole basis of authority for both doctrine and life.

Through the years, customs, rules and regulations
were introduced, that lost nothing in the repeating and
the observing, until the dark mists of traditionalism descended upon the Church and obscured the shining light
of holy Scripture. In view of this condition of affairs, our
Lord's words, addressed to Israel, should come with peculiar emphasis to every believer's heart: "In *vain do they
worship Me*, teaching for doctrines the commandments of
men." As early as A. D. 107, one of these early fathers
named Ignatius wrote: "Let us take heed that we do not
set ourselves against the bishop . . . It is evident that we
ought to look upon the bishop, even as we do upon the
Lord Himself." (Epistle to Ephesus). This was the danger
that Paul foresaw and concerning which he wrote to the
Corinthian assembly: "I fear, lest by any means, as the
serpent beguiled Eve through his subtlety, so your minds
should be corrupted from the *simplicity* that is in Christ"
(II Cor. 11:3). A certain bishop, when speaking to a believer about the many innovations which had been introduced into the ritual of his denomination said: "This is all
part of the *development* of the church since New Testament times." The believer replied: "We call it by a different name: *departure!*"

The tendency of men's traditions is to transform what
was originally a simple scriptural ordinance into a com-
plicated and ornate ritual, until its primary purpose is
completely lost sight of in a host of innovations the Bible

knows nothing at all about. Once the thin end of the
wedge of tradition is allowed to enter, there is practically
no limit to the extent it can develop until, at last, the tradition usurps the place of the Divinely-inspired Scriptures
as the believer's authority and final court of appeal.

The beautiful simplicity of the Lord's supper has degenerated, through the traditions of men, into the sacrifice of the mass. What Christ intended to be a simple
and beautiful memorial of Himself, has become so en-
crusted with the accretions of traditionalism, that its original purpose is lost sight of entirely. The old fable of the
camel and the Arab's tent is well known. We can surely
learn from this that once the camel of tradition is allowed
to put its nose into the tent of Scriptural authority, it will
soon occupy the whole tent and leave no place for the
word of God!

Bunyan, in his allegory: "The Holy War," illustrates
this point well. When Shaddai's (God's) army under
Captain Boanerges, first attacked the rebellious city of
Mansoul, three soldiers of this army (who had volun-
teered while the army was en route) were captured. Their
names were Mr. Tradition, Mr. Human-Invention and Mr.
Human-Wisdom. On being brought before Diabolus (the
Devil), they were asked whether they would serve him,
or be killed. They replied: "We live not so much by the
sense of right, as by the fortunes of war. If you will give
us our wages, we will serve you as we once served Shaddai." Accordingly, they were enlisted in Diabolus' army,
and materially helped Mansoul to continue its rebellion
against Shaddai!

The application is clear. Before the word of God was
given in writing, tradition served the useful purpose of
orally handing down, from father to son, the account of
creation, the fall, the deluge, etc. Once the Divinely in-

spired and authoritative written word of God came into existence, tradition was no longer necessary. But alas, the Devil has now enlisted tradition on his side, not only to blind people to the truth of Scripture, but to substitute it for the word of God itself.

However scripturally a company of believers may seek to assemble themselves together, they will need to be continually on the alert, lest long established modes of procedure, gradually come to be looked upon as though they had scriptural authority for their existence. No assembly of Christians is immune from this danger. The confusion which developed in Israel and, later on, in Christendom because of tradition, began by a *gradual* process. Because it was allowed to continue unchecked, it gathered momentum with the years, until the apostasy set in. We can see its evil fruit today in *modernism* on one hand and *sacerdotalism* on the other. Paul's word to the saints in Colosse are pertinent in this connection: "Beware, lest any man spoil you through philosophy and vain deceit, *after the tradition of men,* after the rudiments of the world, and not after Christ" (Col. 2:8).

(2) Man-made Expediency.
(II Sam. 6:1-8; Num. 4:15; 7:9).

Another false concept of worship is due to this. Instead of following the Divine directions regarding worship, as found in the Scriptures, men imagine themselves to be wiser than the word of God, and seek to introduce various embellishments, which they fondly imagine are an improvement on the Divine pattern.

Such an instance is that which is recorded in II Sam. 6:1-8. David had the laudable desire of bringing the ark of God from the house of Abinadab, in Gibeah, to a place he had prepared for it in Jerusalem. The ark, as we have already seen, was the central object connected with Israel's worship, for it was the place where God had declared He would meet and commune with His redeemed people. Thus it stood for God's presence in the midst of Israel.

Instead of consulting the Scriptures, which gave explicit instructions as to how the ark should be moved from one place to another, David ignored God's directions, and followed the example set by the Philistines some time before, when they sent back the ark to Israel. (See I Sam. 6:1-12). Had he searched the word of God, he would have discovered that plain directions had been given therein as to how the ark should be moved. God had indicated that it was to be borne on the shoulders of the Levites, and was not to be touched by any save the sons of Aaron, the priests. (See Num. 4:15; cp. 7:9). The resultant disaster awakened David to his folly. It was not until three months later that David followed the Divine directions as to how the ark should be moved. It was then safely carried to the place he had prepared for it, with great rejoicing. (See II Sam. 6:11-15).

We must be careful, of course, not to push this illustration of David's resort to human expediency beyond its proper limits. Articles frequently appear in religious magazines in which the writers solemnly assert that anything introduced into an assembly's activities in the gospel that does not have a definite "thus saith the Lord" for it, is on the same plane as the new cart on which David placed the ark! For instance, it has often been asserted that the use of a musical instrument to give the correct pitch, tune and time to a gospel hymn, is on a par with David's act in putting the ark on a new cart! It is hardly necessary to point out that this is sheer nonsense. David, by his act, disobeyed a *distinct* and *definite* "thus saith the Lord;" but we have no Scripture, either pro or con, regarding the use of a musical instrument.

It will be a great help, in deciding any matters of this kind, if we keep three terms distinct in our minds: the *scriptural*, the *unscriptural*, and the *non-scriptural*. By *"scriptural"* we mean that which has a definite "thus saith the Lord" for it. Under this heading would come the preaching of the gospel; the gathering together of believers in assembly fellowship, in the name of the Lord Jesus, etc. By *"unscriptural,"* we mean that which the word of God distinctly prohibits and condemns. Under this classificiation would come the unequal yoke of a believer with an unbeliever, etc. By *"non-scriptural"* we mean that for which we have no definite scriptural authority, but *which does not violate any principle laid down in the word of God*. Under this heading would come the use of a worship hymn book, a gospel hymn book, a gospel chapel, gospel tracts, Sunday Schools, a musical instrument, the use of lantern slides, flannelgraph, object talks, the use of Bible charts, correspondence courses, to give believers a better knowledge of the word of God, Bible Schools, Bible conferences, etc. Much time, paper, energy, tempers and money would have been saved, if this simple distinction had been kept in mind. Often such discussions go to prove the truth expressed by a well known Bible teacher who once remarked: "It is possible, on certain occasions, for believers to appear to be most *solemn* when, in reality, they are merely being most *silly!"*

Let us now return to this act of David, in which he mimicked the worldly-wise strategy of the Philistines, the enemy of God's people, instead of consulting the Scriptures to see what God had to say on the subject. By this introduction of human expediency, God's judgment fell on Uzzah, the worship of God's people was hindered, and David himself was filled with fear. No worship ascended

from the heart of David that day. Instead, there was a
sense of distance from God and a dread of God, for we
read: "And David was afraid of the Lord that day." (II
Sam. 6:9). Not only so, but by this resort to human expediency, God was robbed of His portion from His people,
and His holy word slighted. It was a most unprofitable
business, from every point of view.

What a welcome change is recorded three months later!
David had learned his lesson. He now allowed the *word*
of the Lord to be his guide in his *worship* of the Lord! We
are told: "David, and all the house of Israel, brought up
the ark of the Lord with shouting, and with the sound of
the trumpet . . . And they brought in the ark of the Lord,
and set in his place, in the midst of the tabernacle that
David had pitched for it, and David offered burnt offerings and peace offerings before the Lord." (II Sam. 6:12-
19). Not only so, but David wrote, by Divine inspiration,
a beautiful Psalm to be sung on this occasion in which
these words occur: "Give unto the Lord the glory due
unto His name: bring an offering, and come before Him:
worship the Lord in the beauty of holiness" (I Chron. 16:
29; See also Psalm 96).

We have discussed the effect of Jewish tradition in Israel. In this instance of human expediency, history has
again repeated itself in Christendom. The simple and
scriptural form of assembly gatherings, as pictured in
the Acts and the Epistles, has largely given place, because
of its resort to human expediency, to complex and highly
organized systems of religious belief, all claiming to be
Christian in their composition. It is difficult, in many of
these systems, to *recognize any traces of the scriptural*
pattern revealed in the New Testament. As a direct consequence, there is a dearth of spiritual life which, in turn,
is evidenced by a great lack of real spiritual worship.

This condition of affairs, as in the case of tradition, was not the work of a moment—error seldom is—but was the result of a gradual accumulation of various human expediencies over a considerable period of years, beginning in the early part of the second century. It would be well if every Christian would make himself acquainted with these facts by reading a good book on "Church History." Broadbent's "The Pilgrim Church," would be a good start in this direction.

The first of these departures from the word of God, was the formation of a special caste amongst Christians, who were designated "the clergy." Gradually, those believers who had been gifted by the Lord to either preach, teach, or guide, began to assume a superior air, and claim for themselves a special position, or caste, with exclusive privileges distinct from the rest of the believers. This, in turn, resulted in rivalry amongst this special caste, as each sought to gain the place of chief leader. Ultimately, elections were held, at which the most popular of this class was chosen by a show of hands. He was then formally ordained and placed in charge of the assembly and became "the clergyman." There were not wanting those who opposed this departure from the Divine pattern, but gradually this opposition gave way to toleration and, finally, this new order came to be accepted by the various assemblies of believers.

Thus the scriptural truth of the priesthood of all believers was substituted for the mediation and rule of the clergy. (I Peter 2:5-10; Rev. 1:5-6). The gifts of Christ to the members of His body for their mutual edification were now limited, in their expression in the assembly, to one man. (I Cor. 12:1-14; 40). In this way, the evil of professionalism was introduced into the church of God, and what havoc it has wrought through the centuries which have followed! By this distinct departure from God's word, the way was opened for still more innovations, by which to strengthen the hold of the "clergy" over the "laity."

In due course came the rise of the episcopacy, or the rule of *one* bishop over an assembly. Later, this was extended to the rule of the bishop over a *number* of assemblies in a district, and thus originated the "diocesan bishop." Rivalry arose amongst these diocesan bishops until finally, around the fourth century, the bishop of Constantinople gave himself the title of "universal bishop" over all the churches on earth! Thus we see that David's innovation in putting the ark on a new cart has not lacked for imitators. His act is a typical example of what has happened in Christendom, the evils of which we can see with our own eyes.

Another invention of human expediency, which has contributed much to the spiritual dearth, and consequent lack of worship, is the false theory that infants, when sprinkled with a few drops of water by a clergyman, are then regenerated by the Holy Spirit, and thus made "children of God, and members of the body of Christ!" This, of course, is a flat denial of the scriptural teaching that baptism, by immersion, is only for those who have already been born again through their belief in the gospel message and acceptance of Christ as their personal Savior. (Eph. 1: 13; Mark 16: 16; Matt. 28: 19-20; Acts 10: 47; 18: 8, etc.).

The effect of such a departure from the plain teaching of Scripture is the existence of a vast army of people, who call themselves Christians, but who know nothing whatever of the regenerating power of the Spirit of God in their lives. Lacking spiritual life, they are therefore "dead in their trespasses and sins." While in this condition, they are both unable to understand or impart spiritual truth, to please God, or to render to Him the worship that is His due. As in the case of David's act of putting the ark on a new cart, this evil doctrine of "baptismal regeneration," has resulted in a spiritual tragedy of the worst description.

We could cite many other instances of such innovations introduced through man-made expediency, but these two should suffice. One has only to go to certain so-called "places of worship" to see the baneful and tragic effects of such inventions and additions to the pristine glory that once marked the scriptural simplicity of the assemblies of the saints.

One may well ask when attending such a meeting for "public worship:" "Whence came all these gaudy vestments; these tinkling bells; these burning candles; this smoking incense; these crosses; this sanctuary, reserved only for the clergy; this bloodless altar; this ornate ritual, with the sing-song intonation of its ready-made prayers, and ordered responses of the congregation; and this unholy distinction between clergy and laity? By what authority have all these things been introduced? Have they a Divine origin and a scriptural foundation?" The answer is an emphatic negative. They are the results of man-made expediency, which has substituted the inventions of men for the scriptural and spiritual worship which God's word so clearly enjoins.

CHAPTER TEN

Our Authority For Worship

(Continued)

(3) The Voice of the Church.

Still another of these false concepts of worship is due to the fact that the decrees of Church councils have been given equal authority, and even precedence over the word of God as the sole authority for worship. Many such Church councils have been convened over the years since the Church was formed. The decisions, at which these councils arrived, have been issued in the form of creeds and decrees that all must receive, hold and maintain, upon pain of excommunication. Not only the Roman Catholic Church, but also some Protestant denominations, insist on the authority of the church, as represented by a central governing body, such as a synod to decide, by a majority vote, their church policy. We need hardly say that such a procedure is not according to the principles laid down in holy Scripture.

The objection may be raised: "What about Matt. 16:19, where Christ said to Peter: 'Whatsoever thou shalt bind on earth, shall be bound in heaven, and whatsoever thou shalt loose on earth, shall be loosed in heaven.' Does not this give authority for the church, both to make and enforce its decrees?" Dr. C. B. Williams, in his excellent translation of the New Testament, which emphasizes the tenses of the Greek verb, renders this passage thus: "Whatsoever you forbid on earth, *must be what is already forbidden in heaven,*" etc. Heaven is not in the business of putting its seal of approval on every foolish and wicked decision made by man, or any company of men on earth.

The other Scripture which is often used to bolster the claim of the authority of the church to issue decrees is Matt. 18:17. The words of our Lord are: "If he neglect to *hear the church,* let him be unto thee as a heathen man," etc. The context of these words will be quite sufficient to show that no such thing as the church having authority to issue decrees is taught. The matter in question here is purely a personal trespass of one Christian against another, and the mode of procedure he should adopt to effect a reconciliation with his brother. It has been well said that "text, without context, is a pretext!"

We have only to turn to the Bible to confirm this fact. In the concluding book of the Divine revelation, seven letters are addressed to seven distinct churches, each of which was actually existent at that time. It is not without the deepest significance that each letter contains the same phrase. Let us mark it carefully and allow its truth to grip our hearts: "He that hath an *ear,* let him hear *what the Spirit saith* unto the churches." (See Rev. 2:7, 11, 17, 29; 3:6, 13, 22). Here then, is our sole authority for worship, and for every other form of assembly or Christian activity. It is not what this *Council,* or that *synod* decrees; but only what the *Spirit* says that is authoritative for each assembly of believers, and each believer in that assembly. We have, in the completed word of God, *all that the Spirit has said to the churches,* and we need no other authority than this.

The Lord has not left His Church at the mercy and caprice of councils and synods of men, however sincere, or well versed in theology they may be. We read: "All *Scripture* is given by inspiration of God, and is profitable for doctrine, for reproof, for correction, for instruction in righteousness, that the man of God may be perfect ,thoroughly furnished unto all good works" (II Tim. 3:16). In view of this, we say: "Away with your councils, synods, decrees, bulls, prescribed order of service, prayer books and books of discipline. We need them not, for we have, in the Divinely inspired word of God, what "the *Spirit* saith unto the Churches," and this is enough to fully furnish the assemblies of God's people as a whole and each man of faith in particular!

The formalism and apostasy in Christendom today is due to the *"voice of the Church,"* being allowed to displace the *"voice of the Spirit."* The "order of public worship" has all been previously arranged. The exact wording of each prayer has been determined for each Sunday throughout the year. The service proceeds with machine-like smoothness, with its ready-made prayers and responses, and the hearer is impressed with what the Prayer Book saith, and not "what the Spirit saith." No provision is made for the spiritual Christian to engage in voluntary and spontaneous worship, as led by the Spirit of God. He must proceed along these cut and dried lines until the service has concluded. These prayers with their beautifully worded generalizations, may have their appeal to the esthetic nature which is in all men; but they do not belong in the realm of the Spirit. We read: "Where the Spirit of the Lord is, there is liberty" (II Cor. 3:17).

The New Testament knows nothing of an "order of public worship." The Spirit of God delights to lead out the hearts of believers in spontaneous worship as, with holy boldness, they come by "the new and living way," unfettered by "the voice of the church," or the prescribed prayers that someone else has composed for the occasion. This is the spiritual liberty which is the birthright of every regenerated soul, and for which he must be prepared, if necessary, to give his life. The great need today is for more of those who, like the people of Berea, "searched the

Scriptures daily, whether those things were so," and then
acted on what they found therein, to God's glory in worship, and their own blessing through obedience. (Acts
17:11).

(4) The dictates of one's own conscience.

One often hears the expression: "Each person should
be free to worship God, according to the dictates of his
own conscience." While this sounds very well it is, in
reality, an entirely erroneous conception of what God has
to say regarding true worship. What makes it false is the
failure to mention any authority by which the conscience
is to be guided and regulated in its choice. While every
right thinking person will agree that no one should be
forced to worship God according to the dictates of man-
made laws, whether civil or ecclesiastical; yet the conscience, in itself, is no true guide. By the addition of a
few words, this false concept can become a true one. Let
us put it this way: "Each person should be free to worship
God, according to the dictates of his own conscience, *as it
is enlightened by, and obedient to the revelation God has
given in the holy Scriptures.*"

We have only to turn to the Bible to discover what
utter confusion results when every person acts according
to the "dictates of his own conscience." The book of
Judges contains the sad history of Israel after the death
of their great leader, Joshua. It is a most depressing record of Israel's idolatrous backsliding and punishment, followed by their confession and deliverance, monotonously
repeated, time and time again. Read Judges 2:11-23.
The key phrase, in this dismal recital of failure, is found
in the last verse of the book: "In those days there was no
king in Israel: every man did that which was right in his
own eyes." (Jud. 21:25 cp. 17:6). It is hardly necessary

to point out that, under these conditions, little worship ascended to God from the people of Israel.

The conscience can be likened to a correctly constructed sun dial, which can only tell the time *as the rays of the sun are allowed to shine upon it.* It would be possible for a person to go to that sun dial at night and, by means of a flashlight, get it to indicate any time he wanted! The conscience, therefore, must be enlightened by the word of God if it is to be a contributing factor in our worship. An unenlightened conscience will lead a person, as it did Paul, to "do many things contrary to the name of Jesus of Nazareth" (Acts 26:9). Thousands of Christians have suffered martyrdom at the hands of religious men who acted quite sincerely, and "according to the dictates of their own conscience!" The fact that a person is sincere and conscientious, while acting contrary to the revelation of God's word, only makes the consequences more tragic. It is possible to be quite sincere and, at the same time, sincerely mistaken! The head hunters of Borneo can hunt and kill a man quite conscientiously!

God has not left His people with their conscience as their only guide; but He has given them His word, by which they may adjust their consciences. On the wall that surrounds the Royal Observatory at Greenwich is a large twenty-four hour clock which gives the correct time to the world. Visitors who stand before that timepiece invariably take out their watches, and adjust them to the time indicated by the master clock. Let that great master clock represent God's word, and the watch, the conscience. Thus we have a good illustration of the place and purpose of the conscience, as described in the Scriptures. It is a guide, only in so far as it is adjusted to, and governed by the word of God.

It is this false conception of things that motivates the oft-given advice to new converts to: "join the church of your choice," or to indicate, on the dotted line, one's "Church preference." Scripture does not give to any Christian the right to "join the church of his choice," or to "worship God according to the dictates of his conscience." God has given to the believer, in His word, "*all things* that pertain unto life and godliness." Happy is he who rests not until he knows, on the assurance of Divine revelation, that he is where God wants him to be, and that his worship is with a good conscience that has been adjusted to, and is regulated by the holy Scriptures. (II Pet. 1:3-4).

2. Some wrong estimates of worship.

Having pointed out, at considerable length, some false conceptions regarding worship, let us now look at some wrong estimates of it. A false conception always results in a wrong estimate. We shall think of three of these: (1) The materialistic. (2) The religious. (3) The uninstructed believer.

(1) The Materialistic.
(Exod. 5:1-17).

When Pharaoh was approached by Moses with the demand: "Thus saith the Lord God of Israel: Let My people go, that they may hold a feast unto Me in the wilderness;" the reply of this impious king was: "Who is the Lord that I should obey His voice to let Israel go? I know not the Lord, neither will I let Israel go." This is the language of materialism, which stems from enmity to and ignorance of God. Not only did Pharaoh refuse to obey God's voice, but he made the bondage of Israel more bitter by increasing their burdens. He gave as his reason for this cruel treatment: "They be *idle*, therefore they cry, saying: Let us go and sacrifice to our God" (v. 8). Later on he said: "Ye are idle, ye are idle, therefore ye say: 'let us go and do sacrifice to the Lord.' Go therefore now and work!" (vs. 17-18). To this king, the expressed desire of God's people to obey the call and worship their God was simply an excuse to avoid hard work, and was therefore an indication of their *laziness*. He believed their time would be better spent in laboring for him with their hands.

Egypt, in Scripture, is a type of this materialistic world, which seeks to live its life in independence of God and His Son. The unbelieving and rebellious attitude of Pharaoh to God and His people, well illustrates the opinion of the man of the world today. To him, spiritual things and the worship of God mean nothing at all, except perhaps a useless expenditure of energy and expense. In fact it is boldly affirmed by some that: "Religion is the opiate of the people." By "religion" they mean anything that relates to the spiritual, as compared with the physical. The cynic views any spiritual effort in the gospel, or the worship of God's people, as all part of a huge "racket," by means of which money is mulched from a credulous public. Others adopt the indifferent, "what-do-I-care" attitude of Gallio, the Roman judge. Scripture records of him that he "cared for none of those things" (Acts 18:17).

One can imagine what a worldling, who was accidentally present at a worship meeting, would afterwards report of his impressions to his ungodly friends. He would say: "Why, those people who met inside that building were nothing but a lot of day dreamers! They sat around a table, with their eyes closed most of the time. Every now and then someone would rise and pray, and then, after a while, another would give out a hymn, and thus they wasted a whole hour doing nothing!"

The reason for such a wrong estimate of worship is easy to understand, for we read: "The natural man receiveth not the things of the Spirit of God; for they are foolishness unto him; neither can he know them, because they are spiritually discerned" (I Cor. 2:14). The mind of man, by nature, is "enmity against God." He neither desires, nor can he possibly comprehend spiritual realities. Least of all can he appreciate the tremendous importance and value of the worship of God's people.

(2) The religious.

"This I confess unto thee, that after the way which they call *heresy,* so worship I the God of my fathers, believing all things which are written in the law, and in the prophets" (Acts 24:14). These words were spoken by Paul to Felix in answer to the false charge brought against him by Tertullus. Paul was charged with being: "A pestilent fellow, and a mover of sedition among all the Jews throughout the world, and a ring-leader of the sect of the Nazarenes" (v. 5). From this we learn that, in Paul's day, the estimate placed by the Jewish religionists on what was undoubtedly the true worship of God, was "heresy!" To their prejudiced and religion-blinded eyes, Paul was a heretic. They had already formed their opinion of what constituted "worship;" and because Paul ran counter to their warped and totally erroneous ideas, they designated him a "heretic." With this wrong conception of Scripture, they persecuted him and would gladly have taken his life.

There is no form of persecution quite so bitter and vindictive as that which comes from religious people. Countless thousands of noble, true-hearted, spiritual, and devoted Christians, have had to seal their testimonies with their own blood, because they: "Dared to have a purpose firm and dared to make it known." Let not the believer, who has learned what true worship is, and has acted on what he has learned, be unduly surprised if he is called a "heretic," not only by a materialistic world, but by people who are sincerely and intensely zealous for their own particular religion!

There is actually a religious system in the world today which designates as "heretics" all who refuse to subscribe to its creeds, or bow to its decisions, or join its ranks. In the early days of Christianity, it was *pagan* Rome that persecuted Christians. In the middle ages, it was *religious* Rome that did the same thing! This persecution of the spiritual by the religious is as old as Cain's hatred and persecution of Abel. Cain was a religious man, for he brought an offering unto the Lord; but he refused to come to God in the way God had plainly revealed both to him and his brother. Cain's offering was not the worship of a *false god*, but the *false worship* of the true God. It was not long after God had rejected his offering that Cain stained his hands with the innocent blood of his righteous brother. (Gen. 4:1-15; I John 3:12; Jude 11; Heb. 11:4).

The Christian who seeks, at all costs, to worship God in the Spirit, and in accordance with the truth found in the Scriptures, may find it necessary to sever his connections with the religious system, or denomination, with which he was previously identified. Usually these systems do not tolerate any departure from their organized order, traditions, rituals and commandments of men. This severance of his association with them will bring upon him the wrath of his one-time religious associates. They will not hesitate to revile him and stigmatize him as "a heretic." He will be accused of becoming "a traitor to the faith of his fathers," and have to suffer a measure of ignominy, contempt and persecution; but the price is well worth paying. Our Lord said: "Blessed are ye, when men shall revile you, and persecute you and shall say all manner of evil against you falsely for My sake" (Matt. 5:11). All the popularity, position, power and pelf of this world can never compensate a believer for his failure to obey God's word in this most important matter of worship.

(3) The Uninstructed Believer.
(Matt. 26:6-13)

We have already touched on this incident of Mary's act of devotion. We refer to it again only to draw particular attention to the entirely wrong estimate that even the disciples of Christ placed on this beautiful act of worship which they had witnessed. Their comment was: "To what purpose is this *waste?*" They argued that this costly perfume should have been sold, and the money devoted to a more useful and worthwhile purpose, such as a gift to the poor! They concluded that this exquisite perfume had been merely *wasted* on Christ! Our Lord's comment on the deed has forever immortalized this woman. He said of her: "She hath wrought a good work upon Me . . . Verily I say unto you: wheresoever this gospel shall be preached in the whole world, there shall also this, that this woman hath done, be told for a memorial of her" (vs. 10, 13).

From this incident we can gather that often true Christians do not realize the tremendous importance and priceless value of worship. Many believers have become so occupied with their service for the Lord, that they fail to appreciate the attitude of their fellow believers who insist on the supreme importance of worship, and deliberately take the time and effort to give worship its rightful place in an assembly of the Lord's people. They are inclined to be somewhat critical of those Christians who studiously take time to gather, in scriptural simplicity, to remember the Lord Jesus each Lord's day in the breaking of the bread and the drinking of the cup. They argue that the time and effort which such a worship meeting entails might, with greater advantage, be used either in preaching the gospel to the unsaved, or by listening to a sermon by some gifted teacher of the Word, or by attending and participating in a prearranged service under the guidance of an ordained clergyman, who would see to it that everything ran smoothly from the opening hymn to the benediction.

The reply to such a criticism is first, that we cannot improve on the Scriptural pattern, and second, that the true value of the self-sacrificial worship of those who love the Lord Jesus is rightly estimated by the Savior Himself. It need hardly be said that those who have seen these precious truths for themselves from the word of God should seek, in a humble, loving and gracious manner, to pass them on to their fellow-believers. They should emulate the example of Aquilla and Priscilla. This godly couple saw that Apollos needed fuller instruction in God's word, so they took him aside, and privately expounded unto him the way of God more perfectly" (Acts 18:26).

CHAPTER ELEVEN

Our Authority For Worship

(Continued)

3. The Scriptures alone must be our authority in worship.

Having considered some of the false conceptions of worship, and examined some wrong estimates of it; we now come to a consideration of what constitutes the believer's sole authority regarding worship. This can be stated in three words: *the holy Scriptures.* Just as the word of God alone, without any additions and substractions, is our only authority for the way of salvation and its assurance; so, in every matter pertaining to doctrine, life and godliness, it must also be the sole and final court of appeal.

The need for this will surely be obvious to every right thinking individual. When a person receives an invitation to be presented to a king, or the head of a nation, he immediately consults the regulations governing such receptions in order to conform to the rules of court etiquette. He would be foolish indeed who would argue: "I'll go just when I wish, dress as I please and behave exactly as I want. If the king doesn't like it, he can lump it. I've got my own ideas of how these affairs should be run!" Such a person would soon find himself in disfavor with the king, and quickly conducted outside the palace!

One's conduct in society is governed largely by certain established customs which have been collected and recorded in books of etiquette. Emily Post is the recognized authority on such matters in the U. S. A. All those who desire to succeed in the social world, not only secure, but "read, mark and inwardly digest" all this authoritative information, by which to regulate their social behavior in any given circumstance. One is saved much embarrassment by so doing. Even games must be played accordingly to definite rules, and the authority most quoted is "Hoyle." All disputed matters regarding the playing of certain games are referred to this famous authority. The saying: "It is according to Hoyle," is the final word on any mooted question.

Since certain established rules and regulations are necessary to govern our behavior in the presence of a high dignitary, or our fellow men; what shall be said regarding the transcendingly more important matter of our approach to the great God of the universe, and our behavior in His presence? It is essential that there be a recognized authority on this matter, and God has supplied this need in the Divinely-inspired revelation He has given to us in the Bible. We have not been left to our own devices in this regard, but we possess, in the Scriptures, an authoritative source of information regarding this vitally important question.

(1) As seen in the Old Testament.

God's instructions in the Old Testament regarding the erection of the Tabernacle, with which the worship of Israel was closely identified, were given in particular detail to Moses. He was enjoined many times to take great care that all things should be done "according to the pattern" God had given him. (Exod. 25:9, 40; 26:30; 27:8; Heb. 8:5). The last chapter of Exodus records how completely Moses followed these instructions in the design and erection of the tabernacle. Seven times over the phrase is repeated that he did this or that, "as the Lord commanded Moses." (See vs. 19, 22, 23, 25, 27, 29, 32). It is not surprising, therefore, that we read: "Then a cloud covered the tent of the congregation, and the glory of the Lord filled the tabernacle." (v. 34). It was God's response to a work that had been done according to His directions.

(2) As seen in the New Testament.

When we turn to the pages of the New Testament we discover that worship is no longer connected with a tabernacle, or a temple made by human hands. The Aaronic priesthood, with all its elaborate ritual, came to an end at the sacrifice of Christ. By that one sacrifice, which He offered "once and for all," the question of sin has been settled before a holy God. Every sinner, who now rests in Christ's finished work, receives Him by faith as his own Savior, and owns Him as Lord, is not only saved eternally, but is constituted a priest unto God, with the privilege of coming into His presence to worship. Christ is now the believer's great high Priest and, through Him, each believer may come boldly into the presence of God, and offer to Him the sacrifice of his heart's appreciation in praise and worship. (See Heb. 9:10; 13:15; I Pet. 2:5).

We shall look in vain, in the New Testament Scriptures, for any rules and regulations governing an "order of service" for any meeting of saints for worship. Instead of hard and fast rules, we find certain broad principles laid down, to which we shall do well to take heed and follow as a pattern. As one reads and rereads the pages of the Acts and the Epistles, he will be impressed with certain well defined features which characterized the early assemblies of Christians as, led by the Spirit, they sought to gather in the name of the Lord Jesus in assembly, or church fellowship.

These assemblies, which began as a result of God's blessing on the preaching of the apostles and others, multiplied in a remarkable way, as described in the book of the Acts of the Apostles. In due course letters, penned by Divine inspiration, were addressed to these various companies of Christians. From these epistles we may also learn much of the order that obtained in these assemblies, and the principles that characterized them. Some of these letters were written to correct certain abuses that obtained; as, for instance, the epistles to the Corinthians and the Galatians. Others were written for encouragement, and still others for establishment in doctrine. Thus we have, in the New Testament, all we need in the way of guidance for the worship and service of God's people today.

Now let us consider, very briefly, some of these distinguishing features which marked these New Testament assemblies of regenerated believers, remembering that this is the Divine pattern which has been left for us to follow.

(a) *These assemblies were composed of companies of believers where Christ was acknowledged as Lord.* (I Cor. 1:2).

Christ was the gathering Center. They met in His name alone. (Matt. 18:20). They acknowledged His supreme Headship, not only of the Church as a whole, but of each local assembly of believers. (Rev. 1:12, 13, 20; Eph. 1:22-23). There was no uncertainty in people's minds, in that day, as to who was the Head of the Church. There was no theologically-trained and humanly-ordained "clergyman" to officiate at the Lord's supper, and "administer the sacraments" and, apart from whose presence, the Lord's supper could not be celebrated. Christ was the Host at His own supper and all the believers His privileged guests.

(b) *Each local assembly, wherever it met, was autonomous.* That is to say, each assembly was responsible directly to the Lord alone for its existence, order and discipline. Scripture contemplates no such thing as amalgamations, or combinations of assemblies, with one central governing body, such as is seen in Christendom today. No assembly interfered in the affairs of another assembly, but *each was a distinct unity.* Yet, though outwardly distinct, these assemblies were united to each other by the strong invisible bond of a common loyalty to Christ and His word.

(c) *Each believer in an assembly was recognized as a priest unto God,* with liberty to exercise this priesthood, as led by the Spirit, the brethren audibly and the sisters inaudibly. (I Cor. 14:34; I Pet. 2:9; Rev. 1:6). There is no mention whatever of any prearranged program which was followed in their worship meetings. Nothing is said about appropriate prayers composed and selected by a specially appointed committee and recited during the service. There was a spontaneity about their meetings. Paul could say: "When ye come together, every one of you hath a psalm, hath a doctrine, hath a tongue, hath a revelation. Let all things be done to edifying" (I Cor. 14:26). No distinction is even contemplated between so-called "clergy" and "laity." It did not exist in those days. All believers occupied the same position as being "priests unto God."

(d) *Each assembly recognized and gave liberty for the exercise and development of each spiritual gift,* bestowed by the Lord upon the members of His body (Eph. 4:12; I Cor. 12:8-11; 14:24). These gifts were not confined, in those days, to one man called "the minister." There was a *multiplicity of gifts* which, when exercised under the guidance and power of the Spirit, were used of God to build up the whole assembly and supply all its spiritual needs.

(e) *Each assembly had room for all the word of God.* No assembly "specialized" in a certain truth at the expense or the exclusion of other truths. Their motto was: "All the truth of God for all the people of God." There were no "non essentials," when it came to Divine revelation. (Acts 20:32; II Tim. 3:16-17).

(f) *These assemblies were not divided into a number of different denominations,* as we see in Christendom today. There was no possibility, in those days for a convert to be beseiged by various denominations, all pressing their claims for his church membership, allegiance and support. There was only one membership of the one body, and fellowship was enjoyed with every member of that body. Each person, when saved, associated himself with an assembly of believers in the particular place or district where he lived. Paul, by the Spirit, roundly condemned the rise of factions and parties in the Corinthian assembly. See I Cor. 1:10-15; 3:1-10. The New Testament contemplates neither denominationalism, nor *inter-*denominationalism, but affirms the great truth of *unde-nominationalism.*

(g) *Each assembly was composed of believers only,* or, at least, only those who had professed to believe on the Son of God. These New Testament assemblies did not consist of a mixture of saved and unsaved, as is seen in Christendom today. (Acts 5:13). The letters sent to these churches were addressed to those who were "in Christ Jesus." (Rom. 1:7; I Cor. 1:2; II Cor. 1:1; Eph. 1:1; Phil. 1:1, etc.).

(h) *These assemblies gladly welcomed to their fellowship* all Christians who were sound in doctrine, moral in life, or in good standing with the assembly from whence they came. They did not create artificial "tests of fellowship," but received one another "to the glory of God" (Rom. 15:7). There were no "back seats" for the "dear brother, or sister in Christ," who was "not in fellowship" with them! It was recognized that the Lord's supper was for the Lord's people, and that *life* in Christ, and not *light* on the Scriptures was the essential basis for fellowship (I John 1:3).

(i) *These assemblies were places where godly discipline could be maintained.* It was the disorders in the Corinthian assembly that brought forth Paul's letter of rebuke, in which is contained the well known exhortation: "Let all things be done decently and in order" (I Cor. 14:40). Overt sin must be judged and dealt with in the assembly, if it is to be the holy temple God intends it to be. (I Cor. 3:16-17; 5:1-6).

Thus, as has been before stated, the *worship* of the Lord must be guided by the *word* of the Lord. The holy Scriptures must be read, meditated in and obeyed implicitly, if both the individual believer, or an assembly of believers, is to offer worship that is acceptable to God and the Lord Jesus Christ. Each Christian is responsible to God to "search the Scriptures" for himself, and to "study to show himself approved unto God" in this matter of worship, as also in every other department of his Christian life. (II Tim. 2:15). His motto should be that of a great man of God who said: "Apply thyself wholly to the Scriptures, and apply the Scriptures wholly to thyself."

Chapter Twelve

IV. The Object of Worship.

Having discussed the meaning, importance and authority of worship; let us now consider the vital matter of the *Object* of worship, or whom should we worship? Scripture gives no uncertain answer to this question: "Thou shalt worship the Lord thy God;" "He is thy Lord, worship thou Him" (Luke 4:8; Ps. 45:11). The object of the believer's worship is the triune and eternal Godhead. He is described as being: "Eternal, immortal, invisible, the only wise God, to Whom be honor and glory for ever and ever" (I Tim. 1:17).

Though the actual word, "Trinity," is not found in the Scriptures, yet the truth of the doctrine of the tri-unity of the Godhead is clearly evident as one opens the pages of the Bible. The eternal Godhead is revealed as consisting of three Persons, each equal and eternal with each Other: the Father, the Son and the Holy Spirit. Each Person of the Godhead possesses a distinct Personality, as is seen by the intelligence, emotions and will, which Each evidences; yet these three are but One in *essence*. There are not three Gods, but one Godhead, revealed in three Persons. This tremendous truth is utterly beyond our finite comprehension, but not beyond our apprehension, for it is plainly declared in the word of God.

This fact of the tri-unity of the Godhead is found in the very opening verse of the Bible where we read: "In the beginning God created the heaven and the earth." The word "God," in the Hebrew is the uni-plural noun, "Elohim." Again, in Gen. 1:26, we read that God said: "Let *us* make man in *our* image, after *our* likeness," etc.

This likeness may have reference to the tripartite nature that man possesses, for he is described as being composed of "spirit, soul and body" (I Thess. 5:23). Thus each human being consists of three parts, yet he is but one individual.

In the New Testament, the truth of the tri-unity of the Godhead is still more clearly indicated. We will quote seven out of the many references to this fact. At the baptism of Christ, the *Holy Spirit* descended upon Him in the shape of a dove, while the voice of the *Father* testified: "This is My *beloved Son*" (Matt. 3:17). When our Lord promised His disciples that He would send the Holy Spirit, He made a double reference to the Trinity, for He said: "But when the *Comforter* is come, whom *I* will send unto you from the *Father,* even the *Spirit* of truth, which proceedeth from the *Father, He* shall testify of *Me*" (John 15:26).

Of Christ's redemptive work, which He accomplished on the cross, we read: "If the blood of bulls and of goats, and the ashes of an heifer sprinkling the unclean sanctifieth to the purifying of the flesh; how much more shall the blood of *Christ,* who through the eternal *Spirit,* offered Himself without spot to *God,* purge your conscience from dead works to serve the living *God?*" (Heb. 9:13-14). The believer's salvation is due to the work of the Trinity, for we read that each Christian is: "Elect, according to the foreknowledge of God, the *Father,* through sanctification of the *Spirit,* unto obedience and sprinkling of the blood of *Jesus Christ*" (I Pet. 1:2). The Trinity is also seen in our approach to God in prayer, for we read: "For through Him, (Christ), we both (Jew and Gentile) have access by one *Spirit* unto the *Father*" (Eph. 2:18).

The Trinity is also prominent in baptism. Christ's commission to His disciples was: "Go ye, therefore, and teach all nations, baptizing them in the name of the *Father,* and of the *Son* and of the *Holy Ghost*" (Matt. 28:19). The three-fold ascription of praise in the first chapter of Ephesians is addressed first, to the *Father* for having blessed us; then to the *Son* for His redemptive work; and third, to the *Holy Spirit* for His sealing of the believer (vs. 6, 12, 14). The beautiful benediction of II Cor. 13:14 will be a fitting conclusion to this short summary: "The grace of the *Lord Jesus Christ,* and the love of *God,* and the communion of the *Holy Ghost* be with you all. Amen.

There are no adequate illustrations of the tri-unity of the Godhead, for it transcends all human comprehension, and defies all analysis. God is unique and has declared: "To whom then will ye liken Me, or shall I be equal? saith the Holy One" (Isa. 40:25). Many attempts have been made to illustrate the Trinity, but all fall far short of conveying the actual fact. Nathaniel Wood, in his excellent book, "The Secret of the Universe," sets out to discover this secret, which he affirms is the triunity of the Godhead. He proceeds to demonstrate that each man is a tri-unity, for he is spirit, soul and body, yet he is but one inlividual. Space is a tri-unity, for it is composed of length, breadth and height, yet space is but one. Time also falls into the same category, for it consists of past, present and future, yet it is but one. His book is commended to all who desire to make a study of this particular truth.

Scripture generally presents the Father as *purposing,* the Son as *executing* the Divine counsel, and the Holy Spirit as *energizing* and applying this purpose, and making it operative in the experience of the believer. The *Father* loved the world, and gave His *Son.* The *Son,* obedient to the Father's will, by the eternal Spirit gave Himself as a substitutionary sacrifice to accomplish our redemption.

The *Holy Spirit* convicts the sinner of his need, leads the soul to trust in Christ and then, on his believing, seals him unto the day of redemption (Eph. 1:13; 4:30). The more one contemplates the greatness, majesty and glory of the triune God: Father, Son and Holy Spirit, the greater he is lost in wonder, praise, adoration and worship. It well becomes us, as our thoughts are occupied with this infinitely holy Being; the eternal, omnipotent, omniscient, omnipresent and immutable God, to stand in awe and humbly bow in the presence of the One whom each Christian has been brought to know as "the God and the Father of our Lord Jesus Christ" (Eph. 1:3).

As we did when discussing our authority for worship, we shall first consider the object of worship negatively and then view it positively. Let us therefore see what God has expressly forbidden us to worship.

1. What we are not to worship:

(1) **Idols.** "Thou shalt have no other gods before Me . . . Thou shalt not make unto thee any graven image . . . Thou shalt not bow down thyself to them, nor serve them" (Exod. 20:3). An idol is anything that a person worships in his heart, and which consequently displaces God as preeminent, or relegates Him to a second place in the consciousness. Idolatry is a deliberate turning away from God. It is not, as is sometimes represented, an attempt on the part of man to reach God. Romans 1:19-23 makes this very clear. Mark the words carefully: "That which may be known of God is manifest to them: for God hath showed it unto them. For the invisible things of Him from the creation of the world are clearly seen, being understood by the things that are made, even His eternal power and Godhead, so that they are without excuse; because that, when they knew God, they glorified Him not as God, neither were thankful; but became vain in their

imaginations, and their foolish heart was darkened. Professing themselves to be wise, they became fools, and changed the glory of the uncorruptible God into an image made like to corruptible man, and to birds and four-footed beasts, and creeping things."

The active agent behind all idolatry is Satan and his host of wicked spirits. We read: "What shall I say then? that the idol is any thing, or that which is offered in sacrifice to idols is any thing? But I say, that the things which the Gentiles sacrifice, they sacrifice to demons, and not to God, and I would not that ye should have fellowship with demons" (I Cor. 10:19-20). Satan's chief purpose is first to rob God of the glory and worship that is due to His name, and then to set up *himself* as the object of worship. All idolatry is therefore Satanic in its origin, and evidences the Devil's desire for worship. His fall was due to this very thing. He was created by God as one of His most beautiful and wise creatures. Moreover he occupied a position of close intimacy with Him. He was not content with this, but his heart was lifted up with pride and he aspired to be like God Himself. He said within his heart: "I will ascend into heaven, I will exalt my throne above the stars of God: I will sit also upon the mount of the congregation, in the sides of the north: I will ascend above the heights of the clouds; I will be like the most high God" (Isa. 14:12-15, c. p. Ezek. 28:11-19). For this act of rebellion, he fell.

Not only is idolatry Satanic in its origin, but it is utterly inexcusable on the part of man. This is true also of atheism. God's reality, wisdom and power has been fully demonstrated in creation. In view of this unmistakable evidence of the reality of the Creator, it can be easily appreciated what abysmal folly it is for a person to take something that God has created, fashion from it an idol, and then bow down and worship the work of his own hands! This is graphically pictured for us in Isaiah 44: 9-17. With fine irony and biting sarcasm Isaiah, by Divine inspiration, describes a man making a graven image. First, he cuts down the tree that is to form his idol. With part of this tree he makes a bonfire and warms himself, thus providing himself with the pleasures of life. With another portion he bakes his food, thus supplying himself with the provisions of life. With the residue, or what is left over after providing for his own interests, he makes an idol. Falling down before it, he worships it and prays to it saying: "Deliver me, for thou art my God!"

We have noted before that one does not have to bow down to a visible and material idol in order to become an idolater. Idolatry is a thing that is more of the *heart* than the *hand*. It is possible to commit idolatry while outwardly appearing to be a worshipper of God. Our Lord quoted the words of Isaiah to the religious leaders of His day and said: "This people draweth nigh unto Me with their mouth and honoreth Me with their lips, but their heart is far from me" (Matt. 15: 8). Ezekiel was given a vision of the idolatrous heart-departure of Israel from God. He was shown a hole in a wall which led ultimately to a door through which he was told to enter. Upon entering, he saw all the abominable idols of the heathen pictured on the walls. Before these pictures, seventy of the elders of Israel stood, offering incense to and worshipping these idols. Then said God: "Hast thou seen what the ancients of the house of Israel do in the dark, every man in the *chambers of his imagery?*" (Ezek. 8: 7-18). Every person has this secret chamber in his heart, and the furnishings of this room determine his real spiritual status.

Let us have a look at some of these idols, material and otherwise, which are calculated to turn the believer's heart away from God, deny Him the place of absolute pre-eminence in the life and rob Him of the worship due to His name. In this connection, we need ever to remember the closing injunction of John's first epistle, which was written to Christians: "Little children, keep yourselves from idols" (I John 5:21).

(a) The first idol we shall consider is: *Self.* The fall of man is directly attributed to this idol. Satan's promise to Eve was: "Ye shall be as gods." Thus his temptation was for Eve to exalt herself at the expense of God, and exchange God's rule for self government. We have already seen that this was the cause of Satan's downfall.

Self is a very subtle idol, for it possesses the ability to intrude itself into our holiest moments. It appears in all sorts of disguises, but always for the purpose of displacing God as pre-eminent in every department of the believer's life. Its great appeal is to pride, whether it be pride of race, place, face or grace. It is evidenced in selfishness of every kind: self-exaltation at the expense of others, self-esteem of one's abilities and self-seeking on all occasions. It even masquerades under the name of humility, so that we can become very proud because we are so humble! One often hears the expression: "He is a self-made man and he worships his creator"! We ever need to remember however that, at his best, the self-made man is but a horrible example of unskilled labor! Though self preservation may be the first law of nature, it is certainly not of grace; for Christ said: "If any man will come after me, let him deny *himself,* and take up his cross and follow Me" (Matt. 16:24). This deliberate denial, not merely of "things," but of *self itself,* goes against the natural grain of each person, but it is essential to the spiritual worship of God.

(b) *Money.* How often this idol has been allowed to turn a believer's heart from spiritual realities! From the worship of almighty God, many have degenerated to the secret worship of the almighty dollar, and thus have become "i-dollar-ters." No wonder, therefore, that Paul wrote: "The *love* of money is the root of all evil, which while some coveted after, they have erred from the faith, and pierced themselves through with many sorrows" (I Tim. 6:10). The warning of Col. 3:5 is even more arresting: "Mortify therefore your members which are upon the earth; fornication, uncleanness, inordinate affection, evil concupiscence, and *covetousness, which is idolatry."*

This unholy desire to gain wealth, at whatever cost, is here likened to plain idolatry. These words should be allowed to search all our hearts. God is denied much worship, because those who have the money at their disposal refuse to part with it in order to send forth missionaries of the gospel into the regions beyond, that other souls may be saved, and thus become worshippers of the true and living God. It is tragically possible for Christians to become more interested in stocks and bonds than in the Scriptures. It is a well known fact that too much interest in "stocks" will inevitably result in "bonds," and the believer will soon find his spiritual life has been brought into bondage to wealth.

Money often becomes the acid test of the reality of one's profession of Christianity. It would be well if every Christian tested himself on this score. It is not for nothing that two whole chapters in the New Testament are devoted to the grace of willing, cheerful, systematic, proportionate and bountiful giving (II Cor. 8 to 9). The words of the wise man are in order at this point: "There is that scattereth, and yet increaseth; and there is that withholdeth more than is meet, but it tendeth to poverty" (Prov. 11:24). Peter puts it thus: "As every man hath received the gift, even so minister the same one to another, as good stewards of the manifold grace of God" (I Pet. 4:10).

(c) *Business*. Closely allied to money is this idol, which looms so large on the horizon of many believers and which, in altogether too many cases, has been allowed to drain them of their spirituality and consequent ability to worship. God's word recognizes the necessity for the Christian to be in business, but warns against the danger of business being in the Christian. The Christian business man is exhorted in the Word to be "Not slothful in business, fervent in spirit, serving the Lord" (Rom. 12:11). We may well thank God for the noble army of good business men and women, who do not allow their businesses to run them, but who run their businesses for the glory of God and the blessing of others. Robert Carey, when asked what his business was, replied: "My business is preaching the gospel and I cobble shoes to pay expenses." No Christian should become so busy in his business that he is too busy to do business for and with God. Each believer must be prepared to say to his business what Abraham said to the young men: "Tarry ye here . . . while I . . . go yonder and worship." We must all beware of what has been aptly termed, "the barrenness of a busy life." Each believer should therefore deliberately take time out for this most important matter of worship.

(d) *Pleasure* is still another idol, before whose shrine thousands of devotees prostrate themselves. Scripture indicates that one of the characteristics of the last days is that men shall be "Lovers of pleasure more than lovers of God" (II Tim. 3:4). It is not an exaggeration to say that the world has gone "pleasure-mad." The very word "amuse," simply means to prevent from musing, or meditating. The whole purpose of the goddess of pleasure is to stupify her victims, and prevent them from thinking about God, Christ, sin, salvation, death and judgment. All her pleasures are of the "escapist" variety, which enables her votaries, for a short while at least, to escape from the vital, the spiritual and the eternal realities of life.

It is sadly possible for a Christian to be carried away from heart devotion to God by these pleasures, and thus lose his ability to function as a worshipper of God. It is to be feared that upon the altar of many a Christian's heart, from which there used to ascend fragrant worship that brought delight to the Father; there are now but the cold ashes of formality, and the tragic experience of lost communion through occupation with worldly pleasures. The tendency of the pleasures of this world is to minimize sin, encourage lust, pander to oneself, destroy spirituality, hinder worship and eclipse God.

(e) *Recreation.* It may seem strange to include this in the list of idols, but often that which is *good* is allowed to become the enemy of that which is *best.* No one doubts for a moment the benefits of recreation as a means of maintaining one's physical, mental and spiritual fitness. It is when one's recreations are allowed to encroach on, and even absorb the time and energy that should be spent for Bible study, prayer, service and worship, that it becomes an evil which must come under the category of an "idol." It has been well said that the "abuse of the *best* is the *worst.*" The Scriptures tell us that: "Bodily exercise profiteth for a little time, but godliness is profitable unto all things" (I Tim. 4:8). Time is a precious commodity that must be redeemed (Eph. 5:16). We must therefore be careful to see that recreation is used only for the purpose God intended, and not allowed to become the dominating factor in one's life. Like many other things, recreation can become either a good servant, or a bad master.

(f) *One's family*. This may sound stranger still, yet the fact remains that it is possible to allow one's family to displace God as pre-eminent, and thereby earn His rightful rebuke. Perhaps the classic example of this is Eli, a priest of Israel. Though he himself was a good man who feared the Lord, yet he allowed his two sons, Hophni and Phinehas, to grow up unrestrained by parental discipline, until their vile conduct became a shame and disgrace in Israel. At last God sent a prophet to Eli who rebuked him, and charged him with honoring his sons above God, and said to him: "The Lord saith . . . Them that honor Me I will honor, and they that despise Me, shall be lightly esteemed" (I Sam. 2:27-36). After this, God spoke to young Samuel and, amongst other things, said of Eli: "I have told him that I will judge his house for ever, for the iniquity which he knoweth: because his sons made themselves vile, and he *restrained them not*" (I Sam. 3:11-14).

Many Christian parents have discovered, to their sorrow, the price they must pay for an undisciplined family. These spoiled children have brought disgrace to their name and bitter grief to their hearts. Instead of honoring God and obeying His word by bringing up their children in the nurture and admonition of the Lord, they foolishly allowed their children to dictate the policy of the home, with disastrous results. They failed to take heed to the words of the wise man when he said: "Foolishness is bound in the heart of a child; but the rod of correction shall drive it far from him" (Prov. 22:15). They allowed the family to develop "self expression," at the expense of *God-impression*. They failed to insist on and secure that essential obedience to, and honor of their parents, which God declares should characterize every Christian home. Instead of setting the children an example of godly living, and thus commanding their filial fear and love; they ignored God's plain directions to rule the home and allowed the family to rule them. In this way their children were given preference to God and His word. These children, which should have become blessings to them, were allowed to become idols and developed into a curse.

This bringing up of one's family for God is anything but easy; but it is ten thousand times harder to reap the bitter harvest which results from avoiding one's plain duty, both to God and to them. The tragedy of Eli should speak loudly to all Christian parents, and make them sensible of their solemn obligation to God. There should be a holy determination that their children shall not be allowed to become idols to displace God, but be brought up to fear God, to be obedient to their parents, and thus bring glory to God. Each Christian parent should carefully and prayerfully read and re-read the following scriptures, and be guided by them in bringing up the family for God. Eph. 6:1-4; Col. 3:20-21; Proverbs 17:25; 19:26; 20:11; 22:6; 23:13-14; 29:17; I Tim. 3:2-5.

(g) *Possessions.* This idol is closely allied to money and, in many cases, is allowed to displace God as pre-eminent in the life. The evil of possessions lies in their *possessive* quality. It is one thing to possess possessions, but another to allow one's possessions to possess him. Often it is a believer's house that becomes his all absorbing passion, and which demands all his spare time, energy and money to ensure that it contains every modern convenience and comfort; but alas, to the neglecting of his own spiritual life. Surely it will be agreed that "Better Homes and Gardens" is not the most important thing in life. It is also possible for wives to become "house proud" and go to the extreme in the meticulous care they bestow upon their homes, to the exclusion of all else, including the cultivation of their own spirituality. It is sadly possible for the house to be a marvel of beauty and order; but the *heart* of its occupants empty of that spiritual furniture which makes for worship.

Sometimes it is an *automobile* that occupies the limelight and demands all the attention. It becomes the principal subject of conversation, and the object of the most solicitous care. Many an hour is spent cleaning and polishing it, until it scintillates in the sun, a "thing of beauty and joy for ever," the pride of its owner and the envy of all beholders! No expense is spared to ensure that all the latest features are embodied in its construction, and that it is the finest thing on wheels. If only its possessor was as particular about his spiritual condition as he is about his car, what a volume of worship would ascend from his soul; but, alas, his heart has degenerated into a kind of garage, for every time he opens his mouth, the subject of cars pops out!

Whatever the believer's possessions may be, if they demand a greater place in the life than God, they become idols. Our Lord's own words should be *prayerfully* pondered by all who name His name. He said: "Take heed and beware of covetousness, for a man's life consisteth not in the abundance of the things which he possesseth" (Luke 12:15). It is possible for "things" to eclipse God. Each Christian should remember that he is but a steward, or trustee. All that he has, he is to hold as a sacred trust to be administered for God. The day will come when he will have to "give an account of his stewardship." Happy indeed is he who shall do it with joy and not with sorrow (Luke 16:2).

(h) *Power*. The apostle John had to speak of a man named Diotrephes, as one "who loveth to have the pre-eminence" (III John 9). Power, with this man, had become an obsession. Nothing would suit him but the

highest place of authority in the assembly. It is sad
enough when one sees the mad scramble for power a-
mongst worldlings; but sadder still to see it in a professing
child of God, who claims to be a follower of the One who
was "meek and lowly in heart"; (Matt. 11: 28-29) and
"Who made Himself of no reputation" (Phil. 2: 7). Pride,
with its love of power and pre-eminence, is not the atmosphere where worship is either generated, encouraged or
displayed. Worship belongs to the humble believer, who
is content with the place God has given him, and seeks to
fill it with loving and loyal devotion. An old Christian
used to say: "Why is there such a rush to get to the top
of the ladder, when there is so much room at the bottom?"

(i) *Science*. This is a modern idol which, through
Satan's strategy, has turned many away from the worship
of God. By "science," in this sense, we do not refer to
established facts of creation that are beyond all question,
but to the various theories put forth by men that purport
to account for creation without God. The Bible rightly
terms such: "Science, falsely so called" (I Tim. 6: 20).
Many a young and uninstructed believer has gone to a
place of "higher learning," only to have his faith shaken
in the truth of God's revelation. Some worldly-wise and
unbelieving professor propounds a *theory* as though it
were a *fact*, dubs it "science," and then sneeringly belittles
the Bible as being "unscientific," because it does not support his theory! Thus "Science" is elevated to the position of an idol. There it sits upon a high throne. It has
a mortar board upon its head; an academic gown upon
its body; a diploma for its sceptre, and a halo of letters
around its head, as "B. A., M. A., PH. D., LL. D., B. Sc.,"
etc. At the mention of the name of this sacred idol,
"Science," all students are supposed to prostrate themselves, own it as the supreme lord of their lives, the arbi-

ter of their destiny, and render to it the worship of their hearts, at least until their graduation!

One has only to turn to the sacred page to discover how utterly foolish are these vaporings of ungodly men. Every Christian should carefully read I Cor. 1:17-29. From this he will learn what God thinks of the wisdom of this world, as it is divorced from a knowledge of God and opposed to His revelation of Divine wisdom in the Scriptures. An old scientist, who was also a humble believer in God's word, declared that during his lifetime he had seen the rise and fall of over 300 false theories that loudly claimed to prove the Bible untrue. The false theory of organic evolution, in spite of the fact that there is no scientific evidence to support it, is still put forth as though it was an established fact, and thousands of gullible young men and women swallow it whole because it bears the magical name of "Science," spelled with capital letters!

A young Christian in an infidel college was much shaken in her faith in the integrity of holy Scripture. She decided to shut herself up in her room until she knew where she stood in regard to these matters. At the end of several hours she emerged with the conviction of the truth of Divine revelation. On the flyleaf of her Bible, she had written the words: *"Can time undo what once was true?"* If the word of God was once true, it will *always be true,* for truth is unchangeable and eternal. Some of the greatest *real* scientists, both of the past and the present, are true Christians, who have declared they see no contradiction whatever between what God has been pleased to reveal in His word, and the *established facts* of science.

We have by no means exhausted the list of idols, but surely enough has been written to show that whatever it may be which displaces God, or which hinders our worship of Him is, to that extent, an idol, which we must not tolerate for a moment.

CHAPTER THIRTEEN

The Object of Worship

(Continued)

Now let us consider some other things which we are specifically warned not to worship.

(2) Men. Acts 10:25-26.

Not only is the worship of idols prohibited, whether they be literal or figurative, material or immaterial, but we are also warned against the worship of men. Cornelius the Roman Centurion, was taught this lesson. When Peter, in response to his invitation, came to his house, we read that Cornelius "fell down at his feet and worshipped him, but Peter took him up saying: 'Stand up, I myself also am a man'." There is always the subtle danger of taking one's eyes off God and getting them on man; of allowing the seen to obscure the unseen and of permitting the temporal to eclipse the eternal. God's word to Israel was: "Cease ye from man, whose breath is in his nostrils: for wherein is he to be accounted of?" (Isa. 2: 22). Our Lord's own words to His disciples were even more forceful: "Beware of men, for they will deliver you up to the councils," etc. (Matt. 10:17). It is not for nothing that we are warned: "The fear of man bringeth a snare, but whoso putteth his trust in the Lord shall be safe" (Prov. 29:25).

By nature man has ever been a hero worshipper. He has always been prone to give to man the titles, praise, honor, worship and glory which he denies to God Himself. Part of God's indictment of man is that he has "Changed the truth of God into a lie, and worshipped and served the creature more than the Creator, who is blessed for ever" (Rom. 1:25). The day is coming when the world, which despised, rejected and crucified the Son of God, will welcome as its king, "the man of sin, the son of perdition, who opposeth and exalteth himself above all that is called God, or that is worshipped; so that he as God sitteth in the temple of God, showing himself that he is God" (II Thess. 2:3-4). The number of this man of sin is deeply significant, for it is the number of a man, six hundred, three score and six, or 666.

In the meantime, man largely fills the horizon of the world's thought. They think in terms of humanity: what man is, thinks, says and does: instead of in terms of Deity: what God is, thinks, says and does. At the head of one huge religious system of Christendom is a person to whom the title of "holy father" is actually given. In other circles the titles of "reverend," "right reverend," "very reverend," and "most reverend," are commonly addressed to men. The title, "reverend" is only found once in the Authorized Version, and it is reserved for God alone. We read: "He sent redemption unto His people. He hath commanded His covenant for ever: Holy and Reverend is His name" (Ps. 119). Elihu's words are particularly appropriate in this connection, for he said: "Let me not, I pray you, accept any man's person, neither let me give flattering titles unto man. For I know not to give flattering titles; in so doing my Maker would soon take me away" (Job 32:21-22). One wonders what Elihu's reaction would be today when he heard men addressed as: "holy father," "reverend," "right reverend," "very reverend," and "most reverend!"

Neither do we have any warrant whatever for addressing prayers to men or women and, least of all, to a few so-called "saints," who have been dead for years. The believer is directed to pray to the living God alone, through the sole mediation of Christ, as guided by the

Holy Spirit, through the Word. Our Lord addressed these words to His audience: "How can ye believe, which receive honor one of another, and seek not the honor that cometh from God only?" (John 5:44). Of these same people it is recorded: "They loved the praise of men more than the praise of God" (John 12:43).

The worship of men, whether alive or dead, is thus directly forbidden by God, as also undue reverence paid to man, together with the use of flattering titles, appropriate only to Deity. Like Peter, the Christian must firmly take his stand on this issue and boldly affirm: "We ought to obey God rather than men" (Acts 5:29).

(3) **Angels.**   Rev. 19:10; 22:8-9; Col. 2:18.

Angels are spirit beings, created by God to fulfil His purposes and accomplish His service. (Ps. 104:4). They are described as "ministering spirits, sent forth to minister for them who shall be heirs of salvation" (Heb. 1:14). As created and intelligent beings, they worship their Creator (Rev. 5:11-12). These angels are classified in various orders. We read of "Michael, the archangel" (Jude 9); of "the angel, Gabriel" (Luke 1:19, 26); of the "cherubim and seraphim" (Gen. 3:24; Isa. 6:2); of the "host of angels" (Rev. 5:11-12); and of the "thrones, dominions, principalities and powers," all of which were created by Christ (Col. 1:16). The study of angels is most interesting and instructive, for they have played a large part in the Divine program in the past. Though unseen to human eyes, they are active now in the present, and shall be associated with God's purposes in the future, as is clearly indicated in the book of Revelation.

When the Lord gave to John the wondrous vision that is recorded in the book of Revelation, an angel was deputed to guide him. On one occasion John fell at the feet

of this angel to worship him, but he was immediately rebuked by the angel in these words: "See thou do it not.
I am thy fellow servant, and of thy brethren that have the
testimony of Jesus: worship God" (Rev. 19:10). Later
on, he again lapsed into the same error, for he tells us:
"And I, John, saw these things and heard them. And
when I had heard and seen, I fell down to worship before
the feet of the angel which showed me these things. Then
saith he unto me: See thou do it not, for I am thy fellow
servant, and of thy brethren the prophets, and of them
which keep the sayings of this book; worship God" (Rev.
22:8-9).

The apostle Paul had to combat the false philosophy
of Gnosticism, which taught that Christ merely belonged
to a higher order of angels, and was not the unique Son
of God, equal and eternal with the Father and the Spirit.
He wrote: "Let no man beguile you of your reward in a
voluntary humility and worshipping of angels, intruding
into those things which he hath not seen, vainly puffed
up by his fleshly mind, and not holding the Head" (Christ)
(Col. 2:18-19).

We must keep in mind that angels, however great,
wise and powerful, are only created beings. The worship
of them is absolutely forbidden by God. In the light of
this, it seems strange to hear people addressing prayers to
them and crying: "Michael, help us!" or: "Hear us, O
Gabriel!" Prayers addressed to angels are therefore a
direct violation of the expressed will of God as seen in
His word.

(4) **Nature.**   Deut. 4:14-20; Job 31:24-28.

We hear a great deal today about certain people who
are called: "nature worshippers." Such people affirm
they do not desire to attend "Divine worship in a building
made by human hands;" or to read and study a book called

the Bible; but much prefer to take a walk in the country, in order to "worship the God of nature." As an aid to their devotions, many of these devotees take a fishing rod, others a set of golf clubs, etc. One may see these "worshippers" at their devotions by the hundreds each Sunday! In fact, to many, a "Sabbath day's journey" seems to consist of going around the golf course three times!

While we may rightly admire the beauties of God's handiwork in nature, which combines to reveal His wisdom, power and eternal Godhead; yet to worship His creation is folly in the extreme. God has anticipated this tendency in sinful man to allow creation to obscure the Creator, and has declared: "Take ye therefore good heed unto yourselves . . . lest thou lift up thine eyes unto heaven, and when thou seest the sun, and the moon, and the stars, even all the host of heaven, shouldst be driven to worship them and serve them" (Deut. 4:15-19).

In spite of these plain words, we read that Israel turned aside from the God of heaven to worship the sun god, Baal, and paid the price for its apostasy by being taken into captivity. (See I Kings 18). Amongst the pagan people of the world today, there are still people who worship the sun, moon and stars. David had the right view point when he said: "When I consider Thy heavens, the work of Thy fingers, the moon and the stars which thou hast ordained: what is man that Thou art mindful of him, and the son of man that Thou visitest him? . . . O Lord, how excellent is Thy name in all the earth!" (Psa. 8:3-4, 9). Job referred to the heathenish custom of nature worship that obtained in his day when people, on looking at the sun, kissed their hand as a token of their worship of it. (See Job 31:26-29).

CHAPTER FOURTEEN

The Object of Worship

(Continued)

2. God is to be the Object of our worship.

Having viewed this division of our subject negatively, and learned that God prohibits the worship of idols, men, angels and nature; let us now consider the subject positively and discover, from the Word, Whom we are to worship. We mentioned, at the beginning of this division, that Scripture enjoins us to worship the eternal Godhead, consisting of Father, Son and Holy Spirit. We shall now look particularly at each Person of the Godhead.

(1) We are to worship the Father. John 4:23.

To the regenerated believer, God is not some far off Deity, too high and holy to take notice of him, but He is revealed as a loving Father, into Whose family he has been born, to Whom he has been brought near, and Who has blessed him with all the spiritual blessings in the heavenlies in Christ Jesus (Eph. 1:3; John 1:12-13). The title, "Father," as we have already noticed, suggests intimacy, dearness, love and care. In response to His disciples' request to teach them to pray, our Lord answered: "When ye pray say: 'Our Father, which art in heaven,'" etc. (Luke 11:2-4). In His conversation with the woman at the well, Christ unfolded the great revelation that: "The hour cometh, and now is, when the true worshippers shall worship the Father in Spirit and in truth, for the Father seeketh such to worship Him" (John 4:23). Let us note three reasons why we should worship the Father.

(a) *We should worship the Father because of what He is.*

The New Testament reveals Him as Father in many aspects. He is:

(i) *The Holy Father.* (John 17:16). He loves righteousness and hates iniquity (Heb. 1:9). Never was this holiness of the Father more clearly demonstrated than when, at the cross, He forsook the One who bore our sins and visited all His righteous judgment upon our Divine Substitute. (Read Ps. 22:1-3).

(ii) *The Righteous Father.* (John 17:35). By the righteousness of God we mean God's perfect consistency with His own character. Whatever God performs, He does it on a perfectly righteous basis, either in saving the believer, or condemning the unbeliever. This is Paul's great argument in the epistle to the Romans.

(iii) *The Father of glory.* (Eph. 1:17). By glory is meant displayed excellence. God has displayed all the many perfections and excellences of His character in His Son, and recorded them for us in the holy Scriptures (II Cor. 4:6).

(iv) *The Father of lights.* (James 1:17). We are told that "God is light." Light is that which "makes manifest" (I John 1:5; Eph. 5:13). To Him "all things are open and naked"; for "known unto God are all His works from the beginning of the world" (Heb. 4:13). He is the Father who has manifested Himself, and whose outshining glory is seen "in the face of Jesus Christ."

(v) *The Father of mercies.* (II Cor. 1:3). As such, He is also the "God of all comfort." David sang: "Like as a father pitieth his children, so the Lord pitieth them that fear Him" (Ps. 103:13). As the Father of mercies, He knows all the frailties, fears, failings and faults of His people, and their constant need of His correcting and restoring grace. Truly: "His mercy endureth for ever" (Ps. 107:1). Every need of His children is not only anticipated, but abundantly supplied "according to His riches in glory by Christ Jesus" (Phil. 4:19).

(vi) *The Father of all* (Eph. 4:6). This does not mean that God is the universal Father of all humanity, and that all people are His children. The false theory of "the universal Fatherhood of God and brotherhood of man," has no foundation whatever in Scripture. The reference here is to the fact that all regenerated believers have "One God and Father of all, who is above all, and through all, and in you all." In other words, there is no aristocracy in His family. All God's children are equally near and dear to Him, so there is no occasion for spiritual pride, or the exhibition of snobbery amongst Christians.

(vii) *The Father of our Lord Jesus Christ.* II Cor. 1:3; Eph. 1:3; I Pet. 1:3. What an inexpressibly precious title this is! He is not only the Father of the whole family of the redeemed; but He is also the Father of the One whose precious blood has made such a family relationship possible! Christ is the "only begotten of the Father." This phrase, "only begotten," literally means "unique," or "the only one of His kind." The term "eternal Father" necessitates an "eternal Son;" and an "eternal Son" necessitates an "eternal Father." We cannot have one without the other. For all eternity He was the Son of God, equal in every respect to the Father and the Holy Spirit. When Christ became incarnate and was born in Bethlehem, He did not enter into existence, but only unto another *form* of existence, that of man. Thus Deity became Humanity and "without controversy, great is the mystery of godliness: God was manifest in the flesh" (I Tim. 3:16).

As the incarnate Son of God, He lived His life as a Man on earth, in voluntary submission to all the will of His Father. This will led Him all the way to Calvary, where He accomplished perfectly all the work the Father gave Him to do. The Father indicated His complete approval of this work of redemption by raising His Son from the dead, and glorifying Him at His own right hand. Every sinner, trusting in His finished work and receiving Him as Savior, is that moment, by the Spirit's regenerating power, born into the family of God. From thenceforth he is called a "child of God," an "heir of God," and a "joint heir with Christ." (Rom. 8:14-17). Thus we have the unspeakable privilege and honor of addressing God by the same name as did His Son while on earth, and we may now call Him, "Father." Our Lord, in resurrection, associated Himself with all who loved Him and said: "Go to My brethren and say unto them: I ascend unto My Father and your Father; and to My God and your God" (John 20:17).

(b) *We should worship the Father because of what He has done.*

(i) *He has loved us.* (John 3:16). Why He set His love upon us is a mystery we shall never solve, but we rejoice because of its glorious reality. God's love is described as being: Eternal (Jer. 31:3), Revealed (John 3:16), Manifested (I John 4:9), Bestowed (I John 3:1), Believed (I John 4:16), Reciprocated (I John 4:19), and Inseparable (Rom. 8:38-39).

(ii) *He has given the unspeakable gift of His Son.* (I John 4:14). "And we have seen and do testify that the Father sent the Son to be the Savior of the world." The greatness of God's love can only be estimated by the gift He gave, for love is ever measured by the sacrifice made on behalf of its objects. We do well to sing:

> "Blessed be God, our God!
> Who gave for us His well beloved Son,
> That Gift of gifts, all other gifts in One!
> Blessed be God, our God!"

(iii) *He has chosen us in Christ* (Eph. 1:3-4). "Blessed be the God and Father . . . according as He has chosen us in Him (Christ) before the foundation of the world, that we should be holy and without blame before Him in love." Before the world was called into being by His creative word, and flung into space to follow its pre-destined orbit, the believer was foreseen and chosen in Christ. This is a stupendous and breath-taking thought. It would be incredible but for the fact that God has told us so in plain, unmistakable language.

(iv) *He has saved us by His grace.* (Col. 1:12-13). "Giving thanks unto the Father . . . Who hath delivered us from the power of darkness, and hath translated us into the kingdom of His dear Son." What a marvellous translation and transformation God has wrought in the life of each believer! How can Christians possibly estimate the depth of sin, degradation and spiritual darkness from which they have been mercifully delivered by God's matchless grace! It becomes them, therefore, to sing:

> "Great God of wonders! All Thy ways
>   Display Thine attributes Divine;
> But the bright glories of Thy grace,
>   Above Thine other wonders shine:
> Who is a pardoning God like Thee?
> And Who has grace, so rich and free?"

(v) *He has blessed us.* (Eph. 1:3). "Blessed be the God and Father of our Lord Jesus Christ, who hath blessed us with all spiritual blessings in the heavenly places (heavenlies) in Christ Jesus." How can we possibly enumerate these blessings, or "name them one by one," seeing they are innumerable? Our Father is not only the "blessed God," but He also is the God of blessing. The believer's wealth is untold, for God has said: "All things are yours; whether Paul, or Apollos, or Cephas, or the world, or life, or death, or things present, or things to come; all are yours; and ye are Christ's, and Christ is God's" (I Cor. 3:21-23). There is not a blessing we possess that has not come to us from the loving hand of our

Father in heaven. With the hymn writer, we can lift our voices in worship to Him and sing:

> Praise ye the Father—Source of all our blessing,
>   Before whose gifts earth's richest boons wax dim!
> Resting in Him, His peace and joy possessing,
>   All things are ours, for we have all in Him!"

(vi) *He has made us His children* (I John 3:1). "Behold, what manner of love the Father hath bestowed upon us, that we should be called the sons of God." How wonderful it is to think that we, who "were sometimes alienated and enemies in our mind by wicked works," are now not only reconciled but, by the regenerating power of the Spirit of God, actually made the "sons and daughters of the Lord God almighty!" (Col. 1:21; II Cor. 6:18; John 1:12). Thus we have the inestimable birth-right privilege of calling Him, "Abba, Father" (Rom. 8:15-17).

As "the Father" He has revealed Himself in the Scriptures as the One who *knoweth* our needs (Matt. 6:8); who *loveth* us (John 16:27); who *keepeth* us (John 17:11); Who *disciplineth* us (Heb. 12:7-9); who *supplieth* all our necessities (James 1:17); who *comforteth* us (II Thess. 2:16); and who *heareth* and answereth our prayers (Matt. 6:4).

(vii) *He has made it possible for us to worship Him.* (John 4:23-24). Not content with all the other things He has done for us, He now both seeks and appreciates the worship of His children. To this end "a new and living way" has been provided, by which each believer, by faith, may enter the holiest of all. In His blessed presence, he may now fall before Him and worship Him as the Father. May each one of us seek to take full advantage of this privilege and thus fulfil the Father's gracious purpose in our redemption and regeneration (Heb. 10:19-22).

CHAPTER FIFTEEN

The Object of Worship

(Continued)

(2) We are to worship the Son. Heb. 1:6; Rev. 5:8, 13;
Phil. 2:10.

We have already drawn attention to the triunity of
the Godhead, and seen that each Person in the Godhead
possesses full Deity and Personality, and each is equal and
eternal with the Other. There is abundant evidence in
Scripture that the Son of God is to be worshipped. The
Father Himself has declared it, and issued the decree:
"Let all the angels of God worship Him" (Heb. 1:6). It is
important to notice that our Lord, during His lifetime on
earth, as Son of Man, received the worship of men. At His
birth (Matt. 2:11); during His ministry (Matt. 8:2; 9:18;
14:33; 15:25; Mark 5:6; John 9:38); at His resurrection
(Matt. 28:9, 17); at His ascension (Luke 24:52). He now
receives worship in heaven (Rev. 5:9-10; 12, 13). He shall
receive worship in the future (Phil. 2:10). He Himself
claimed equal honor with the Father, and declared that
"All men should honor the Son, even as they honor the
Father. He that honoreth not the Son, honoreth not the
Father which hath sent Him" (John 5:23; cp. John 14:
10-11).

(a) *We should worship the Son because of what He is.*

(i) *He is the Son of God.* As such, He is equal with
the Father (John 1:1). He possesses full and absolute
Deity, for we read: "In the beginning was the Word, and
the Word was with God, and the Word was God." In this
magnificent prologue to John's gospel, three things are affirmed of Christ. First, the eternity of His Being: "In
the beginning." Second, the distinction of His Person:

He was "the Word." Third, His essential Deity: "The Word was God." In Heb. 1:8 we find the Father speaking to the Son and addressing Him as Deity: "But unto the Son He saith: Thy throne, O God, is for ever and ever; a scepter of righteousness is the scepter of Thy kingdom."

(ii) *He is the Creator of all things.* (Col. 1:16; John 1:3).

Though the apostle's creed may affirm: "I believe in God the Father, Maker of heaven and earth," yet the New Testament puts the emphasis for Creation, not on the Father, but on the Son as the One Who created all things. We read: "For by Him (Christ) were all things created, that are in heaven, and that are in earth, visible and invisible, whether they be thrones, or dominions, or principalities, or powers: all things were created by Him, and for Him: and He is before all things, and by Him all things subsist" (or hold together). It was His hands that fashioned man from the dust of the earth and gave him life. The universe around us came into being by His creatorial power and all things are now sustained by Him.

(iii) *He is the alone Revealer of the Father.* (John 1:18). We are told that "No man hath seen God at any time; the only begotten Son, which is in the bosom of the Father, He hath declared Him" (or told Him out). The invisible God has become visible in Christ. All that can be seen of the Father is in the Son. In fact, Christ Himself declared: "He that hath seen Me, hath seen the Father" (John 14:6-11). He is described as being "the brightness of God's glory, and the express image of His Person" (Heb. 1:3).

Josiah Condor, in his magnificent hymn, has caught something of the glories of the Person of the Son of God.

"Thou art the everlasting Word,
　　The Father's only Son,
God manifest, God seen and heard,
　　And heaven's beloved One.

In Thee, most perfectly expressed
　　The Father's glories shine,
Of the full Deity possessed,
　　Eternally Divine.

True image of the Infinite,
　　Whose essence is concealed;
Brightness of uncreated light,
　　The heart of God revealed.

Throughout the universe of bliss,
　　The center Thou, and Sun,
The eternal theme of praise is this,
　　To heaven's beloved One.

Worthy, O Lamb of God, art Thou,
　　That every knee to Thee should bow!"

(b)   *We should worship the Son because of what He has done.*

(i)   *For His incarnation.* I Tim. 3:16; Isa. 9:6. From the infinite heights of eternal Godhead, He came to the simplicity of a human body, and thus Deity clothed Himself with Humanity! No finite mind can possibly comprehend the wondrous mystery and miracle of the incarnation; but we can believe and, believing, fall at His feet in worship as did the wise men of old (Matt. 2:1-12). By His incarnation God became Man, not part God and part Man, but wholly God and wholly Man. Thus absolute Deity and perfect humanity were combined in one Person, when the Son of God became the Son of Man.

"Thou wouldst like sinful man be made,
　　In everything but sin;
That we, as like Thee might become;
　　As we, unlike had been."

By His incarnation the Lord Jesus bridged the gulf that separated man from God. Six hundred years before His advent, Isaiah wrote concerning Him: "Unto us a Child is born;" here in His humanity. "Unto us a Son is given;" here is His Deity. (Isa. 9:6). Conceived of the Holy Spirit, born of a virgin, the mighty Creator became the Babe of Bethlehem. No wonder His birth was accompanied by the heavenly demonstration of a multitude of the angelic host who praised God and chanted: "Glory to God in the highest, and on earth peace, good will toward men!" (Luke 2:14). As God, He fulfilled all the obligations that perfect righteousness demanded. As Man, He met the deepest and direst need of lost humanity and, by the blood of His cross, secured their reconciliation to God.

It truly becomes us to sing:

> "Worthy, incarnate Word, to be adored!
>   All things were made by Thee, and for Thee, O Lord!
> Yet Thou didst leave Thy bright throne for earth's shame
>   And, clothed with humanity, our Savior became!"

(ii) *For His holy life of perfect obedience,* by which He glorified the Father on earth. He could say: "I have glorified Thee on the earth: I have finished the work which Thou gavest Me to do" (John 17:4). During His earthly sojourn He displayed those perfect moral qualities and glories that so delighted the heart of His Father, and which brought from heaven the testimony: "This is My beloved Son, in Whom I am well pleased" (Matt. 3:17). Our Lord could say: "And He that sent Me is with Me, the Father hath not left Me alone, for I do always those things that please Him" (John 8:29). The Father's eye rested on the Son of His love in absolute complacency as, for thirty-three years, He perfectly translated all the will of His Father into the terms of a sinless, holy and harmless life.

What infinite humility and gracious condescension marked His steps as He moved in the midst of a crooked and perverse generation, which neither desired nor appreciated the beauty of His holy character! Think of Him as "He went about doing good." (Acts 10:38). He gave sight to the blind, cleansing to the leper, healing to the sick, hearing to the deaf and even life to the dead. Such was the character of His spoken ministry that those sent to arrest Him returned empty handed and testified: "Never man spake like this Man!" (John 7:46).

By His holy life, His matchless words and His marvelous miracles, Christ demonstrated His essential and eternal Deity. At the same time, He evidenced His perfect humanity. Thus essential Deity and sinless humanity were harmoniously blended and perfectly expressed in the Person of our blessed Lord. His whole life was redolent with the glory of God. One has only to read the inspired account in the four Gospels, which combine to give us a fourfold view of Him as Israel's King, Jehovah's Servant, the Son of Man and the Son of God, to be carried away with wonder, praise and worship, and exclaim with the hymn-writer:

> "What grace, O Lord, and beauty shone
>   Around Thy steps below!
> What patient love was seen in all
>   Thy life and death of woe!
>
> For ever on Thy burdened heart
>   A weight of sorrow hung;
> Yet no ungentle murmuring word
>   Escaped Thy silent tongue.
>
> Thy foes might hate, despise, revile,
>   Thy friends unfaithful prove;
> Unwearied in forgiveness still,
>   Thy heart could only love."

These moral glories of our Lord have been the subject of countless books. One of the best of them is by J. G.

Bellett and is entitled: "The Moral Glories of our Lord Jesus Christ." This little book, which can be read at a sitting, beautifully presents the perfect combination of the Deity and Humanity of Christ, as seen in His life on earth. It has been used to lead many to a fuller appreciation of the earthly life and ministry of our Lord Jesus Christ.

(iii) *For His voluntary and substitutionary sacrifice on our behalf.* This was the supreme purpose of His incarnation. He clothed Himself with humanity in order that He might die for man, His creatures' sin. We read that He was made "a little lower than the angels for the suffering of death" (Heb. 2:9). He informed His disciples of His purpose to be a vicarious and substitutionary sacrifice and said: "The Son of Man came not to be ministered unto, but to minister, and to give His life a ransom for many" (Mark 10:45). On another occasion He declared: "Therefore doth My Father love Me, because I lay down My life, that I might take it again. No man taketh it from me, but I lay it down of myself. I have power (or authority) to lay it down, and I have power to take it again" (John 10:17-18).

The cross was ever before Him. At the outset of His ministry He said: "The Son of Man *must* be lifted up." He allowed no person or circumstance to turn Him aside from His lonely path to Calvary. He exclaimed: "The cup which My Father hath given Me, shall I not drink it?" (John 18:11).

> "It was a lonely path He trod,
>   From every human soul apart;
> Known to Himself, and God alone,
>   Was all the grief that filled His heart.
> Yet, from the track, He turned not back,
>   'Till where we lay, in sin and shame,
> He found us—blessed be His name!"

The classic passage on this subject is Phil. 2: 5-8, where we read that Christ: "Being in the form of God, thought it not robbery (or a thing to be grasped at) to be equal with God: but made Himself of no reputation, and took on Him the form of a Servant, and was made in the likeness of men; and being found in fashion as a man, He humbled Himself, and became obedient unto death, even the death of the cross." It becomes us therefore to adore Him for His redemptive work and sing:

> "Worthy, O Lamb of God, worthy art Thou:
> Low at Thy blessed feet, Lord Jesus, we bow!
> For Thou wast slain for our sins, blessed Lord;
> And Thou hast redeemed us to God by Thy blood!"

As the believer thinks of Calvary, and of the holy Son of God, who had no sin, knew no sin and did no sin, being made sin for him; there can be no room for pride, but only for humble and reverent worship of the Savior. It becomes him to sing with Isaac Watts:

> "When I survey the wondrous cross,
> On which the Lord of glory died;
> My richest gain I count but loss,
> And pour contempt on all my pride."

All alone, in that "dark, mysterious hour," despised and rejected of men and forsaken of His God, our blessed Lord bore our sins and drained, to its last, dark, bitter drop, the awful cup of God's judgment. By that one sacrifice, which He offered to God, He has satisfied, *once and for ever,* all the demands of a holy God against the believing sinner, who can now testify:

> "Because the sinless Savior died,
> My sinful soul is counted free;
> For God, the Just, is satisfied
> To look on Christ, and pardon me!"

The substitutionary sacrifice of Christ is the basis of all the believer's blessings. As he concentrates his mind's attention and his heart's affection upon the Son of God, who loved him, and gave Himself for him, worship is generated in his soul. F. Allaben's beautiful hymn seems to sum up this appreciation of the believer's heart:

> "Life, life of love poured out, fragrant and holy!
>   Life, 'mid rude thorns of earth, stainless and sweet!
> Life, whence God's face of love, glorious, but lowly,
>   Shines forth to bow us, Lord, low at Thy feet!
>
> Grief, grief of love, that drew hate's every arrow!
>   Grief that Thy suffering heart only could meet.
> Grief, whence Thy face of love, shining in sorrow,
>   Draws us, adoring, Lord, low at Thy feet!
>
> Death, death of stricken love, wrath's sea exploring!
>   Death, life's mysterious death-deep meeting deep;
> Death, whence Thy bursting heart fills ours, outpouring
>   All, all in worship, Lord, low at Thy feet!"

(iv)   *For His glorious resurrection and ascension.*

We must ever link, in our thoughts, "the sufferings of Christ" with "the glory that should follow" (I Pet. 1:11). We do not worship a dead Christ, but One who rose again triumphant, and now is glorified at God's right hand. As the believer thinks of this he sings:

> "Rise, my soul, behold, 'tis Jesus!
>   Jesus fills thy wondering eyes,
> See Him now, in glory seated,
>   Where thy sins no more can rise!"

To John, the glorified Lord made the triumphant proclamation: "I am He that liveth and was dead; and, behold, I am alive forevermore!" (Rev. 1:18). The transaction at Calvary will never be repeated, for we read: "Christ, being raised from the dead dieth no more; death hath no more dominion over Him. For in that He died, He died unto sin once: (for all) but in that He liveth, He liveth unto God" (Rom. 6:9-10). Not only did Christ rise, henceforth to live in the power of an endless life, but He ascended to take His place "on the right hand of the majesty on high" (Heb. 1:3). More wonderful still, He has declared to the believer: "Because I live, ye shall live also" (John 14:19). Thus he unites all His redeemed people in Himself, and secures for them and assures to them the prospect of their eternal glory with Him.

(c) *We should worship the Son of God because of what He is doing.*

(i) *As the Advocate, Intercessor and great high Priest of His people.*

Having accomplished all the work necessary for our salvation by His death and resurrection; He now ever lives at God's right hand as the Intercessor, Advocate and great high Priest of the believer. He sits upon the throne in order to make good *in* us all He accomplished *for* us on the cross. As the Advocate, He represents us before the Father (I John 2:1). As the Intercessor, He pleads for us with the Father (Heb. 7:25). As the great high Priest, He presents our worship to the Father (Heb. 8: 1-3). Hence we sing:

> "Much incense is ascending
>   Before the eternal throne;
> God graciously is bending
>   To hear each feeble groan;
> To all our prayers and praises
>   Christ adds His sweet perfume,
> And love the censer raises,
>   Its odors to consume.
>
> O God, we come with singing,
>   Because our great high Priest,
> Our names to Thee is bringing,
>   Nor e'er forgets the least:
> For us He wears the mitre,
>   Where holiness shines bright,
> For us His robes are whiter
>   Than heaven's unsullied light."

(ii) *As Head of the Church, which is His body.*

Christ is now the "Head over all things to the Church, which is His body, the fulness of Him that filleth all in all" (Eph. 1:22-23). As such, He lives to supply every need of the members of His body on earth. For this cause He gives gifts unto men. In the beginning of the Church's history He gave: "apostles and prophets." Now he gives: "evangelists, pastors and teachers, for the perfecting of the saints, for the work of the ministry, and for the edifying of the body of Christ." (Eph. 4:8-12). By these gifts from the risen glorified Head, "The whole body, fitly joined together, and compacted by that which every joint supplieth, according to the effectual working in the measure of every part, maketh increase of the body unto the edifying (or building up) of itself in love" (Eph. 4:15-16).

As the Head, He is described as walking in the midst of the local churches, appraising the true spiritual worth of each (Rev. 1:13). He graces, with His presence, each gathering of believers who meet in His name (Matt. 18:20). He is the Host at the table of remembrance, and invites each blood-bought one to eat of the bread and drink of the cup saying: "This do, for a remembrance of Me." The Lord Himself revealed to Paul that "as often as ye eat this bread, and drink this cup, ye do show the Lord's death till He come" (I Cor. 11:23-26). When His saints, in scriptural simplicity, gather in His name alone to thus remember Him; what hallowed experiences are theirs as they sense the presence of the Lord in their midst!

> "What food luxurious loads the board
> When, at His table, sits the Lord!
> The wine how rich, the bread how sweet,
> When Jesus deigns the guests to meet!"

Believers are called upon to worship the glorified One, at God's right hand, for all He is doing on behalf of those He has made forever His, at such infinite cost.

(d) *We should worship the Son of God for what He is yet to do.*

The remembrance feast points forward to a time when the Lord shall return, for we eat the bread and drink the cup only "till He come." The great hope of the Church is the literal and personal coming again of the Lord Jesus Christ. It is a significant fact that about one-sixth of the New Testament is taken up with this great event and its far reaching consequences to the Church, to Israel and to the world. We shall concern ourselves only with the first.

We are left in no doubt as to the certainty of His coming, for we have a three-fold testimony concerning it. First of all, there is our Lord's own *proclamation* to this effect (John 14:1-3). Next, there is the angelic *confirmation* of it (Acts 1:10-11). Third, we have the apostolic *revelation* concerning it (I Thess. 4:13-18; I Cor. 15:51-58). These Scriptures alone are sufficient to prove the truth of the literal and personal second coming of Christ.

Nor are we left in doubt as to the *purpose* of His advent. We are told: "The Lord Himself shall descend from heaven with a shout, with the voice of the archangel, and with the trump of God: and the dead in Christ shall rise first: then we which are alive and remain shall be caught up together with them in the clouds, to meet the Lord in the air" (I Thess. 4:16-17). Thus the bodies of those Christians who have died, shall be raised and reunited to their spirits which are already with Christ. This is called the first *resurrection*. Those Christians who are alive at His coming shall have their bodies changed, and then be caught up to be with Christ. This is referred to as the *rapture*. This is the event to which every true Christian looks forward with the keenest expectation and sings:

"O joy! O delight! should we go without dying,
  No sickness, no sadness, no dread, and no crying;
Caught up through the clouds with our Lord into glory,
  When Jesus receives His own!"

Think what this will mean for the Lord! He will have,
in His presence, and clothed with bodies "like unto His
own body of glory," all those for whom He suffered, bled
and died! (Phil. 3:21). The believer's corrupt nature,
called "the flesh," will be left behind for ever, no more
to hinder communion with Him. All the redeemed shall
then appear before His judgment seat for review and reward (I Cor. 3:12-15; Rom. 14:10-12; II Cor. 5:10). In
that day the Lord shall present "to Himself a glorious
Church, not having spot or wrinkle, or any such thing"
(Eph. 5:27). Throughout the vast, eternal ages, the redeemed shall worship the Lamb that was slain and that
liveth again; and He, the Lord of all, "shall see of the
travail of His soul, and shall be satisfied!" (Isa. 53:11).

Whether we think of what our Lord is, in Himself,
or what He has done, or what He is doing, or what He
will yet do; every aspect of our Lord's person and work
calls forth, from the believer, the worship and adoration of
his redeemed spirit. It well becomes us to sing:

"Lord of glory, we adore Thee,
  Christ of God, ascended high!
Heart and soul we bow before Thee,
  Glorious now beyond the sky:
Thee we worship, Thee we praise,
  Excellent in all Thy ways!

Lord of life! To death once subject;
  Blesser, yet a curse once made;
Of Thy Father's heart the Object,
  Yet in depth of anguish laid:
Thee we gaze on, Thee recall,
  Bearing here our sorrows all.

> Royal robes shall soon invest Thee,
>   Royal splendours crown Thy brow;
> Christ of God, our souls confess Thee,
>   King and Sovereign, even now!
> Thee we reverence, Thee obey,
>   Own Thee Lord and Christ alway!"

Sometime ago we were informed that, among certain circles of Christians, it was being taught that prayer, praise and worship should *never* be addressed, *directly* to the Lord Jesus Christ, but should only be addressed to the Father through the Son.

To combat this erroneous idea, a pamphlet was issued, bearing the title: "Direct Address to the Lord Jesus." This has now been added, as an appendix, to this book and should be consulted at this point. (see page 250).

May God be pleased to use it to clarify the mind of each believer as to the Scripturalness of addressing the Lord Jesus Christ *directly* in prayer, praise and worship!

(3) We are not instructed to worship the Holy Spirit.

There is no precept, or example in the Scriptures, either for addressing the Holy Spirit personally in prayer, or of directly offering to Him our worship. We are enjoined to pray *in* the Spirit, that is, as guided by the Spirit; but are not told to pray *to* the Spirit. Our worship is to be *in* the Spirit, but we are not told to offer it *to* the Holy Spirit (Eph. 6:18; John 4:23). Apart from the Holy Spirit's leading, we can neither pray as we ought, nor worship as we should. He alone makes both these possible to the believer. We shall deal more fully with this subject later, under the heading, "The power for worship."

A great deal of misconception as to the Person and work of the Spirit of God is due to incorrect hymnology. Many hymns present the Spirit's work as though He were *outside* the believer, and as One who must be entreated to come in. The Scriptures plainly indicate that the Holy Spirit indwells the believer the moment he trusts in

Christ, and thereby seals him unto the day of redemption. (Eph. 1: 13-14; 4: 30; I Cor. 6: 19-20; John 14: 16-17; etc.)

While there is no precept or example, either of prayer or worship to the Spirit, this does not, for one moment, mean that He is less important, or that He occupies a subordinate place to the Father and the Son. On the contrary, He is equal and eternal with both. The Son of God, for the purpose of securing our redemption, became incarnate. As the Son of Man, He voluntarily submitted Himself to a life of absolute submission to the will of His Father, of complete obedience to the holy Scriptures, and to the empowerment and guidance of the Holy Spirit. Likewise, in this present dispensation, the mission and delight of the Holy Spirit is to occupy the believer with Christ, and to draw forth from the Christian's heart, worship to the Father and the Son. *There is no jealousy in the eternal Godhead.* Each Person in the Trinity delights to glorify the Other. When we worship the eternal Godhead, we therefore include, in our thought, each Person in the Divine Triunity. That grand old doxology can and should be sung by each believer:

> "Praise God from whom all blessings flow,
>   Praise Him, all creatures here below;
> Praise Him above, ye heavenly host,
>   Praise Father, Son, and Holy Ghost!'

We have learned, from the Scriptures, that the object of our worship is the Father and the Son, as empowered by the indwelling Holy Spirit, and guided by the word of God. The words of our Lord Jesus seem fitting to conclude this particular section of our subject: "If ye know these things, happy are ye if ye do them" (John 13:17). It is one thing to have *light* on this subject and be perfectly orthodox in our views; and another to *live in the good of it,* and to experience the great privilege and joy of worshipping the Father and the Son in the power of an ungrieved Holy Spirit. May each of us know much of this!

CHAPTER SIXTEEN

V. The Ground of Worship.

We now come to a consideration of the ground, or basis of worship. In this, as in everything else pertaining to life and godliness, we should know just where we stand. We shall think of three things which are fundamental to worship: redemption, relationship and representation.

1. Redemption.

The infinite holiness of God demands that all those who approach Him, with a view to worship, must be acceptable to Him. Holiness possesses two qualities, a love of righteousness and a hatred of iniquity (Heb. 1:9). We read that God is "of purer eyes than to behold evil, and canst not look upon iniquity" (Hab. 1:13). His intense hatred of sin is revealed everywhere upon the pages of Scripture. Because of His intrinsic and absolute holiness He must punish sin. We read that: "The wrath of God is revealed from heaven against all ungodliness and unrighteousness of men;" and that: "He can by no means clear the guilty" (Rom. 1:18; Exod. 34:7).

In view of this, the question may well be asked: "How can a person, who is both a sinner by nature and practice, be made fit to stand accepted in the presence of a holy God, and offer worship that delights His heart? The answer, in one word, is *redemption*. God has revealed in His word, that the only way a sinner can approach Him, and be accepted before Him, is *on the ground of a God appointed, scripturally presented, and divinely accepted substitutionary sacrifice.*

This fact is everywhere evident in Scripture, from Genesis to Revelation. Over the pages of the Old Testament are written the words: "The life of the flesh is in the blood; and I have given it to you upon the altar to make an atonement for your souls; for it is the blood that maketh an atonement for the soul" (Lev. 17:11). Over the pages of the New Testament appear the words: "Without the shedding of blood, there is no remission" (Heb. 9:22). There can be no approach to God, no standing before God, no acceptance with God, no pardon from God and no worship to God, apart from an acceptable substitutionary sacrifice which bears the sinner's sins, takes his place, died in his stead and is accepted by God on his behalf. No person can ever be accepted before God on the basis of his own merits, such as his morality, good works, religious observances, prayers, or good resolves. Both by nature and practice, every person is a sinner and, as such, deserves only eternal banishment from God's presence.

A beautiful illustration of the necessity for and the provision of God's redemption is found in Exod. 20:22-26. The law had just been given from Mount Sinai, consisting of ten commandments, which combined to reveal the righteous requirements of Deity. God well knew that the people of Israel were incapable of keeping this law, in spite of their proud avowal: "All that the Lord hath spoken, we will do" (Exod. 19:7-8). On God's instructions, Moses then re-ascended the mount, and received a further revelation from the Lord. This gives us a beautiful picture of both His holiness and grace.

Mark carefully the words God spake: "An altar of earth shall thou make unto Me, and shalt sacrifice thereon thy burnt offerings, and thy peace offerings, thy sheep and thine oxen. In all places where I record My name, I will come unto thee and I will bless thee." The meaning of this is plain. God knew that Israel would never be able to approach Him, or be blest by Him, on the basis of their law keeping, or because of human merit. Therefore, in His grace, He provided a means by which they could approach to Him, be blessed by Him and worship before Him. This trysting place between God and Israel was an *altar*. On that altar a substitutionary sacrifice was to be offered, by which the offerer was to be accepted by God *in his offering*. Thus he was enabled to worship God, not on the basis of his own efforts at law keeping, but on the ground of the sacrifice God had provided for him.

Notice God's desire for His people's blessing: " I will come unto thee and bless thee." There could have been no blessing for Israel *then,* nor can there be any for us *now,* if this blessing is to be conditioned on our obedience to the law, or on the ground of human merit. Blessing can only flow out from God to man on the ground of a substitutionary sacrifice. Let us illustrate. Here is an Israelite who has broken the law. He realizes that God is holy, righteous and just, and that his sin must be punished, unless he approaches God in the way He has indicated in His word. He therefore comes to the altar with a lamb for a substitutionary offering. He kneels down and places his hands on the head of the lamb, thus identifying himself with his offering and transferring, in picture, his guilt from himself to the offering. That lamb is now viewed by God as bearing the sins of that sinner. He next takes a knife and slays the lamb. As he watches the blood flowing from the spotless sacrifice, he can truthfully say: "Though I am a sinner, and therefore condemned by the law to die for my sins; yet that lamb has borne my sins, taken my place and died for me, to be accepted by God on my behalf." He is now in the position to worship God because of his acceptance before Him on the basis of redemption by the blood (or death) of the lamb. The language of Scripture is: "It (the offering) shall be accepted for him" (Lev. 1:4). Thus the offerer is accepted in and through his offering.

We have drawn attention to only one of very many pictures, or types of Christ in the Old Testament Scriptures. It required all these types and offerings to illustrate the great work which He, as the Lamb of God, accomplished on the altar of Calvary. It was there that "once in the consumation of the ages, He appeared to put away sin by the sacrifice of Himself" (Heb. 9:26). Upon that cross Christ willingly allowed Himself to be crucified, for He knew it was the only way by which a just and holy God could righteously pardon a guilty, but repentant and believing sinner. Each person who comes to God upon the sole basis of Christ's substitutionary sacrifice, rests simply in the finished work of Christ, and receives Christ as his own Savior and Lord is, that moment: "Justified freely by His (God's) grace, through the redemption that is in Christ Jesus" (Rom. 3:24).

Let every reader make certain that this is the only ground upon which he approaches God to worship, for there is no other way. Albert Midlane wrote a hymn that clearly and beautifully presents this glorious truth:

> "The perfect righteousness of God
>   Is witnessed in the Savior's blood;
> 'Tis in the cross of Christ we trace
>   His righteousness, yet wondrous grace.
>
> God could not pass the sinner by,
>   His sin demands that he must die;
> But in the cross of Christ we see,
>   How God can save us righteously.
>
> The sin is on the Savior laid,
>   'Tis by His blood the debt is paid;
> Stern justice can demand no more,
>   And mercy can dispense her store.
>
> The sinner who believes is free,
>   Can say: 'The Savior died for me!'
> Can point to the atoning blood,
>   And say: 'This made my peace with God'."

2. Relationship.

The second essential, or ground for worship, is relationship. Those who approach God do so with the word, "Father," upon their lips. Our Lord taught his disciples to say: "Our Father, which art in heaven, hallowed be Thy name" (Matt. 6:9). It is "the Father" that seeketh worshippers, and the worshippers are those who have become "the children of God by faith in Christ Jesus" (Gal. 3:26). This relationship, as we have previously seen, is brought about by the regenerating power of the Holy Spirit through the word of God. We read: "Being born again, not of corruptible seed, but of incorruptible, by the word of God which liveth and abideth forever" (I Pet. 1:23).

In the Old Testament, it was Aaron and his sons who were called upon to act as priests in connection with the place of worship; first, in the tabernacle and later, in the temple. It was their *relationship to Aaron* that qualified them for this privileged position. In the New Testament, it is "the sons and daughters of the Lord Almighty" who are called, fitted and privileged to worship. Over "the new and living way," which leads into "the holiest of all," are written the words: "For the children of God only."

Happy indeed are those who have come to know what it means to "have redemption through His blood, the forgiveness of sins, according to the riches of His grace" (Eph. 1:7). Such are assured, by the Word, that they have been born from above, and that this birth was "not of blood, (or heredity) nor of the will of the flesh, nor of the will of man, but of *God*" (John 1:13). It is as "brethren," or those in the family of God, that we are said to have "boldness to enter into the holiest by the blood of Jesus" (Heb. 10:19). The Christian comes not to a strange cold, distant and impersonal God to worship, but to One whom he knows and loves as his Father. One of the evidences of regeneration is that the believer receives the spirit of sonship, whereby he cries; "Abba, Father" (Rom. 8:15). Thus between God and those who worship Him, is the precious and permanent link of heaven-born relationship.

3. Representation.

The third essential for worship is representation. This means that the worshipper must have a high Priest as his Representative in the presence of God for him. Through the mediation of this great high Priest, his worship is presented and made acceptable to God.

Once more we must turn to God's picture book, the Old Testament, to learn from the "types," "figures" and "patterns" which God has given, just why the mediation of Christ, as our great high Priest, is absolutely essential if our worship is to be acceptable unto God. The two Old Testament books to read and study in connection with this truth are Exodus and Leviticus. The true significance of these, in turn, cannot possibly be understood apart from the New Testament book, the Epistle to the Hebrews. Should the reader desire a fuller knowledge of these truths, he will find George Soltau's: "The Tabernacle, The Priesthood, and The Offerings," a veritable gold mine of spiritual profit. C. H. M.'s "Notes on Leviticus," and "Notes on Exodus" will also yield its quota of wealth.

After God had redeemed His people by the sprinkled blood of the Passover lamb, and delivered them from Egypt's power through the divided waters of the Red Sea, He gave instructions to Moses to prepare a Tabernacle, by means of which He might dwell in the midst of the people of His choice. Elaborate instructions were given in regard to this Tabernacle and its furniture, and also concerning the selection, clothing, consecration and anointing of Aaron, together with a description of his varied duties. Aaron was the Divinely selected, called and appointed high priest of this tabernacle. While in this capacity, he acted as Israel's representative before God. Associated with Aaron were his sons, who acted as priests. Minute directions were also given as to the various kind of offerings, and the ritual in connection with each, as it was brought before and offered to God.

The last chapter of Exodus records the erection of the Tabernacle, the installation of the Aaronic priesthood, and concludes with God's approving response to all that which had been done in obedience to His instructions. We read that: "A cloud covered the tent of the congregation, and the glory of the Lord filled the tabernacle . . . The cloud of the Lord was upon the tabernacle by day, and fire on it by night, in the sight of all the house of Israel, throughout all their journeys" (Exod. 40: 34, 38).

What we wish to draw particular attention to is the high priestly ministry of Aaron, as he performed his duties, as Israel's representative, in the presence of God. In the epistle to the Hebrews, Christ, as "the great high Priest of our profession," is *contrasted* with Aaron, and *compared* with Melchisedec. In fact, the key word of this epistle is "better." Christ is seen as superior to Aaron in every respect, both as to His Person and His work. Christ offered a "better sacrifice" (Heb. 9: 23), by which He brought in a "better covenant" (8: 6), which contained "better promises" (8: 6), of "better things" (12: 24), resulting in a "better hope" (7: 19), and leading to a "better country" (11: 16).

Undoubtedly the outstanding event of the year to the children of Israel was the great day of Atonement, which is described in Leviticus 16. On this occasion all the sins, transgressions and iniquities of the nation were brought to remembrance, and a substitutionary sacrifice was offered for them by means of which an atonement, or covering for them, was made. This was the only day of the year that the high priest was allowed to pass through the veil and enter into the holiest of all.

The ceremony connected with this day of Atonement is full of spiritual significance. First of all, Aaron had to make an atonement for his own sins, before he could do anything on behalf of the people whom he represented before God. Accordingly, he took a young bullock for a sin offering and a ram for a burnt offering. After laying his hands on the bullock, he killed it at the brazen altar. He then took his censer which was filled with burning coals and placed incense thereon. With the blood of the sin offering, he now entered within the veil into the holiest of all. With the incense rising in clouds, Aaron proceeded to sprinkle the blood both on and before the mercy seat seven times, and thus made atonement for *himself*.

After this he took two goats and presented them before the Lord at the door of the tabernacle. Next, he cast lots upon the goats, one lot for what was called "the Lord's goat," and the other for what was termed, "the scapegoat." He then slew the goat of the Lord and, with its blood and his censer, again entered the veil and sprinkled the blood seven times on and before the mercy seat, and thus made atonement for *the people*. After this, he returned to the gate of the tabernacle, laid his hands upon the head of the scapegoat, and confessed over it "all the iniquities of Israel, and all their transgressions in all their sins," and thus transferred them, in picture, to the head of the scapegoat. This goat was then led away, by a fit man, into the wilderness and there turned loose, to return no more.

This ceremony, like all the others in connection with

the worship of Israel, is utterly meaningless apart from the New Testament. When we turn to the epistle to the Hebrews, all this involved ritual becomes beautifully clear and redolent with Christ. The fact that Aaron had to present an offering for his own sins is used to show, by *contrast*, the superiority of Christ as our great high Priest. We read: "He needeth not . . . to offer up sacrifice, first for His own sins, and then for the people's, for this He did *once*, when He offered up Himself" (Heb. 7:27). The two goats constitute a double type of Christ's sacrifice, illustrating the fact that He not only died for our sins to meet every claim of a holy God, but also bore them away from God's presence for ever.

The infinite superiority of Christ's sacrifice to that of Aaron's is further seen in the fact that the Lord Jesus is not only described as the *Offerer*, but also the *Offering*. Moreover, this offering on the day of Atonement had to be repeated each year, so that there was a continuous remembrance of sins (Heb. 10:3). In contrast to this we are told that: "*Once* in the end of the world (the consummation of the ages) hath He (Christ) appeared to put away sin by the sacrifice of Himself" (Heb. 9:26). We are further assured that believers "are sanctified through the offering of the body of Jesus Christ, once for all" (Heb. 10:10). We are further informed that there had to be many high priests in Israel, "because they were not suffered to continue by reason of death; but this Man, (Christ, the great high Priest) because He continueth *ever*, hath an *unchangeable Priesthood*" (Heb. 7:23-24).

Just as Aaron, with the atoning blood and the fragrant incense, entered through the veil into the holiest of all, as Israel's representative, and sprinkled the blood before and on the mercy seat, thus satisfying all the demands of God's holy throne; so Christ, by virtue of His own blood has "entered in, once (for all) into the holy place, having obtained eternal redemption for us" (Heb. 9:11-12). Now, as our Representative, He ever lives in the presence of God on behalf of His people, with all the eternal virtue and value of His divine Person and perfectly accomplished redemption!

Not only has our Lord entered heaven to engage in His work as our great high Priest, but He has also opened up the way for all His redeemed people to enter into the holiest through Him, there to engage in their highest occupation—the worship of God. Just as Aaron, within the holiest, caused clouds of incense to rise before the blood-stained mercy seat; so now Christ, our great high Priest, because of the eternal virtue and value of His Person, and the efficacy of His precious blood, causes the incense of our worship to rise before God's holy throne and be acceptable unto the Father.

Mark carefully what God has to say in this regard: "For by one offering He hath perfected forever them that are sanctified . . . Their sins and iniquities will I remember no more. Now where remission of these is, there is no more offering for sin. Having therefore, brethren, boldness to enter into the holiest by the blood of Jesus, by a new and living way, which He hath consecrated for us, through the veil, that is to say, His flesh; and having an high Priest over the house of God; let us draw near with a true heart, in full assurance of faith, having our hearts sprinkled from an evil conscience and our bodies washed with pure water" (Heb. 10:14-22). No wonder the inspired writer, as he contemplated the super-excellency of the priesthood of Christ, as contrasted with Aaron, said simply: "Now of the things which we have spoken, this is the sum: We have such an high Priest, who is set on the right hand of the throne of the Majesty in the heavens" (Heb. 8:1).

What a wealth of meaning is compressed into those six monosyllables: "We have *such* an high Priest." The whole epistle is taken up with this theme. Christ is described as being a *powerful* high Priest, for "In that He Himself hath suffered, being tempted, he is able to succour them that are tempted" (Heb. 2:18). He is a *merciful* high Priest, for He knows all the frailties of His people, and meets their every need (Heb. 2:17). He is a *faithful* high Priest, both to God and man. Unlike Aaron, He is incapable of failure. He never fails in the fulfilment of His promises, or in the execution of His duties. He never slumbers nor sleeps, but ever lives to accomplish His gracious purposes (Heb. 2:17). He is a *sympathetic* high Priest, for He is touched with all the "feeling of our infirmities"; and was "in all points tempted like as we are, yet without sin" (Heb. 4:15). Christ was "the Man of sorrows and acquainted with grief" (Isa. 53:3). He knows what it means to be weary, to hunger and thirst, to be betrayed and forsaken, to suffer agony and to die. The child of God is therefore assured of both a sympathetic ear and an understanding heart from his Representative. He is an *ever-living* high Priest. "Death hath no more dominion over Him" (Rom. 6:9). He lives in "the power of an endless life;" and is therefore untiring and unceasing in His activities on behalf of His own. Thus His people are being "saved to the uttermost" through His ceaseless intercession on their behalf. (Heb. 7:25). Then He is an *exalted* High Priest, for He is described as "a *great* high Priest," and One who has been "made higher than the heavens" (Heb. 4:14; 7:26). How great He is, no finite mind will ever comprehend:

> "The Father only—glorious claim—
> The Son can comprehend."

Lastly, He is an *eternal* high Priest, for He is made "an high Priest for ever after the order of Melchisedec" (Heb. 6:20).

It is grand indeed to see how full and complete is this high priestly ministry of our Lord. His *heart* is occupied for us, for He loves His own with a tender and unceasing sympathy (John 11:33-36). His *mind* is occupied for us, for His people are the subject of His constant thought (Ps. 40:17). His *eyes* are constantly upon us, to anticipate and provide for all our needs, for "He that keepeth . . . shall neither slumber nor sleep" (Ps. 121:3-4). His *hands* are busy for us, guarding, guiding and protecting the sheep of His pasture (John 10:26-30). His *ears* are ever open to His people's cry (Ps. 34:15). His *lips* are constantly used as He pleads for His people and, by His ceaseless advocacy and intercession, maintains their cause before the Father's face (Heb. 7:25; I John 2:1). His *feet* are not idle, for He companies with His own, and promises never to leave or forsake them. The two disciples on the Emmaus highway discovered, to their delight, the blessedness of the Savior's companionship (Luke 24:15). Yes, we can truthfully testify: "We have *such* an high Priest!"

Christ is thus our divine Representative in the presence of God for us. He has secured our *redemption* by His own most precious blood. He has made our *relationship* actual with God. He now, "in the power of an endless life," as our great high Priest, *represents* us before the Father's throne. Thus the three-fold ground of worship, which the holiness of the triune God demanded, has been perfectly and gloriously provided. The redeemed child of God need not stand outside in fear but, with holy boldness, may draw near into the holiest of all. He is assured that his Representative, the great high Priest, will present his worship before the Father in all the perfection of His own Person. All believers may now reverently and adoringly repeat: "We have *such* an high Priest!"

CHAPTER SEVENTEEN

VI. The Power For Worship.
(John 4: 23-24)

We have noted the meaning, importance, authority, object and ground of worship. We now come to a consideration of the power for it. How is the believer to be made spiritually capable of true worship? The answer is simple: The power for worship is the Holy Spirit, the third Person in the Godhead. It may be helpful to take a brief survey of His Person and work, so as to better appreciate how essential He is, not only to the believer's worship, but also in every department of his life. We shall think first of

1. His Person.

There is a great deal of misconception regarding the Holy Spirit. Sometimes He is referred to as though He was merely an "influence," or an "atmosphere," and is often mentioned as "it." Others seem to create the impression that the Spirit is but an emmanation from God, and not a distinct and Divine Personality, equal and eternal with the Father and the Son.

The personality of the Holy Spirit is everywhere evident in the word of God. Christ's own words should be sufficient to establish this fact. Mark the personal pronouns used by Christ in referring to Him: "It is expedient for you that I go away: for if I go not away, the Comforter will not come unto you; but if I depart, I will send *Him* unto you. And when *He* is come, *He* will reprove the world of sin, and of righteousness, and of judgment: . . . When *He* the Spirit of truth, is come, *He* will guide you unto all truth: for *He* shall not speak of (from) *Him-*

self; but whatsoever *He* shall hear, that shall *He* speak: and *He* will show you things to come. *He* shall glorify me: for *He* shall receive of mine, and shall show it unto you" (John 16:7-8; 13-14). In this short passage alone, Christ used twelve personal pronouns to describe the Holy Spirit and the work He should do.

Personality necessitates the possession of three qualities: *knowledge,* or intelligence; *feelings,* or emotions; and *will,* or volition. Scripture bears record that the Holy Spirit possesses each of these qualities, as also does the Father and the Son. He has *intellect,* for we are told He "knows" (Rom. 8:27), "teaches" (John 14:26), "testifies" (John 14:26), "guides" (John 16:13), "hears" (John 16:13), and "speaks" (John 16:13).

He has *emotions,* for it is said He can be "grieved" (Eph. 4:30), "quenched" (I Thess. 5:19), "resisted" (Acts 7:51), and "despised" (Heb. 10:29).

He has a *will,* for He "strives" (Gen. 6:3), "lusts (or desires) against the flesh" (Gal. 5:17), "reproves" (John 16:8), "makes intercession" (Rom. 8:26), and "shows" (John 16:13).

He has many titles in the word of God. Each title is full of spiritual significance and indicates the various aspects of His character and work. He is the "Holy Spirit," which emphasises His absolute holiness. He is "the Spirit of *truth,*" because of His perfect trustworthiness. He is the *"Comforter,"* or "Paraclete," which means: "one called alongside to help." He is "the Spirit of God," stressing His Deity. He is "the Spirit of *grace,*" pointing to the unmerited favor He shows. He is "the Spirit of *Christ,*" indicating His mission to glorify the Son of God. He is "the Spirit of *glory,*" in that His excellencies are displayed in the Word. He is "the Spirit of *promise,*" which points to His sealing of the believer as the guarantee of his eternal blessedness. These, and many other titles, all combine to show forth the Deity of His Person, the dignity of His character and the glory of His displayed attributes.

This brief glance into the Scriptures should be sufficient to clearly indicate that the Holy Spirit is a Person, possessing full, equal and eternal Deity with both Father and Son. How we should praise God for this "holy, heavenly Guest," apart from whose presence and power we could never have been saved, or brought into God's presence, or enabled to worship! Now let us consider

2. His Work.

(1) **In relation to Creation.** (Gen. 1:2). Here is the first mention of the Spirit. He is seen as moving (literally, "brooding") over the face of a chaotic earth, until darkness gave place to light, and chaos was succeeded by order and beauty. Here is a striking picture of His work today in the awakening, conviction and regeneration of a ruined, guilty and helpless sinner!

(2) **In relation to the Scriptures.** We owe the written revelation of God's word to Him, for we are told: "Prophecy came not in old time by the will of man: but holy men of God spake as they were moved by the Holy Ghost" (II Pet. 1:21). David testified: "The Spirit of the Lord spake by me, and His word was in my tongue" (II Sam. 23:2). Paul declared: "All Scripture is given by inspiration of God" (Literally, "is God breathed") (II Tim. 3:16). The Spirit of God so came upon and possessed these Old Testament prophets that what they wrote, under His Divine control, were the very words of God.

The Spirit's inspiration of the New Testament record is indicated by Christ Himself. The *four gospels* are accounted for by the words: "He shall bring all things to

your remembrance, whatsoever I have said unto you"
(John 14:26). The *Epistles* are provided for by the
words: "He shall teach you all things" (John 14:26).
The book of *Revelation* is taken care of by the words:
"He shall show you things to come" (John 16:13). Thus
the entire range of holy Scripture has come to us through
the Spirit of God.

(3) **In relation to Christ.** The Holy Spirit is prominent in the life of our Lord.

(a) In Christ's *incarnation.* Gabriel was instructed
to tell Mary: "The Holy Spirit shall come upon thee, and
the power of the Highest shall overshadow thee: therefore also that holy Thing which shall be born of thee shall
be called the Son of God" (Luke 1:25).

(b) *In His life on earth.* He descended as a dove
upon Christ at His baptism (Matt. 3:16). He led the
Savior into His *temptation,* and empowered Him during
His testing, from which He emerged more than conqueror
(Matt. 4:1-14). The same was true of our Lord's minis-
try, for we are told it was in the power of the Spirit that
Christ spake (Luke 4:18-22; John 3:34).

(c) *In His death.* Scripture informs us it was
"through the eternal Spirit" that Christ offered Himself
to God. (Heb. 9:14).

(d) *In His resurrection.* Furthermore, it is revealed
that Christ was "declared to be the Son of God with
power, according to the Spirit of holiness by the resurrection from the dead" (Rom. 1:4).

(e) *In His post-resurrection ministry.* Christ, during the forty days after His resurrection, companied with
His disciples. Nor did He ascend back to heaven until
"He, through the Holy Ghost, had given commandments
unto the apostles whom He had chosen" (Acts 1:2).

(4) **In His relation to the world of men.** (John 16: 8-11). He was sent to convict it of *sin,* because of its unbelief of Christ, as evidenced by its rejection and crucifixion of the Son of God. He convicts of *righteousness,* because God has indicated, by the resurrection of Christ, that all His righteousness claims have been met by His substitutionary sacrifice for sin. He convicts of *judgment,* because Satan, the prince of this world, has been defeated and judged. The Devil now awaits the execution of his sentence, banishment to the lake of fire.

Thus the Spirit's work in relation to the unsaved is to produce within them, through the preaching of the Word:

(a) *A sense of their need,* as unbelieving sinners.

(b) *A realization that God's righteousness* has been revealed in the redemptive work of Christ, in proof of which He has been raised to sit at God's right hand.

(c) *That inasmuch as Satan has been judged,* all who die rejecting Christ, must share his eternal doom. In other words, He convicts the sinner of his need, unfolds God's remedy in Christ, and warns of the certainty of judgment. In this day of shallow preaching and professional evangelism, with its "guaranteed results," there is a great need to so preach the word that, through it, the Spirit may do His work of conviction and conversion.

(5) **In relation to the believer.**

(a) *He awakens the soul and leads to faith in Christ.* See Acts 2:37; 7:54. He opens the *ears* of the sinner to hear with the hearing of faith. He then opens the spiritual *eyes* of the sinner's mind to see his guilty and undone state, and the remedy Christ has provided. He next opens the *heart* of the believer to trust Christ's finished work, and to receive Him as his own Savior. Lastly, He opens the *mouth* of the child of God to confess Christ as the Lord of his life. This is the Divine "quickening," which only the Spirit of God can produce. (Eph. 2:1-2).

(b)   When the truth of the gospel is believed and Christ is received, *He indwells the believer,* and thereby seals him unto the day of redemption (Eph. 1:13; Eph. 4: 30; I Cor. 6:19-20).

(c)   *He enlightens the Christian.* This He does by creating a capacity for spiritual things, and imparting spiritual discernment, thus enabling him to understand what previously he could not comprehend. (I Cor. 2: 10-16, cp. II Pet. 1:4).

(d)   *He guides the believer into all truth.* (John 16: 13; 14:26). As the believer reads, meditates and studies the pages of Scripture, and then seeks to walk in obedience to what he sees written therein; the Holy Spirit will lead him further into the truth of God, so that he will "grow in grace and in the knowledge of the Lord Jesus Christ."

(e)   *He empowers the Christian for service.* Christ's promise to His disciples before Pentecost was: "Ye shall receive power after that the Holy Spirit is come upon you: and ye shall be witnesses unto Me" (Acts 1:8). As the Spirit is allowed to dwell ungrieved within the believer, He will impart power to testify, either privately or publicly, and use him both to bring other souls to Christ, or to lead his fellow believers into a better knowledge of the word of God.

(f)   *He produces fruit in the Christian's life.* As the Spirit is allowed to have His way in the believer, others will see "the fruit of the Spirit" manifested in his life. This fruit has a nine fold quality. *Godward,* there will be "love, joy and peace." *Manward,* there will be seen "long suffering, gentleness and goodness." *Selfward,* there will be "faith, meekness and temperance" (or self control). (Gal. 5: 22-23).

(g) *He glorifies Christ.* (John 16: 14). That is to say, He displays to the believer the many excellencies of the Son of God. He takes of the "things of Christ," and so impresses the mind and heart of the Christian with all the virtues and value of the Savior, that he is carried away and exclaims: "He is the chiefest amongst ten thousand!" Thus it is the Holy Spirit's delight to make Christ more precious to the soul, and thus glorify Him in and through the believer.

(6) **In relation to the Church.**

We are told that: "By one Spirit are ("were" R. V.) we all baptized into one body, whether we be Jews or Gentiles, whether we be bond or free; and have been all made to drink into one Spirit" (I Cor. 12: 13). This is the event which took place on the day of Pentecost. He came, in accordance with the promise of Christ, and united all believers in Christ into one body, the Church. Paul also likens the Church to a building, and says: "In Christ, all the building fitly framed together groweth unto an holy temple in the Lord: in Whom ye also are builded together for an habitation of God through the Spirit" (Eph. 2: 21-22). Again, Paul exhorts the saints in Ephesus and says: "I . . . beseech you that ye walk worthy of the vocation wherewith ye are called. With all lowliness and meekness, with long suffering, forbearing one another in love; endeavoring to keep the unity of the Spirit in the bond of peace" (Eph. 4: 1-3). Thus the Spirit of God seeks to lead the people of God to maintain the unity that He Himself has formed.

In chapters 12-14 of I Corinthians, the Spirit of God is seen in His relation to the operations of a local assembly. Here He is described as imparting to, encouraging the development of, and empowering the manifestation of the

various spiritual gifts which Christ has bestowed on believers. (Eph. 4:8-16). When these are exercised according to His leading, they will result in the edifying, or
building up of the assembly, so that it will present a united
testimony for Christ. As each believer responds to His
guidance in the exercise of his gift, a spiritual atmosphere
is created which will cause an unbeliever, who comes into
such an assembly, to fall upon his face and "worship God,
and report that God is in (among) you of a truth" (I Cor.
14:24-25).

It cannot be too strongly emphasized that spiritual
gifts must be exercised in the power of the Spirit of God.
Apart from this, all the ecclesiastical machinery in the
world is worse than useless. Scriptural principles require
spiritual power for their operation, and this spiritual
power comes only through the Holy Spirit of God.

(7) In relation to worship.

The work of the Spirit of God, in connection with worship, is to lead each individual believer, through the word
of God, to an ever increasing apprehension and appreciation of the Father and the Son. Therefore the need for
each Christian to be both a reader and a student of the
holy Scriptures. The Holy Spirit will never lead anyone
to believe, or to do anything contrary to the word of God.
As the believer is taught by the Spirit, through the Word,
and is obedient to what he learns, the Spirit will lead him
on to a deeper knowledge of Divine things and particularly in the matter of worship.

We have already learned that worship is, first of all,
an individual matter. It is not primarily something that
is to be stored up to be presented at a meeting; but that
which should rise continually from the believer's soul,
day by day, as he appreciates all God is and has done, as
revealed in His Son. When a company of believers, in this

spiritual condition, meet together as an assembly, what a volume of Spirit-led worship there will be!

The leading of the Spirit is particularly evidenced as a number of believers gather, in a scriptural manner, to remember the Lord Jesus. One can mark the definite guidance of this "holy, heavenly Guest," as He impresses one and another, either to give out a hymn, or to lead the assembly in worship, or to read a portion from the Word. Each hymn or spoken word is seen to be in perfect harmony with the particular theme of the meeting. This makes for a gradual, but steady progression of worship, which rises higher and higher, until the bread is broken and the cup passed. One has only to attend such a meeting to be convinced of the absolute necessity for, and the reality of the power and presence of the Spirit of God, as He occupies the hearts of the believers with the Father and the Son, and leads them out, as a company of royal priests, in adoring worship.

Each believer must therefore see to it that he does not *grieve* the Holy Spirit by any misconduct on his part, or else his worship will be hindered. Should he do so, prompt confession of, and the forsaking of that sin will restore the communion. Each assembly, in turn, must be careful not to *quench* the Spirit. This may be done in many ways. (a) By denying or despising the ministry He would seek to give through one and another whom He has gifted. (b) By being disobedient to His leading. (c) By refusing to welcome to the Lord's supper each exercised believer who desires to thus remember the Lord Jesus, and who is known to be sound in his life and doctrine. (d) By permitting sin to remain unjudged in its midst. (e) By allowing a sectarian, or party-spirit, to be fostered within it. (See Eph. 4:28-30; I Thess. 5:19-21; I Cor. 5:1-8; 3:1-5; 14:40).

For the gift of the Holy Spirit we do well to praise God. Arthur Cutting's beautiful and scriptural hymn is appropriate in this connection:

"O God our hearts are lifted
    To Thee, in grateful praise,
Responsive to Thy Spirit,
    A joyful song we raise;
For He, Thy gracious purpose
    In Christ to us has shown,
That now, as sons before Thee,
    His favor is our own.

In nature's darkness shrouded,
    And dead in sins we lay,
Until Thy Holy Spirit
    Transformed our night to day;
Awakened needs within us,
    Begetting us anew,
And by love's strong compelling,
    Our souls to Jesus drew.

We trusted Him as Savior,
    When rest and peace we sought,
And now Thy Spirit seals us,
    As those His blood has bought.
Made Thine, He ne'er will leave us,
    For He is pledged to stay,
As earnest of our portion,
    Until redemption's day.

O may Thy Holy Spirit,
    Blest unction from on high,
With all His rich infilling,
    Lead us to glorify
The risen Christ our Savior,
    By loyal witness true,
Constraining us to serve Him
    In all we say and do."

(8) In relation to Service.

True, Spirit-led *worship,* will lead the believer to render loyal Spirit-led and Spirit-empowered *service* for the Lord. The Acts of the Apostles might better have been entitled: "The Acts of the Holy Spirit." It is He who is seen throughout the entire book, empowering believers for the preaching of the gospel, and granting them an abundant harvest of precious souls.

Believers are described therein as being "full of the Holy Spirit and of faith." These Christians knew what it meant, by experience, to "walk in the Spirit," to "pray in the Spirit," to "live in the Spirit," and to be "led by the Spirit." Truly, those who worship most will serve God best, and only the Spirit can supply the power for both.

In view of these things, may each of us see to it that, by the grace of God, we also shall be included in the number of those who "worship in Spirit, and in truth."

Chapter Eighteen

VII. The Manner of Worship.

By this is meant those inner spiritual qualities which must always characterize the believer if his worship is to be acceptable to God. It is possible for one to draw nigh to God with his lips, and yet be far removed from Him in heart. God had to say of Israel: "This people draw near Me with their mouth, and with their lips do honor Me, but have removed their heart far from Me" (Isa. 29:13). Through His prophet Ezekiel God declared: "They hear Thy words, but they will not do them, for with their mouth they show much love, but their heart goeth after their covetousness" (Ezek. 33:31). The tendency of everything, with which man is in any way associated, is to degenerate, and worship is no exception. In the case of Israel, that which was described in the beginning as a "feast unto Jehovah," came to be referred to, hundreds of years later, as a "feast of the Jews" (Exod. 13:6; John 6:4). Thus, in the process of time, the spiritual emphasis was transferred from God to man.

It will be readily appreciated that anything presented to God must fulfil certain Divine requirements, if it is to meet with His approval. Not only must the offerer and the offering be acceptable to God, but the *spirit in which it is offered* must also be pleasing to Him. Though correctness of doctrinal belief and outward conformity to certain scriptural principles is necessary, it is not enough. The *spiritual condition* of the worshipper is a contributing factor, as to whether or not his worship is to be acceptable to the Father.

God taught Samuel this lesson, when He sent him to anoint one of the sons of Jesse to be king in place of Saul.

As Eliab, the eldest of the family stood before him, Samuel's inward thought was: "Surely the Lord's anointed is before me!" But God said to him: "Look not on his countenance, or on the height of his stature; because I have refused him; for the Lord seeth not as man seeth; for man looketh on the outward appearance, but the Lord looketh on the heart" (I Sam. 16:6-7).

Our Lord pressed this truth home upon His hearers. Addressing the Pharisees, who were most punctillious in the *outward* observance of the many ceremonials of their religion, He said: "Ye are they which justify yourselves before men; but God knoweth your hearts: for that which is highly esteemed among men is abomination in the sight of God" (Luke 16:15). How this should search the heart of every Christian! It is sadly possibly to sing, most melodiously, a beautiful hymn of worship, and even audibly express, in well chosen and scriptural language, the worship of an assembly; and yet fail to reach God's ear, or draw forth Divine approval. The *quality* of the worship is determined by the *spirituality* of the worshipper. What may appear to be worship may, in reality, be only a "fair show in the flesh" and, as such, only an "abomination in the sight of God."

Let us, therefore, consider the manner of worship, or those spiritual qualities that must be the essential accompaniment if we are to worship God as we should. We shall think of three of these essential qualities: Worship must be spiritual, sincere and intelligent.

1. Worship should be spiritual.

Our Lord declared emphatically: "God is a Spirit, and they that worship Him must worship Him in Spirit and in truth" (John 4:24). In these words Christ indicated that only that worship which was prompted, led and empowered by the Holy Spirit would be acceptable to God. It is tragically possible for one who has been born of the Spirit, and who is indwelt by the Spirit, to be anything but spiritual.

Paul divided all humanity into three distinct classes. First, is the *natural man*. By this is meant man as he is by nature; unregenerate, and therefore incapable of understanding Divine things, or of pleasing God. Second, is the *spiritual man*. He is one who has been born from above, is indwelt by the Spirit of God, and consequently possesses the capacity for discerning and appreciating Divine truth, and who seeks to live a life well-pleasing to God. Third, is the *carnal man*. This person, though born from above, and indwelt by the Holy Spirit, lives his life on earth in the energy of the flesh, instead of in the power of the Spirit. There were many such believers in the assembly at Corinth and he had to say of such: "I . . . could not speak unto you as unto spiritual, but as unto carnal, even as unto babes in Christ . . . for ye are yet carnal" (I Cor. 2:14-3:2).

It is important to note that Paul does not, for one moment, question the salvation of these carnal believers, for he addresses them as "brethren," and as being "sanctified in Christ Jesus, and called saints" (I Corinthians 1:2, 10). What he does draw attention to is the fact that they were not "spiritual." That is to say, they were not living in the energy of the Spirit, or in the enjoyment of Divine things. Their lives were characterized by God-dishonoring manifestations of the flesh, as evidenced by their divisions, indifference, selfishness and lack of spiritual growth.

While in this carnal condition of soul, their worship had been adversely affected. The Lord's supper, which should have been characterized by Spirit-led worship, harmony and power, had degenerated into a thing of

shame and confusion. In fact, many of these carnal believers had suffered the extreme punitive discipline of
God, for Paul had to say: "For this cause, many are weak
and sickly among you, and many sleep (or have died) (I
Cor. 11:23-30). Their carnality had grieved, quenched
and limited the Spirit of God in their assembly gatherings, so that little worship had ascended from their midst.
Instead of a spiritual atmosphere which was conducive
to worship, there was the cold, clammy spirit of formalism
and carnality which stifled any spiritual exercise of the
soul in worship.

Let us not imagine, for one moment, that this spirit of
carnality died with the Corinthian assembly. It is a
danger to which every Christian has been exposed since
the Christian era began. It is greatly to be feared that
there is altogether too much of it in the present day. It
well becomes each believer to pray as David did: "Search
me, O God, and know my heart: try me, and know my
thoughts: and see if there be any wicked way in me, and
lead me in the way everlasting" (Ps. 139:23-24). The
price of spirituality is high. It may cost us all we have,
but it is not too much, for nothing can compensate the
believer for its loss. The high cost of spirituality is only
exceeded by the higher cost of carnality! The price one
pays for spirituality is the same as that of peace, namely,
eternal vigilance. We shall note later some of the evidences of carnality under the heading, "Hindrances to
Worship."

We have seen that worship, to be acceptable, must be
spiritual, and that this necessitates the spirituality of the
worshipper. The believer must therefore resolutely and
assiduously discipline himself, so as to cultivate his spiritual life on a high plane. The Devil and his wiles must
be withstood, as the believer stands panoplied in all the
armor of God. The world, with all its allurements, must

be definitely declined. The flesh, with all its evil desires, must be constantly denied. See Eph. 6:10-18; I John 2: 15-17; Rom. 13:14. Thus the Christian must rule himself with an iron hand, saying "no" to self in all its many forms, and "yes" to God in all that He demands. The result of this will be spirituality, in the atmosphere of which he can worship God acceptably, with reverence and godly fear.

Carnality would fain counterfeit spirituality, by substituting artificial enthusiasm for holy zeal; mere fleshly emotionalism, for the joy of the Lord; organization, for the unity of the Spirit; religious externals, for inward reality; and cold orthodoxy of doctrine, for the warm experience, power and enjoyment of its truth in the soul. The best preventative against artificiality is spirituality. There will be no need to pump up worship when the soul is in conscious communion with God, and living in the enjoyment of spiritual realities. There will be no call to force oneself to worship. It will rise spontaneously from the soul, even as the smoke of the burnt sacrifice of old ascended to the One to whom it was offered.

2. Worship should be sincere.

Christ declared it must not only be in "spirit," but "in truth." This is to say, our worship must not only be guided by the truth of God's word, but it must be presented in a truthful, or sincere way. There must be no sham in worship, or the pretence of claiming a greater spirituality than we really possess. God hates hypocrisy in any shape or form. Our Lord's reference to the Pharisee's prayer, with its five capital "I's" bears eloquent testimony to His detestation of religious humbug (Luke 18:9-14). Someone has defined hypocrisy as: *"pretending to be, what we don't intend to be."*

The word "sincere," means "without wax." In the olden days sculptors sometimes used wax to fill up a flaw in the stone images they had carved. When the purchaser exposed this image to the rays of the sun, the wax melted and the imperfection was thus disclosed. Often a dealer in images would proclaim his wares as being "sine cere," or "without wax." Thus he guaranteed the purchaser against sham and pretense. Paul's desire for the Philippian believers was that they might be "sincere and without offence till the day of Christ" (Phil. 1:10). God wants the sincere worship of a sincere heart.

The history of Israel can again furnish us with an example of how God views the absence of sincerity in worship. In the last book of the Old Testament we find God saying, through His prophet Malachi: "Ye offer polluted bread upon Mine altar; and ye say, 'Wherein have we polluted thee?' In that ye say, 'The table of the Lord is contemptible.' And if ye offer the blind for sacrifice, is it not evil? and if ye offer, the lame and sick, is it not evil? Offer it now unto thy governor; will he be pleased with thee, or accept thy person? saith the Lord of Hosts . . . I have no pleasure in you, saith the Lord of Hosts, neither will I accept an offering at your hand . . . Ye said also, 'Behold, what a weariness is it!' and ye have snuffed at it, saith the Lord of Hosts; and ye brought that which was torn, and the lame, and the sick; thus ye brought an offering: Should I accept this of your hand? saith the Lord?" (Mal. 1:7-14).

The prophet Amos, the herdsman of Tekoa, was sent by God to both expose and denounce the apostasy and hypocrisy of Israel. Amongst other things, God said through him to Israel: "I hate, I despise your feast days, and I will not smell in your solemn assemblies. Though ye offer Me burnt offerings, and your meat offerings, I will not accept them: neither will I regard the peace offerings of your

fat beasts. Take thou away from Me the noise of thy
songs; for I will not hear the melody of thy viols. But let
judgment run down as waters, and righteousness as a
mighty stream" (Amos 5:21-24). Thus the very feasts
which God had given them explicit directions to observe
became, through their hypocrisy and double dealing, an
offence to Him! Though Israel maintained an outward
orthodoxy in their observance of these feast days and the
offerings which God had commanded, yet their unright-
eous lives gave the lie to their profession.

From it we can surely learn that orthodoxy of belief
and correctness of religious observance is a poor substitute for righteous living. It is possible for a person's
head to be in the clouds of orthodoxy, while his feet are
in the mire of unsavory practices. God's advice to Israel
was: "Seek good and not evil, that ye may live; and so the
Lord, the God of Hosts, shall be with you, as ye have
spoken. Hate the evil, and love the good, and establish
judgment in the gate: it may be that the Lord God of hosts
will be gracious unto the remnant of Joseph" (Amos 5:
14-15). God looks for consistency between standing and
state; between creed and conduct; between lip and life;
between belief and behavior; between profession and expression. It was this that David had in mind when he
said: "Thou desireth truth in the inward parts" (Ps. 51:
6).

Through the great prophet Isaiah, God exposed the
double dealing of Israel in these soul searching words:
"To what purpose is the multitude of your sacrifices unto
Me? . . . I am full of the burnt offerings and rams, and
the fat of fed beasts; and I delight not in the blood of
bullocks, or of lambs, or of goats . . . Bring no more vain
oblations; incense is an abomination unto Me; the new
moons and sabbaths, the calling of assemblies, I cannot
away with; it is iniquity, even the solemn meeting. Your

new moons and your appointed feasts My soul hateth; they are a trouble unto Me; I am weary to hear them. And when ye spread forth your hands, I will hide Mine eyes from you: yea, when ye make many prayers, I will not hear: your hands are full of blood. Wash you, make you clean; put away the evil of your doings from before Mine eyes; cease to do evil; learn to do well; seek judgment, relieve the oppressed, judge the fatherless, plead for the widow" (Isa. 1:11-20). This is simply another way of saying: "They that worship Him must worship Him in Spirit and in truth."

Our Lord twice quoted God's word through the prophet Hosea: "For I desired mercy, and not sacrifice" (Hos. 6:6). The word mercy is literally, "goodness," or rectitude of conduct and decency of life. Christ quoted it, first in connection with the Pharisees' criticism that He ate with publicans and sinners. The Pharisees were a sect of separatists who prided themselves on their meticulous outward observance of the ceremonial part of the law; but on the whole were utterly inconsistent in their lives. These people were Christ's bitterest enemies. They desired nothing more than to kill Him, because of His searching analysis of their character, and bold denunciation of their hypocrisy. Our Lord's words to them were: "Go ye and learn what that meaneth, 'I will have mercy, and not sacrifice:' for I am not come to call the righteous, but sinners to repentance" (Matt. 9:13). It was not that God did not *desire* sacrifices, for He Himself hath ordained them. What our Lord emphasized here was that the act of sacrificing and offering of animals must ever be accompanied by the consistent life and sincere attitude of the offerer, if his worship was to be acceptable. If the choice is to be between strict observance of ritual, and goodness and sincerity of life: then the latter must always take the precedence.

Christ's second reference to Hos. 6:6 was in connection with the Pharisees harsh and unjust judgment of His disciples, as they plucked and ate some grains of wheat on the Sabbath day. The Pharisees argued that the plucking of these grains constituted "reaping;" and the rubbing of them in the hands constituted "threshing." They affirmed that both these acts were a direct contravention of their tradition regarding the sacredness of the Sabbath. Our Lord rightly pointed out to them the error of their judgment. From the very Scriptures, which they affirmed were their authority, He showed them the shallowness of their argument and the inconsistency of their judgment. He then added the deeply significant words: "But I say unto you that, in this place, is One greater than the temple. But if ye had known what this meaneth, 'I will have mercy, and not sacrifice,' ye would not have condemned the guiltless" (Matt. 12:1-8).

The very fact that this message is given to us three times in Divine revelation, should be enough to cause all believers to seriously ponder its spiritual import. While the scriptural principles governing the *order* of worship are important, equally so must be the *manner* of our worship. One must not be held at the *expense* of the other, but each should be maintained as the *complement* of the other. Goodness and sacrifice must ever go hand in hand into the presence of God if we are to worship as we should.

If our worship is to be both spiritual and sincere, there must be heart dealings with God. All known sin must be mercilessly judged, confessed to God and resolutely turned from with abhorrence. All subterfuge, equivocation and hypocrisy must be avoided like a plague. Transparent honesty must characterize the believer, both in thought, word and deed. Clean hands, a pure heart and sincerity of purpose, must ever be the necessary accom-

paniments of the worship of God if it is to bring delight to
His heart. The holiness of the One worshipped, demands
a corresponding holiness of life on the part of the one who
worships. See I Peter 1:13-16.

CHAPTER NINETEEN

The Manner of Worship
(Continued)

3. Worship should be intelligent.

God places no premium on ignorance. One of the purposes of the Holy Scriptures is to make the believer "wise" as to what God has to say, and to give him a proper understanding of both his privileges and responsibilities in this matter of worship. Spirituality and sincerity in worship must therefore be accompanied by an intelligent apprehension as to what God has revealed regarding this important subject. Paul, in his epistles, repeatedly uses the expression: "I would not have you to be ignorant." See I Cor. 10: 1; 12: 1; II Cor. 1: 8; I Thess. 4: 13; Rom. 1: 13; 11: 25. It is both interesting and instructive to observe the various subjects on which he would not have the believers to be ignorant.

Perhaps one of the greatest liabilities in Christendom today, is the vast number of ignorant Christians, who seem to know little or nothing of the great fundamental truths of their most holy faith. They seem quite content to let others do their thinking for them and decide what they shall, or shall not believe. Particularly is this true in the matter of worship. Ignorance as to what constitutes worship is evidenced by the hazy expressions of it that one sometimes hears in meetings convened for this particular purpose. This confusion of thought and expression is due to the failure of each believer to read, discover and meditate on what God has to say on the subject. We are told that: "God is not the Author of confusion, but of order." The believer who undertakes to study the Scriptures will soon be able to arrive at an intelligent apprehension of what worship really is and govern his words and actions accordingly.

In thinking of "intelligent" worship, we must not confound it with a mere theoretical, or head-knowledge of its definition. What we have in mind is the believer's heart *apprehension* and *appreciation* of God's estimate of it, that results in an upward flow of spiritual, sincere and intelligent worship to God. Paul tells us that mere "knowledge puffeth up" its proud possessor, and imparts to him an exaggerated idea of his own importance (I Cor. 8:1). This kind of knowledge is a *liability,* for it hinders a person from either desiring or acquiring the wisdom that only God can give. Let us think particularly of three ways by which the believer may be enabled to become a spiritually intelligent worshipper.

(1) **He should acquire an intelligent knowledge of Scripture truth.**

This, of course, necessitates both the reading and study of the word of God. This is the price each must pay for spiritual intelligence. While it is good to read expositions of the Scriptures by sound and able men, this must never be allowed to become a substitute for one's own personal reading and study of the Word. What the believer discovers for himself, as a result of his own Bible searching, will mean much more to him than what others give him. This implies that:

(a) *He should be clear as to his own position in Christ.* That is, he should learn he has been foreknown, predestinated, chosen, called, saved, justified, sanctified, accepted and "blessed with all the spiritual blessings in Christ Jesus." As he is brought to realize these glorious truths from the word of God, his heart will be tuned to sing the praises of the One who has done such great things for him.

(b) *He should be clear as to the tri-unity of the eternal Godhead.* Many do not seem to be able to distinguish between the Persons in the Godhead. One sometimes hears believers thanking the Father for having died for them on the cross, or asking the Holy Spirit to come into them. A knowledge of the Word would enable them to appreciate the distinction of Persons in the Godhead, and deliver them from such confusion of thought and expression.

(2) He should seek to get an intelligent grasp of Church truth.

Surely that which Christ "loved," and for which He "gave Himself," is worthy of each Christian's most serious and earnest consideration (Eph. 5:25). Many believers seem to know little or nothing of this tremendous truth, and seem content to live in a haze of uncertainty regarding this great doctrine of the word of God.

(a) *He should be clear as to his position as a member of the body of Christ,* which is the Church of God. (Eph. 1:22-23; 4:16, etc.) He should know that he has been joined to this mystical body by the Spirit of God, and thus united to Christ, the Head, in heaven, and also to every other believer on earth. This is "the unity of the Spirit" which God has made (Eph. 4:3). As he is brought to realize that there is but one body, with one Head; he will clearly see that there is no need for him to join some other "body" with another "head." Thus he will endeavor to "keep the unity of the Spirit (which has already been made) in the bond of peace."

(b) *He should be clear regarding his position as a priest unto God.* (I Peter 2:5-9; Rev. 1:5-6). As such, he is privileged to offer the "spiritual sacrifices" of his praise and worship to God (Heb. 13:15). He will realize that the present distinction between "clergy" and "laity" has no foundation in the word of God, but is purely an invention of man and which has wrought untold evil. He will recognize that he has been "ordained" of the Lord and, with this assurance, will not only enter into the holiest as a worshipper, but also go forth to witness for Him as a servant and herald. (Heb. 10:19-23; John 15:16).

(c) *He should be clear as to what worship really is,* and its place and importance in his life, for this is his highest occupation. We have already referred to this fact in the previous pages.

(3) **He should endeavor to gain an intelligent apprehension of the purpose of a meeting** convened for the remembrance of Christ and for the worship of the Lord's people. Many believers apparently seem unable to sense the purpose of such a gathering. This meeting does not exist for the preaching of the gospel, or of supplicating the throne of grace, or for Bible Study, or for testimony, or for the awakening and encouragement of missionary effort. The gospel meeting, the prayer meeting, the Bible reading, and the missionary meeting serve these purposes most admirably. The meeting for the remembrance of Christ and for worship exists for that purpose only. In spite of this obvious fact, one often hears believers, whose spoken ministry before the breaking of bread, clearly indicates they have never really grasped the main purpose of the gathering. Confusion breeds in the atmosphere of ignorance.

(a) *He should be clear as to the words he utters.* Words are, or should be, the result of thought. If the thought is hazy, the utterance will be correspondingly so. It surely is not too much to expect that when one rises to express the worship of the assembly, he should know why he is there, and what is the purpose of the meeting. Anything that does not rightly belong to such a gathering should therefore be left unsaid. This simple test would eliminate much of the confusion that is sometimes evidenced at such a gathering.

(b) *He should be clear as to the theme of hymn he gives out.* The hymn book may be a very good one, but all the hymns in it are not suitable for the immediate purpose. The selection of the right hymn at the right time therefore calls for spiritual intelligence, so that the hymn fits in with the particular theme of the meeting. Surely one would not give out a marriage hymn at a funeral! Each hymn has a distinct thought, presents a particular message and serves a definite purpose. Therefore the need for an intelligent knowledge and use of the hymn book for, by it, an assembly is enabled to express its own aspiration, praise and worship. *

(c) *He should be clear as to the time the meeting begins,* and be there *well in advance* of that time. How often such a meeting has been disturbed because of late comers who, by a little exercise of common sense, Christian courtesy, and loving consideration, could easily have been there on time. A time of quiet meditation, before the meeting is due to begin, is an excellent preparation for the season of worship that follows. There should be no rushing into the presence of God but, instead, a quiet waiting upon Him, as the believers concentrate their minds' attention and their heart's affection upon the One they have come to remember.

(d) *He should be clear as to his deportment* in such a gathering. The very purpose of such a gathering should determine the kind of clothes he wears, and his behavior during the meeting. It is not a dress parade, at which one attracts attention to himself, nor does it exist for the

---

* See Author's booklet: "Hymns, Their Use and Abuse."

display of gift and, least of all, for irreverent behavior. The bread and the cup upon the table should remind all who are present that the One they have come to remember died to make their salvation possible, rose again and ascended to make it actual. Furthermore, the Lord Jesus is the Host at His own supper. An intelligent grasp of this fact will do much in determining one's deportment at such a meeting.

These practical and common sense suggestions regarding worship, and the believer's behavior in a meeting for this purpose, may appear to be unnecessary to some; but we need ever to remember that "God hath not given to us the spirit of fear; but of power, and of love, and of a *sound* mind" (II Tim. 1:7). The believer's possession of a Divine nature does not rob him of his common sense, but ennobles it and enables him to use it for the glory of God.

Thus the *manner* of the believer's worship is not the least important thing in regard to this great subject. Each Christian should therefore see to it that the worship he presents to God, through Christ, in the power of the Holy Spirit, is both spiritual, sincere and intelligent.

CHAPTER TWENTY

VIII. The Hindrances To Worship.

Having looked at the manner in which we should worship God, if it is to be acceptable to Him; let us now view the subject in the negative way, and note some of the hindrances to it. Seeing that worship is the Christian's highest occupation, we may be quite certain that both the Devil, the *infernal* enemy, the world, the *external* enemy, and the flesh, the *internal* enemy, will combine to hinder the believer as he seeks to worship God. It will be impossible to enumerate all these hindrances, for they are legion. We can do no more than name a few of the better known.

These hindrances will be experienced, not only by an individual in his own personal spiritual life, but also by a gathering of believers, in assembly capacity. The spiritual tone of such a worship meeting is determined by the spirituality of each person present. This spiritual tone is difficult to describe, but it is nevertheless very real, and can be readily discerned by spiritual believers. There is a sense of the presence of God, of the reality of the unseen but eternal verities, and the hush of reverent awe that quiets the spirit and prepares the soul for worship.

Anything that tends to hinder this spirit of worship in a believer, or in an assembly of believers, should be avoided. Should the hindrance exist, it should be judged, confessed and turned from. Now let us look at a few of these hindrances.

1. Self-will.

Self, in all its varied forms, will ever seek to intrude itself into the presence of God, and the Scriptures recognize this fact. In Exodus 28:36-38 we are given the description of the mitre which Aaron was to wear when, as high priest of Israel, he went into the presence of God. On the front of the mitre was a plate of gold, on which was inscribed the words, "Holiness unto the Lord." The purpose for this mitre is then given: "And it shall be upon Aaron's forehead, that Aaron may bear the iniquity of the holy things, which the children of Israel shall hallow in all their holy gifts, and it shall always be upon his forehead that they may be accepted before the Lord."

What a strange expression this is: "the iniquity of the holy things." How can iniquity be associated with that which is holy? The answer is quite simple. Everything that man touches, he contaminates. Iniquity is present, even in the Christian's holiest moments. Peter's grand confession of Christ's eternal Deity was scarcely out of his mouth before the Lord had to rebuke him as the mouthpiece of Satan! (Matt. 16:15-23). The nearer the believer gets to God, the more conscious he becomes of his own unworthiness and iniquity. How good, therefore, to have One in the presence of God who bears the iniquity of our holy things!

Perhaps the classic example of self-will intruding itself in the worship of God is the case of Nadab and Abihu, the sons of Aaron the high priest (Lev. 10:1-11). These two men, probably under the influence of strong drink, (v. 9) a sign of their lack of self control, took fire of their own making, placed it in their censers, together with incense which they had manufactured and, in direct disobedience to God's distinct command, offered it before the Lord at the golden altar of incense. God's reaction to this act of self-will was summary judgment, for we read: "And there went out fire from the Lord and devoured them, and they died before the Lord" (v. 2). Any objection that

Aaron might have offered was silenced by God's word to him, for we read: "This is it that the Lord spake, saying: I will be sanctified in them that come nigh Me, and before all the people I will be glorified" (v. 3).

Thus God, by this act of judgment, clearly indicated that there must be no self-will in connection with the worship of Himself. Worship must be in accordance with the instructions He has given in His word. The "strange fire" of self-will cannot be tolerated for one moment. From this we may gather that no person can worship God as he pleases, or act in defiance of the known will of God as revealed in His word, and expect the smile of His approval, or that his worship will be accepted. Self-will is, therefore, definitely *out* in worship. However cunningly the "strange fire" and incense may be concocted; or however ornate may be the ritual of its presentation; it is doomed to be rejected by the God who "will be sanctified in them that come nigh" Him, and who must be "glorified before all the people." The believer can best worship when he has proposed, seconded and carried unanimously a vote of no confidence in himself. Both self-will and self-expression have no place in the worship of One who must, because of Who He is, have "the pre-eminence in all things."

2. Worldliness.

This has proved to be an effectual bar to worship. By the world, in this sense, is meant the sum total of all those things in the world from which God is left out, whether they be pleasures, persons, places or pursuits. Though the believer is "in the world," as to the sphere of his physical life; yet he is most emphatically "not of the world," as to the sphere of his spiritual life. See John 17:11, 14-15. The worldling is of the world, worldly. He not only lives *in* it, but he lives *for* it, and is quite content to live his life with no reference whatever to God, Christ, the Holy Spirit, the word of God and eternal realities. He wants nothing better than to be left alone to enjoy its pleasures, popularity, fashions, politics, riches, etc.

The moment such a worldling is awakened by the Spirit of God to a sense of his need as a guilty sinner, led to rest in Christ's redeeming work, and receive Him as his Savior and Lord, a great transformation takes place. Instead of the world and its vanities being the center of his existence, Christ becomes both the Center and Circumference of his life, and he becomes "other worldly." Instead of living for the kingdom of this world, he orders his life in relation to the kingdom of God. Instead of living for self, he lives for Christ. Instead of living in the realm of the seen and the temporal, he lives in the light of the unseen and the eternal. Instead of his interests being earthly, they are now heavenly. Thus he is "delivered from this present evil world" (Gal. 1:4). Through the new birth, he becomes a "stranger and a pilgrim" in the land of his natural birth. In this way he demonstrates the truth of that Scripture which affirms: "If any man be in Christ, he is a new creature: (creation) old things are passed away; behold, all things are become new" (II Cor. 5:17). As a member of this new creation, he now becomes a worshipper of God.

It would be pleasant to record that, having become a new creature, the Christian never again manifests any desire for the world and its ways; but alas, this is not true. That evil nature, the flesh, is still within him, and only requires encouragement to evidence itself in worldliness of thought, word and conduct. This was the tragedy of Demas, one of Paul's fellow helpers, of whom he had to say: "Demas hath forsaken me, having loved this present world" (II Tim. 4:10). The apostle John realized the subtle appeal that the world makes on the child of God. He faithfully warned believers concerning it and wrote: "Love not the world, neither the things that are in the world. If any man love the world, the love of the Father is not in him. For all that is in the world, the lust of the flesh, and the lust of the eyes, and the pride of life, is not of the Father, but is of the world" (I John 2:15-16). It was the worldliness of the Corinthian saints that prompted the letter of rebuke which Paul addressed to them.

Let us not confine worldliness, in our thoughts, to the *visible* and *outward* manifestations of it. The lust of the eyes, the lust of the flesh, and the pride of life may never be outwardly seen in a believer, or even be suspected by his fellow-saints; and yet it may be there, artfully concealed and in abundant measure. Though a Christian may never outwardly darken the door of a theater, or dance hall, or engage in any of the visible and admittedly worldly amusements, he can *inwardly* be just as worldly in mind as the one who does. The brother in the meeting who sits with his eyes shut, and apparently engrossed in worship, may be planning a business deal in his mind. That sister, who sits so prim and proper, and who would never dream of being seen in any questionable place of amusement, or be guilty of doing anything that "simply isn't done," may be filled with self-complacency at the high degree of her attainment of "separation," and be quite proud of her humility and unworldliness of manner! Worldliness, therefore, may consist of *thought* and *attitude,* as well as outward behavior.

One thing is certain, whether it is worldliness of thought or behavior, both combine to hinder the believer from worshipping in Spirit and in truth. Worship cannot function in an atmosphere of worldliness. If the believer is to experience what it means to be:

"Shut in with Thee, far, far above
    The restless world that wars below;"

then he must also know what it means to be unworldly in thought, attitude and deed. Before he can be "shut in," he must "go forth" unto Christ from all that denies Him the place of absolute preeminence (Heb. 13:13). The Christian must view the world, in all its aspects, as being "crucified unto him," and he to the world (Gal. 6:14). He must take his stand with Christ, in separation from that which is "of the world," and stedfastly *maintain* this separation.

The child of God must not confuse *isolation* with *separation*. A monk may isolate himself in a monastery and yet not be separated unto God in heart and mind. It is not a case of shutting oneself up from any contact with the world and the people of the world, but of keeping oneself "unspotted from the world" (James 1:27). The extent of the believer's *separation* will be determined by the measure of his *occupation* with Christ. As the Lord Jesus is allowed to fill his vision, occupy his thoughts, control his words and actions and satisfy his heart; in that degree the believer will be unworldly, and thus spiritually fitted to offer acceptable worship to God. The poet has expressed it in the following lines:

" 'Tis the treasure I've found in His love
    That has made me a pilgrim below."

3. A critical spirit.

The fostering of a fault-finding attitude of mind in a believer is fatal to worship, for it occupies the Christian with his fellow believers, instead of with God. This critical frame of mind may begin in a small way, but if it is encouraged, and thus allowed to develop unjudged and unchecked, it will ultimately sour his whole life. It will dry up the milk of human kindness in his heart, blind his vision, warp his understanding and render him useless, either to God or his fellow believers.

When a person looks at things through the spectacles of censorious criticism, everything becomes distorted to his vision. Due to prejudice, he is unable to appreciate the viewpoint of others. Prejudice has been wittily defined as: "being *down* on what you are not *up* on!" Thus, with a warped mind, he imputes ulterior to the actions of others. Instead of looking for something to commend, the critic is always on the look out for something to condemn. Unfortunately, the critic is usually quite blind to his own many imperfections and shortcomings! He demands from others what he is not prepared to give himself. He is so intent on removing what he thinks to be a splinter in his brother's eye, that he does not realize it is but the reflection of a huge plank in his own eye! What he refers to as "rudeness" in others, he dubs "frankness" and "faithfulness" in himself. What he calls "bad temper" in others, becomes "righteous indignation" in himself. What he alludes to as "stinginess" in others, is viewed as "sound economy" in his own life. What he designates "duplicity" in others, becomes "diplomacy" in himself!

It is bad enough when only one believer in an assembly is possessed by such a censorious spirit; but it is ten-thousand times worse when all those composing it are similarly affected. It is hardly necessary to say that no worship can rise in such an environment. God's word says: "If ye bite and devour one another, take heed that ye be not consumed one of another" (Gal. 5:15). Such a spirit of criticism acts as a corrosive and eats away the spirituality, both of an individual and an assembly.

It was this critical spirit, doubtless prompted by envy, that caused Korah and his companions to approach Moses and Aaron with the complaint: "Ye take too much upon you, seeing all the congregation are holy, every one of them, and the Lord is among them. Wherefore then lift ye up yourselves above the congregation of the Lord?" God left the people of Israel in no doubt as to what He thought of this act, first, by vindicating Moses and Aaron with the miracle of the budding rod; next, by visiting His summary judgment upon the malcontents (See Numbers 16). These things, "written for our learning" (Rom. 15: 4), should speak loudly to all our hearts of the evil of a critical spirit.

The remedy for such a spirit is first of all a realization of its sinfulness and hatefulness in the sight of God. Next, humble and frank self-judgment and acknowledgment of it to God. Third, a holy determination never to allow it to have a place in one's life again. Fourth, an apology to any who have been grieved by the unjust criticism. Fifth, much prayer on behalf of one's brethren. There is no better cure for a critical and jealous spirit than to pray earnestly for God's richest blessing on the one who is the object of the criticism. Sixth, a resolve to look for something to *commend* in one's brethren. We read that "love thinketh no evil . . . beareth all things, endureth all things" (I Cor. 13: 5-7). We must look at them through the eyes of Christ, and see how much of *Him* is evident in them. Seventh, to put the knife of self-judgment to all the future uprisings of this critical and censorious spirit. The believer must ever keep in mind what he is in himself. This will cause him to be deeply thankful to the Lord that his fellow believers have exhibited so much grace in extending their fellowship to him, and for their great forbearance in putting up with him for so long!

The result of such repentance will be a restoration of soul, an enlargement of heart-capacity for God, a freedom of spirit, an appreciation of all Christ is and has done, and a consequent pouring forth of adoring worship to the One who has done all things well.

4. Slothfulness.

By this is meant the failure to use the means God has provided to enlighten the believer as to the value of worship and to stimulate it in a believer's heart. Many shrink from a study of this subject because of the effort such preparation involves. We have noted, earlier in this book, the high cost of worship. Worship is not an easy thing, but is developed as the believer, in holy energy, lays hold of what God has provided for him in Christ. Worship is not generated by *lounging,* nor is it developed in the atmosphere of spiritual apathy and neglect. The fruit of worship does not grow in the field of the slothful, but comes by persistent cultivation, and this necessitates the determined application of mind and will. (Prov. 24: 30-34). The fire of worship needs the constant renewing of fuel if it is to rise, like the smoke of the morning sacrifice to God. The fuel needed is the study of, meditation in and obedience to the word of God, plus a life of prayer and devotion. If this fuel is not forthcoming, then the fire of worship on the altar of the soul will die, and God will be denied the worship He seeks.

The awkward and poverty-stricken silences, that sometimes occur in a gathering of believers for worship, is the sad consequence of this particular hindrance of slothfulness. The saints have nothing to *give* God, because they have not gathered anything *from* God. Instead of their baskets being full of their appreciation of God and His Son, as a result of their individual study of the Word; they have neglected their Bibles, wasted their time on trivialities, and consequently appear before God empty. Such Christians often complain that they do not get the spiritual food they desire. The truth is they do not spiritually *desire* the food God has provided for them. The lack is not in *the food* provided, but in the lack of *appetite* for it. Ruth diligently gleaned in the fields of Boaz, with the result she had something to give. See Ruth 2:15-18. As the believer gleans in the rich fields of holy Scripture, and beats out by meditation what he has gathered, there will be no lack of worship in his heart, for he will be full of appreciation of all God is and has done.

This spiritual preparation of Bible study and prayer, so essential to worship, calls for both systematic and persistent effort, often of the heroic order. Life today proceeds at an ever increasing tempo. Business and domestic duties cry insistently for more and more of the believer's time. Unless he is very careful, the Christian will soon discover that the secular has crowded out the sacred. He must therefore both *make* time and *take* time for the cultivation of his own private devotional life. It may require getting up half an hour before the usual time, and spending that period in systematic Bible reading, meditation, study and prayer. He must jealously guard this period against the encroachment of business or household duties, and devote it sacredly and exclusively to the Lord.

Spiritual laziness must be viewed as the thief it is, for it will steal away the worship that should be offered to God. Each believer needs to heed the soul stirring exhortation: "It is high time to awake out of sleep: for now is our salvation nearer than when we believed. The night is far spent, the day is at hand: Let us therefore cast off the works of darkness, and let us put on the armor of light" (Rom. 13:11-12). Spiritual lethargy must therefore give place to spiritual alertness, if our worship is to be what it should.

CHAPTER TWENTY-ONE

The Hindrances To Worship
(Continued)

5. Impatience.

By this is meant the believer's failure to wait for God and upon God. This, of course, is the opposite of the former hindrances of self will and slothfulness. We are naturally creatures of extremes and quickly swing, like a pendulum, from one side to the other. While we must avoid the danger of lagging behind God, we must also beware of rushing ahead of Him. There is not only a time when we must be up and doing, but also a period when it is essential that we "rest in the Lord and wait patiently for Him" (Ps. 37:7).

There is a verse of Scripture which combines to reveal the two fold danger of these extremes of impatience and slothfulness. It reads: "Be ye not as the horse, or as the mule, which have no understanding" (Ps. 32:9). The horse is noted for its *spirited impetuosity*. Without any thought of the consequences ahead, it "rusheth into the battle" (Jer. 8:6). The mule is famous for its *stubborn inertia*. The mule draws back when it is urged to go on. God wants neither extreme in His people. He has promised: "I will instruct thee and teach thee in the way thou shalt go: I will guide thee with Mine eye" (or "with Mine eye upon thee") (Ps. 32:8).

The sad case of King Saul will furnish us with an illustration of how impatience can hinder worship. The prophet Samuel had anointed Saul as king over Israel, and prophecied that the Spirit of the Lord should come upon him, that he should prophesy, and that God should turn him into another man (I Sam. 10:1-13). Then Samuel gave Saul definite instructions regarding his future actions and said: "And thou shalt go down before me to Gilgal; and behold, I will come down unto thee, to offer burnt offerings and to sacrifice sacrifices of peace offerings: seven days shalt thou tarry, till I come to thee, and shew thee what thou shalt do" (v. 8). Thus instructed, Saul returned to his home, and the signs which Samuel had foretold came to pass. In Chapter 13 we find Saul at Gilgal, waiting impatiently for the coming of Samuel, while the Philistines gathered together to attack the Israelites. Instead of waiting for Samuel to appear, to do what only he could do as a priest unto God, Saul, in his impatience and impetuosity, commanded his servant to bring him the burnt offering and the peace offerings, and he offered them to God.

Scarcely had he completed the task, which he had absolutely no right or authority to perform, than Samuel appeared and inquired the reason for his act. Saul replied that he saw the people of Israel were scattered from him, and that the Philistines seemed about to attack him, and that Samuel had not yet come to him, and ended by saying: "I *forced myself* therefore, and offered a burnt offering" (I Sam. 13:11-12). Upon this explanation Samuel charged him with folly and disobedience and concluded: "But now thy kingdom shall not continue: the Lord has sought him a man after His own heart, and the Lord hath commanded him to be captain over His people, because thou hast not kept that which the Lord commanded thee" (vs. 13-14). Therefore, because of his failure to wait God's time, and do things in accordance with God's way, Saul was rejected for his "forced" worship.

God wants no "forced" worship from his people, for worship is essentially a voluntary thing. It rises from the soul of him who waits patiently in His presence and takes time to meditate in His word. Saul learned, to his cost, that "the flesh profiteth nothing" (John 6:63). Saul, in his impatience, committed the folly of intruding where he did not rightly belong. He rushed ahead of God and offered that which he was not Divinely qualified to do, and consequently both merited and received Divine disapproval. Each believer is in the same danger of trying to accomplish, in the energy of the flesh, what can only be done acceptably in the power of the Holy Spirit. That unholy and fleshly impatience, which would prompt the believer to rush unprepared into the presence of God and offer artificial worship, must be curbed and judged in the light of God's word. He must heed the Divine injunction: "Be still, and know that I am God" (Ps. 46:10). Like David, he must say to himself: "My soul, wait thou only upon God; for my expectation is from Him" (Ps. 62:5).

Often, in a meeting for worship, there comes a period of silence, when hearts are too full for vocal expression. A holy, but eloquent hush of worship and adoration descends upon the gathered saints. Sometimes an impatient brother will interrupt this golden silence by giving out an inappropriate hymn, and thus break in upon the worship of the people of God. Worship calls for spiritual discernment of the highest order, and each believer should be exercised before the Lord as to this, lest he interrupt the worship of the people of God. It is far better to keep silence than to act in an impatient manner in such a gathering. It has been well said: "When you don't know what to do, don't do it!"

6. Sectarianism.

By this is meant a narrow, bigoted, party-spirit, which does not include, in its thought and scope, *all* the people of God. It focusses its attention upon a small section of believers and refers to them piously as "the Lord's gathered-out people," to the *exclusion* of other truly born again and godly believers, who are sound in doctrine and moral in life. Such a distinction between the Lord's people is a virtual denial of the unity of the Spirit which God has formed, and to which every Christian belongs. It is therefore hateful to God and a hindrance to worship. Paul, writing to the believers at Corinth, who had been guilty of nourishing a sectarian spirit said: "The cup of blessing which we bless, is it not the communion (or fellowship) of the blood of Christ? The bread which we break, is it not the communion of the body of Christ? For we, being many, are one bread, and one body: for we are all partakers of that one bread" (I Cor. 10:16-17). Thus the cup and the bread are not only the emblems of Christ's sacrifice for us, but they also set forth the oneness of all true believers. This should be sufficient to rebuke all thought of sectarianism, and reveal it to be the shameful thing that it really is in the sight of Him who died, rose and ascended to make such a unity possible.

What shall be said of an assembly of believers that refuses to welcome, at the Lord's supper, one who desires to remember the Lord, and who is known to be a godly Christian, sound in doctrine and consistent in his life? Such a shameful and God-dishonoring thing has happened more often than one cares to think about. Needless to say, this always results in loss to that assembly, whose collective worship is thus hindered by its refusal to recognize the unity that God has made. To these same sectarian-minded Corinthians, Paul, by the Spirit wrote: "God is faithful, by Whom ye were called unto the fellowship of His Son, Jesus Christ our Lord" (I Cor. 1:9). It is to be feared that many limit the term "fellowship," which here applies to *all believers,* to a small section of such who have seen certain scriptural truths and acted upon them. Sometimes one hears the statement: "He is

a dear brother in Christ who is not in fellowship with us!"
What a contradiction of terms! If he is a "dear brother in
Christ," and desires to remember the Lord in this way,
then woe betide that company of believers which refuses
him a place at the Lord's supper, and thus limits "the fellowship of His Son" to a little circle of its own making.

No wonder the worship of the believers at Corinth was
hindered, and confusion reigned in the assembly when
they exhibited such sectarianism of spirit! Some were
saying: "I am of Paul; and I of Apollos; and I of Cephas;
and I of Christ" (I Cor. 1:12). Note carefully the argu-
ments Paul used to show them the utter falsity and folly
of their wretched divisions, which constituted a virtual
denial of the unity of the body.

History, as we have seen before, has a bad habit of
repeating itself. The individual believer must beware of
becoming sectarian in heart, and limiting his affection and
care to a small coterie, or clique, instead of to all those
who "belong to Christ." An assembly of believers must
also beware lest it grieves the Holy Spirit by refusing to
welcome to the Lord's supper one who has been "called
unto the fellowship" of God's Son, and who desires to
meet with them. Such an assembly will be characterized,
not by the warmth of its spiritual worship, but by its
coldness, legalism and sectarian spirit.

It is sadly possible for an assembly, which claims to be
unsectarian in its constitution, to act in a far more sectarian manner than a group which makes no such claim.
It is indeed good to sing as we meet together:

> "Here every one who loves Thy name,
>   Our willing hearts embrace;"

but there is something far better than merely *singing* it,
and that is, actually *doing it!* Thus the hindrance of sectarianism will be removed, and worship can unhinderedly

ascend to the One who has united all His people into one body, and has brought them all into fellowship with Himself and with each other.

7. Formalism.

By this is meant the substitution of scriptural simplicity and the liberty of the Spirit, for a scrupulously meticulous and exact observance of certain outward forms, rules and regulations, without the inward spiritual reality. One does not have to go far to see a demonstration of this in Christendom. In many places, the whole meeting for "public worship" is prearranged from beginning to end and proceeds, with clocklike precision, from the opening hymn to the benediction. The hymns to be sung are all previously arranged. The prayers that are offered are all read from a book and have been composed by persons who have long since died. To add to the confusion, in many cases, the person who conducts this "worship service" has never been born again by the Spirit of God, and is consequently "dead in his trespasses and sins!" What a travesty this is on the pattern given in the New Testament scriptures! The coming together of believers for worship in those days was marked by spirituality, simplicity, equality, liberty and spontaneity. The result was much worship and much blessing.

It all goes to demonstrate the fatal tendency of the flesh to introduce human regulations as a substitute for God's pattern, imagining, by so doing, that the Divine plan is improved thereby! No company of believers, however scripturally gathered, is free from this danger of drifting into formalism. For instance: a mode of procedure is introduced which, by constant observance over a period of years, comes to be looked upon as being of Divine authority, and therefore "scriptural." This par-

ticular mode of procedure may be perfectly all right, but
*it must ever be kept distinct from what the word of God
actually authorizes. Rutualism* can become as great a
menace to worship as *ritualism!* We must beware of forc-
ing our customs on our fellow believers, and depriving
them of their "liberty in Christ Jesus" (Gal. 2:4).

The tendency of formality is to substitute *uniformity,*
for *unity.* It seeks to produce, through its rules and regulations, what only the Spirit of God can accomplish when
He is given His rightful place. Formality may produce
an outward harmony and order, but it is a *mechanical*
one, and is dependent entirely upon the strict and continued observance of the prescribed form of service. The
Holy Spirit, as He is allowed to lead the assembled saints,
will produce harmony and order of a *vital* character.
This will result in true worship ascending to God and
bringing delight to His heart.

8.   An Unforgiving Spirit.

What a blighting effect this has upon the worship of
an individual, or an assembly of believers! Our Lord
made a special reference to this hindrance and provided a
remedy for it. He said: "If thou bring thy gift to the altar,
and there rememberest that thy brother hath ought
against thee; leave there thy gift before the altar, and go
thy way; first be reconciled to thy brother, and then come
and offer thy gift" (Matt. 5:23-24). So long as a grudge
is cherished in one's heart against a fellow believer, so
long will that believer remain in darkness. So wrote
John, the apostle of love (I John 2:11). He goes further
and says: "If a man say, 'I love God,' and hateth his brother, he is a liar; for he that loveth not his brother whom
he hath seen, how can he love God whom he hath not
seen? And this commandment have we from Him, That

he who loveth God, love his brother also" (I John 4:20-21).

Paul's words should come home with peculiar force to each believer's heart: "Let all bitterness, and wrath, and anger, and clamour, and evil speaking, be put away from you, with all malice: and be ye kind one to another, tender hearted, forgiving one another, even as God, for Christ's sake, hath forgiven you" (Eph. 4:31-32). Well did Paul know the fatal effect an unforgiving spirit has upon worship. An old Christian used to say that the best way to kill a grudge in one's heart, was to pray for the person against whom the grudge was formed, and *keep on praying* for him until the grudge was gone! We must all beware lest little misunderstandings are allowed to develop into big feuds, which act as a blight upon our worship and hinder our testimony for God.

9. Pride.

One thing is certain: worship and pride of heart are mutually exclusive, unless it be self-worship, and this is really what pride is. Pride ill becomes a child of God, or an asembly of His people; yet alas, it is often seen, and its baneful effects are only too plainly evident in the lack of spiritual worship. Pride is a subtle thing and often exists where it is least expected, for one can even be proud of his humility! Pride in one's own personal appearance leads that individual to give undue attention to himself, or herself. Pride of gift leads to an ostentatious display of it and a secret craving for applause. Pride of position leads its owner to adopt a condescending air to his fellow believers. Pride of possession shows itself in self-complacency and boasting. Pride of one's ecclesiastical position evidences itself in smugness and sanctimoniousness. We could add to the sordid list, but enough has been said to indicate what a hindrance these forms of pride are to the worship of either an individual or an assembly.

God leaves us in no doubt as to how He views pride, for we read: "God resisteth the proud, but giveth grace unto the humble" (James 4:6). The best cure for pride is to "look off unto Jesus," of Whom it was said He: "made Himself of no reputation, and took upon Him the form of a servant, and was made in the likeness of men: And being found in fashion as a Man, He humbled Himself, and became obedient unto death, even the death of the cross" (Phil. 2:7-8). It is only as a believer, or an assembly, in true humility of spirit seeks the face of God, and contemplates the blessed Lord Jesus, that worship will be the inevitable outcome. May we, by God's grace, see to it that none of these things shall be allowed to hinder our worship to the One who alone is worthy.

CHAPTER TWENTY-TWO

IX. The Place of Worship.

A confused idea exists in Christendom as to the place of worship. Certain buildings, of an ecclesiastical design, are often called "places of worship." These are duly and formally "consecrated," and often such a building is referred to as "the house of God." This, of course, is entirely foreign to the New Testament, which is the believer's sole authority in the matter of worship, or any other matter on which it speaks.

The woman of Samaria was puzzled regarding the matter of the correct geographical location for worship. She said to Christ: "Our fathers worshipped in this mountain; (Mt. Gerizim); and ye say, that in Jerusalem is the place where men ought to worship" (John 4:20). Our Lord's reply to her makes perfectly clear that the geographical situation, or the kind of building, is *utterly immaterial to worship*. Mark His words well: "Believe Me, the hour cometh, when ye shall neither in this mountain, nor yet at Jerusalem, worship the Father ... But the hour cometh, and now is, when the true worshippers shall worship the Father in Spirit and in truth; for the Father seeketh such to worship him" (Vs. 21-23).

In these words our Lord completely swept away the common idea that one locality, or one building, is more sacrosanct than another; or that worship is more acceptable to Him when offered in one place than another. The place, or the building, *has nothing whatever to do with worship*. It is the *spiritual condition* of the worshipper, and not his *physical location* that determines whether or not his worship is acceptable to the Father. Once this fundamental fact is really grasped by the believer, it will deliver him from a great deal of the misconception regarding this matter, that abounds in Christendom. Let us consider this subject of the place of worship under two aspects, the spiritual and the physical.

1. Spiritually, Worship Is In the Holiest of All.

The Christian worships, spiritually, where his great high Priest is. This is heaven, or the holiest of all. This fact is set forth for us in the epistle to the Hebrews. In it the writer uses the illustration of the Tabernacle as the "pattern of things in the heavens" (Heb. 9:23). He proceeds to describe how Aaron, the high priest of Israel, entered once a year into the holiest of all, with the blood of the sin offering which he had offered for his own sins, and also for the sins of the people of Israel (Heb. 9:1-10).

He then proceeds to contrast Aaron's high priestly work with that of Christ, the great high Priest. He says: "But Christ, being come an high Priest of good things to come, by a greater and more perfect tabernacle, not made with hands, that is to say not of this building; neither by the blood of goats and calves, but by His own blood, He entered in once (for all) into the holy place, having obtained eternal redemption for us" (Heb. 9:11-12). As the holiest of all, in the tabernacle, was a type of heaven and the presence of God; so Christ, by virtue of His substitutionary sacrifice, and the eternal value of His precious blood, has entered into heaven as the great high Priest of His redeemed people. The writer then goes on to say: "For Christ is not entered into the holy places made with hands, which are the figures (or types) of the true, but into heaven itself, now to appear in the presence of God for us" (Heb. 9:23).

Not only has Christ entered into heaven as our Divine Representative, but He has opened up, for all His people, "a new and living way," by which they are en-

abled, spiritually, to enter the holiest also and pour out
their worship in the presence of God.

It will be recalled that the veil of the temple, which
shut men out from the presence of God, was rent in twain
at the death of Christ. By this God signified that the
perfect sacrifice of His Son had met all His holy claims,
and that access into His presence and favor could now be
the portion of all who trusted in Christ and His finished
work. The Word is quite clear as to this fact, for we read:
"Having therefore brethren, boldness to enter into the
holiest by the blood of Jesus, by a new and living way,
which He has consecrated for us through the veil, that
is to say His flesh; and having an high Priest over the
house of God, let us draw near, with a true heart, in full
assurance of faith," etc. (Heb. 10:19-22). Thus every
born-again believer, being constituted a priest unto God,
is both spiritually fitted and Divinely invited to come by
faith into the very holiest of all and worship.

What is true of an individual is also true of an assembly of believers. As they meet in the name of the Lord
Jesus, they form a God-constituted company of priests.
As such, through their great high Priest, they may lay
hold, by faith, upon God's provision and spiritually enter
within the holiest of all, to present their worship to the
Father and the Son. Christian hymn writers have beautifully expressed this truth in song, and believers delight
to join in the following hymn by J. G. Deck:

> "The veil is rent, lo, Jesus stands
>   Before the throne of grace;
> And clouds of incense from His hands
>   Fill all that glorious place.
>
> His precious blood is sprinkled there,
>   Before and on the throne;
> And His own wounds in heaven declare
>   The work that saves is done.

> Within the holiest of all,
>   Cleansed by His precious blood,
> Before the throne we prostrate fall,
>   And worship Thee, our God."

While believers are physically on earth yet, in the energy of faith, they enter spiritually into the reality of this blessed truth. Thus their spirits are bathed in celestial atmosphere, so that they can sing in verity and truth:

> "Shut in with Thee, far, far above
>   The restless world that wars below;
> We seek to learn and prove Thy love,
>   Thy wisdom and Thy grace to know."

A saintly believer, who lived in the enjoyment of this truth, was once asked: "How far is heaven from earth?" He replied: "It cannot be far, for I spent half an hour there this morning!" There is only a veil between heaven and earth. The child of God may enter within that veil by faith, and prostrate himself before the throne of grace in worship. With his fellow-believers he can truthfully sing:

> "Through Thy precious body broken, inside the veil;
>   O what words to sinners spoken, inside the veil;
> Precious as the blood that bought us,
>   Perfect as the love that sought us,
> Holy as the Lamb that brought us, inside the veil.
>
> Lamb of God, through Thee we enter, inside the veil;
>   Cleansed by Thee, we boldly venture, inside the veil;
> Not a stain, a new creation,
>   Ours is such a full salvation;
> Low we bow in adoration, inside the veil!"

Thus, by faith, guided and empowered by the Holy Spirit, and through the great high Priest of their confession, believers are enabled, spiritually, to enter the holiest of all, and worship God in the beauty of holiness.

2. Physically, Worship May be Anywhere, or in Any Building.

There are no *geographical limits* to worship. One can worship just as truly at the North Pole as at the South Pole. Nor is any *building* required for this purpose, though such may be a great convenience to a company of believers, particularly in bad weather. The size, cost and architectural design of such a building has *nothing whatever to do with the worth,* or otherwise, of worship. Our Lord's words should dispel any false ideas as to the value of one building, or place, as against another: "Where two or three are gathered together in My name, there am I in the midst of them" (Matt. 18:20).

It is the *presence of Christ,* in the midst of His people, that sanctifies the gathering, and not the *kind of building* that encloses them. The huge ornate and costly buildings that men have erected add not a whit to the value, or acceptability of the worship offered therein. In fact, many of these buildings merely represent a great waste of time, labor and money. In the early days of the history of the Church, believers frequently met for worship in the home of a fellow believer; so that we often read of "the church, which is in his house." (Col. 4:15; Rom. 16:5; etc.). This does not imply, of course, that any old ramshackle building should be erected and used as a meeting place for believers. Such a building should at least meet the requirements of common decency, and be a suitable place to which others may be brought to hear the gospel. Thus the physical *location* of the worshipping believer, or believers, is utterly immaterial.

Nor is there any virtue in the physical *posture* he adopts: whether he kneels, sits, or stands. The believer can worship as he lies upon his bed, as he walks to work, as he rides in the street car, train, or auto, as he works, or as he kneels in his bedroom, etc. It is the spiritual *quality* of the worship of the individual believer, or of a company of believers, that determines its worth to God. Nor is the time of day material to worship. Any time of the day or night is equally fitting. It can be offered in the flush of early morning, in the brightness of the noon, in the soft velvet of the evening, or in the blackness of midnight. All times are equally appropriate for this highest of all occupations.

It is not the physical place *where,* or the time *when;* but the spiritual *how,* that is the important factor in worship. Though *physically* on earth, the Christian, with Divine fitness and holy boldness, worships in heaven. May it be ours to experience much of its reality in our own lives!

CHAPTER TWENTY-THREE

X. The Results of Worship.

Having discussed the meaning, the importance, the authority, the Object, the ground, the power, the manner, the hindrances, and the place of worship; it may be appropriate to conclude the study of this subject with a consideration of the results of worship. These results will be seen to be far reaching, affecting both God, the believer, the assembly and the unsaved.

1. God Shall Be Glorified.

Worship gives to God His rightful place of absolute pre-eminence in everything. It presents to Him the praise, honor and glory that is His rightful due, by virtue of what He is and what He has done. It has been well said that: "Man's chief end is to enjoy God and glorify Him for ever." As the Christian concentrates his attention upon the triune God, and the exceeding greatness of the Divine attributes, as displayed in creation, redemption and regeneration; he will be lost in wonder, awe, adoration and worship. Thus he displays the excellencies (or glorifies) of the One who has made it all possible.

As Robert Hall has finely said: "Were we capable of comprehending the Deity, devotion would not be the sublimest employment to which we can attain. In the contemplation of such a Being, we are in no danger of going beyond our subject: we are conversing with an infinite Object, in the depths of Whose essence and purposes, we are forever lost. This will probably give all the emotions of freshness and astonishment to the raptures of the beatific vision, and add a delightful zest to the devotions of eternity. This will enable the Divine Being to pour in continually fresh accessions of light; to unfold new views of His character, disclose new parts of His perfections, open new mansions in Himself, in which the mind will find ample room to expatiate. Thus we shall learn, to all eternity that, so far from exhausting His infinite fulness, there will remain infinite recesses of His nature unexplored; scenes in His counsels never brought before the view of His creatures; that we know but 'parts of His ways,' and that, instead of exhausting our theme, we are not even approaching nearer to the comprehension of the eternal All."

God's purpose, behind all the display of His attributes, has been revealed. Mark carefully the Divine utterance: "I will be sanctified in them that come nigh Me, and before all the people, I will be glorified" (Lev. 10:3). There can therefore be no greater occupation for man than the glorification of God, and this is what worship does. We have already seen that God desires the worship of man, His creature. At infinite cost He has provided a way by which man may be redeemed by Him, accepted before Him, approach to Him, be blessed by Him and become a worshipper of Him. When His blood-redeemed people fall down before Him in worship, the purpose of the triune God is thus fulfilled and He is thereby glorified. The Father will be glorified in the revelation He has given of Himself in the Son of His love. The Son will be glorified in the work He accomplished by the sacrifice of Himself. The Holy Spirit will be glorified, for it was through Him the written revelation came, and His indwelling presence makes possible the worship of the believer. Thus worship redounds to the glory of Father, Son and Holy Spirit.

2. The Believer Will Be Blest.

No one loses by giving to God, for God will be no man's Debtor. He will pour multiplied joy into the heart of the worshipper, in "good measure, pressed down, and shaken together and running over" (Luke 6:38). God delights to give, and reveals Himself as possessing both the ability and willingness to "do exceeding abundantly above all that we ask or think" (Eph. 3:20). God is described as "the blessed God." Consequently, all who bless Him in worship are blessed by Him in return. Luke's Gospel concludes in a very beautiful way. After describing the ascension of our Lord we read: "And they worshipped Him, and returned to Jerusalem with great joy; and were continually in the temple, praising and blessing God" (Luke 24:52-53). Notice the close connection between their worship of Christ, and the resultant great joy of their own hearts! The worship of God ever results in the great joy of man.

The worshipping believer is a joyous believer, for joy comes through obedience. Christ said: "If ye know these things, happy are ye if ye do them" (John 13:17). Worship enables the believer to know God better, and to appreciate Him more; and this knowledge causes God to become his "exceeding joy" (Ps. 43:4). He who fulfils God's desire for worship, shall have his own desire fulfilled for joy. There is no joy so exquisite as that which comes from the contemplation of God, as He has revealed Himself in the Person of His beloved Son. While the believer does not worship God *in order* to obtain this resultant joy; yet the fact remains that this "joy of the Lord" is but one of the many by-products of worship. Thus the adoration that ascends to God from the believer, to delight God's heart, will be more than recompensed by the blessing descending from God to the believer, which will rejoice his heart. God's definite promise is: "Them that honor Me, I will honor" (I Sam. 2:30).

Not only does worship minister joy to the worshipper, but it results in his deep soul-satisfaction. This is the very antithesis of self satisfaction, which is the result of favorable occupation with oneself. This is exemplified in the Pharisee's so-called prayer. (Luke 18:11-12). Worship occupies the soul with God, and the believer who spends time in the presence of God proves the truth of David's statement: "They shall be abundantly satisfied with the fatness of Thy house; and Thou shalt make them to drink of the river of Thy pleasures. For with Thee is the fountain of life: in Thy light shall we see light" (Ps. 36:8-9). The "broken cisterns" of this earth can never satisfy the one who has experienced the regenerating grace of God. With the hymn writer he sings:

> "Jesus, Thou joy of loving hearts,
> Thou Fount of life, Thou Light of men;
> From the best bliss that earth imparts,
> We turn, unfilled, to Thee again."

We might mention other blessings which the believer is caused to experience as a result of worshipping God; but enough has been written to prove that all those who bless God shall be blessed by God. He who from his heart exclaims: "Bless the Lord, O my soul: and all that is within me, bless His holy name!" shall also prove, with David, that: "Blessed is the man whom Thou choosest, and causeth to approach unto Thee, that he may dwell in Thy courts: we shall be satisfied with the goodness of Thy house, even of Thy holy temple" (Ps. 103:1; 65:4).

3. The Assembly Will Be Edified.

Not only does worship glorify God and bring blessing to the worshipper himself; but a company of believers, who give worship its proper place, is blessed and edified thereby; for it is fulfilling its God-given function. It will be recalled that God, in the tabernacle and, later, in the temple, responded to the worship of His people by filling the place with His glory (Exod. 40:34; I Kings 8:11). Wherever believers gather together for worship today and, with one heart and voice, join to worship God spiritually, sincerely, and intelligently, they too shall be made to experience what it means for the place to become redolent with the glory of the Lord. There is no spot nearer heaven than when the united worship of an assembly of Christians ascends, like fragrant incense, before the face of God.

We have already seen that this calls for spiritual preparation of the highest order, but such an exercise of heart is not in vain. The Divine purpose in constituting each believer a priest will be fulfilled when such, audibly or inaudibly, join as an assembly to present their appreciation to God of all He is and has done. When an assembly of believers thus puts "first things first," the saints are thereby built up in their most holy faith. This, in turn, fits and enables them to fulfil the other purposes God has in mind for His gathered people. An assembly that allows its service for the Lord to crowd out its worship to the Lord, not only comes short of God's purpose for it, but the effectiveness of its service is curtailed thereby. Both the desire and ability for true service flows from spiritual worship. It was after Isaiah had seen the glory of the Lord, and been impressed with the majesty of His presence, that the call and commission for service came, and to which he gladly responded: "Here am I; send me" (Isa. 6:8).

4. The Unsaved Will Be Reached.

As the worshipping Christian moves amongst his fellow men, he will unconsciously carry with him something of God. We are told that Moses, when he returned from the interview he had with God upon the mount, "Wist not that . . . . . his face shone" (Exod. 34:29). The Bible points out that "None of us liveth to himself" (Rom. 14:7). Each life touches some other life, either for good or evil. Each Christian, by the impact of his personality, makes an impression upon others. Only as God, through worship, impresses the believer with Himself, can the believer impress others with God. It is this unconscious influence that counts for so much in one's contact with the world.

It was when the Lord turned the captivity of His people, and their mouth was "filled with laughter," and their "tongue with singing," that the heathen were moved to testify: "The Lord had done great things for them" (Psalm 126:2). The world is looking for reality, and rightly holds in contempt all religious sham, humbug and pretence. An ostentatious display of sanctimoniousness only awakens its ridicule. The believer, who knows what it means to worship the true and living God, is best fitted to present the gospel to the unsaved, both by commending it in his life and proclaiming it with his lips.

It is not an uncommon thing for the worship of an assembled company of God's people to be used by the Lord to impress unsaved people who happened to be present, of the reality of eternal things, so that they were led to trust the Savior. Such certainly are prepared to fall upon their faces, "worship God, and report that God is in you of a truth" (I Cor. 14:23-25). Thus worship is seen to have far reaching and blessed effects, beginning with God Himself, and flowing out to His own people and, through them, to a world that sits in darkness and the shadow of death.

*   *   *   *

May the Lord be pleased to use this study of worship to both the awakening, encouragement and edification of His people; so that from each believer individually, and from each assembly collectively, there may flow up, to the triune God, a constant volume of adoring worship which shall bring delight to His heart and glory to His name!

APPENDIX

DIRECT ADDRESS

to the

LORD JESUS

Direct Address To The Lord Jesus

Introduction

THE title of this paper may appear strange to those Christians who, from their conversion, have been rightly taught that it is their scriptural privilege to address both the Father and the Son *directly* in worship, praise and prayer. It will therefore come as an unpleasant surprise for such to learn that in certain circles there are Christians who would strongly object to a believer directly addressing the Lord Jesus. Some have gone so far, in their erroneous belief, to remove from their hymnbooks all those songs of worship and praise which are addressed directly to the Son of God!

The writer recently heard of a company of believers where certain brethren were taken to task because they had addressed the Lord Jesus directly. They were solemnly informed that all worship, praise and prayer must be addressed *only* to the Father through the mediation of the Son. Such scriptures as John 4:23 and 16:23 were quoted to support the assertion, as though this represented the entire revelation of the word of God regarding the matter of worship, praise and prayer!

Unfortunately, such an incident is by no means an isolated one. Periodically, this question is raised at Bible readings and conferences of believers, and there seems to be a little confusion in the minds of some as to this question of *direct address* to the Son of God, in either worship, praise or prayer. In view of this, it will be profitable to look into the matter, and see what the word of God has to say concerning it.

It is well to remember that one of the fundamental principles governing the correct understanding of any text of Scripture is that it must be interpreted in the light of all the other scriptures which refer to the same subject. This is the meaning of II Peter 1:21-22, which reads: "Knowing this first, that no prophecy of the Scripture is of any private interpretation. For the prophecy came not in old time by the will of man, but holy men of old spake as they were moved by the Holy Ghost." This simply means that no single text of Scripture can be interpreted wholly in the light of itself, but must be understood in the light of *all* that the Divinely inspired word has to say regarding the subject as a whole.

Almost any mistaken theory can be based on an *isolated* text, or even a skillfully arranged *collection* of texts, as the claims of scriptural support by false cults will demonstrate; but no wrong theory can possibly stand up to the test of *all* that the Bible has to say concerning any *doctrine*. Therefore, in discussing any scriptural theme, the *full revelation* of it must be taken into consideration ere a right conclusion can be reached. It has been well said: "Learned and gifted men can make what is only a human theory look so like a Divine principle that the honest, but unwary person, is led into a snare without being aware of it."

When we apply this sound principle of interpretation to the subject now under consideration, we shall discover that the Bible gives ample authority for the believer to address both the Father and the Son directly in worship, praise and prayer.

*   *   *   *

We shall begin our study of this subject by a short consideration of the great truth of

I. The Triunity of the Eternal Godhead.

The Bible clearly teaches that the Object of the believer's worship is the triune and eternal Godhead, who is described as: "Eternal, immortal, invisible, the only wise God, to whom be honor and glory forever and ever" (I Tim. 1:17).

1. *The meaning of the term.*

While the word, "trinity," is not found in the Scriptures, yet the truth of the tri-unity of the Godhead is clearly evident as one opens the pages of the Bible. The Godhead is revealed as consisting of three Persons: Father, Son and Holy Spirit, each equal and eternal with the Other, each possessing all the essentials of Deity, as omnipotence, omniscience, omnipresence and immutability, and each possessing all the essentials of personality, as intelligence, emotions and will.

Yet these Three are One in nature and essence. Thus there are not three Gods, but one Godhead revealed in three Persons. "God is a trinity of Persons in a unity of nature." This tremendous truth is utterly beyond our finite *comprehension,* but not beyond the *apprehension* of faith, for we implicitly believe what God has been pleased to reveal concerning this fact.

2. *What this triunity of the Godhead involves.*

The late W. E. Vine wrote: "The word, 'trinity,' was used as early as the second century to express conveniently the scriptural doctrine that, in the undivided unity of the Divine nature of the Godhead, there are the personal distinctions of Father, Son and Holy Spirit, each possessed of complete and perfect personality." Campbell Morgan puts it thus: "In one essential Godhead there co-exists three Persons, con-substantial, co-equal and co-eternal. This mystery cannot be explained, or defined, because it is beyond the grasp of the finite, and no explanation is given in the inspired word."

In the fourth century, Athanasius, who so valiantly defended the doctrine of the essential and eternal deity of the Lord Jesus against the attack of Arius, who denied the Deity of Christ, stated his conception of the trinity in this magnificent passage: "We worship one God in Trinity, and Trinity in Unity. There is one Person of the Father, another of the Son, another of the Holy Spirit; but the Godhead of the Father, and of the Son and of the Holy Spirit is all One, the glory equal and the majesty co-eternal. Such as the Father is, such is the Son, and such is the Holy Spirit; the Father eternal, the Son eternal, and the Holy Spirit eternal. And yet there are not three Eternals, but one Eternal. So likewise the Father is Almighty; the Son, Almighty; and the Holy Spirit, Almighty. And yet there are not three Almighties, but one Almighty. So the Father is God, the Son is God, and the Holy Spirit is God. And yet there are not three Gods, but one God."

3. *Some attempted illustrations of the Trinity.*

There are no adequate illustrations of the Triunity of the Godhead, for it transcends all possible human comprehension and defies all philosophical analysis. Many attempts have been made to illustrate the Trinity, but all fall far short of conveying the actual fact. Nathaniel Wood, in his excellent book: "The Secret of the Universe," declares that this secret is the triunity of the Godhead. He proceeds to demonstrate that this triunity is reflected in man himself, who was made in the image of God, and who is composed of spirit, soul and body, yet he is but one individual. Space also is a triunity, consisting of length, breadth and height, yet space is but one. Time also falls into this same threefold category, for it consists of past, present and future, yet time is but one thing.

4. *The distinctions in the Godhead.*

Scripture generally presents the Father as *purposing,* the Son as *executing* the Divine purpose, and the Holy Spirit as *energizing* and applying this purpose, and making it operative in the experience of the believer. The *Father* loved the world, and gave His Son. The *Son,* obedient to the Father's will, gave Himself as a substitutionary sacrifice to accomplish our redemption. The *Holy Spirit* convicts man of his need as a sinner, leads him to repentance and faith in the Person and work of the Son of God and, on his trusting in the Lord Jesus, seals him unto the day of redemption. (Eph. 1:13; 4:30). It has been well said: "All that can be *seen* of God is through the Son, and all that can be *experienced* of God is through the Holy Spirit." (John 1:18; 14:9; 15:26; 16:7-15).

We need ever to keep in mind the fact that there is no jealousy in the eternal Godhead. Each person delights to glorify the Other. The Bible does not even maintain a fixed order of sequence when mentioning their names. For the purpose of convenience of identification we usually speak of the Father, Son and Holy Spirit as: "The first, second and third Persons of the Godhead." Scripture, however, varies the order of their names. Sometimes the order is: "Father, Son and Holy Spirit" (Matt. 28:19). At other times the order is: "Spirit, Father and Son" (John 15:26). Then again, the order reads: "Son, Spirit and Father" (Heb. 9:13-14; Eph. 2:18). Once more, the order is "Son, Father and Holy Spirit" (II Cor. 13:14).

Let each reader carefully ponder the wonderful revelation of the Father which His beloved Son gave, as recorded in the fifth chapter of John. Let the full significance of Christ's own words sink deep into his heart, for it reveals a tremendous truth: "All men should honor the Son even as they honor the Father. He that honoreth not the Son, honoreth not the Father which hath sent Him" (John 5:23). What does this mean? There is only one answer: it means exactly what it says. The same honor that we give to the Father must be given equally to the Son. In whatever way we honor the Father, then in that same way we are to honor the Son. We shall have occasion to refer more fully to this passage later on.

The more a believer contemplates the infinite greatness, majesty, holiness, righteousness, truth, mercy, love and grace of the triune God: Father, Son and Holy Spirit, the more he will be lost in reverential awe, wonder, praise and worship. It becomes us, therefore, as our thoughts are occupied with such a glorious Being, to prostrate ourselves before Him in humble adoration for all He has revealed Himself to be, and for all He has done in the wondrous work of our redemption.

Each Christian should keep in mind the distinction between the Persons of the Godhead. This will enable him to be spiritually intelligent, not only in his private devotions, but also as he audibly takes part in a gathering of believers for worship or prayer. Sometimes one hears a believer thanking the Father for dying for him on the cross. This person would never have expressed himself thus if he had been clear in his conception of this distinction of the Persons in the Godhead. Confused thinking must inevitably issue in confused speaking. While we would not "make a man an offender for a word" (Isa. 29: 21), yet we should heed the injunction to "hold fast the form of sound words" (II Tim. 1:13). Sound *doctrine,* when grasped by a sound *mind,* will result in sound *thoughts* which, in turn, will find expression in sound *words.* (See II Tim. 1:7, 13; Titus 2:1).

Often the word, "God," includes in its scope both Father, Son and Holy Spirit in their undivided Unity, as Gen. 1:1; Rev. 19:10; 22:9, etc. Sometimes the word has the *Father* particularly in mind, as John 3:16; 4:24; 5:44, etc. At other times it is the *Son of God* who is in view, as Rom. 9:5; Heb. 1:8, etc. At still other times it is the *Spirit* who is emphasized, as Acts 5:4. Let us ever keep in mind the fact that each Person is equally "God," with all that this term implies.

5. *The approach to the Father and the Son.*

The Bible makes it abundantly clear that the believer, as a member of the family of God (Eph. 3:15), is to approach *the Father* in worship, praise and prayer *through the mediation* of the Son of God. See John 14:6; 4:23; 14:13; 16:23; I Peter 2:5; Heb. 10:19-22; Eph. 2:18, etc. The same Divine revelation, however, makes it equally clear that the believer may approach the Son of God *directly* in worship, praise and prayer, *without any mediation* whatever. See Luke 24:50-53; Heb. 1:6; Rev. 5:9-10; Eph. 5:19; Acts 7:59-60; 9:5-6; 9:10-17; II Cor. 12:8-10; Acts 22:10; Rev. 22:20.

Romanism has introduced, amongst other false teaching, the unscriptural theory of the mediation of Mary. They argue that inasmuch as the Father must be approached through the mediation of the Son, therefore the Son must be approached through the mediation of Mary. The scripture reveals that *there is no mediator* between the believer and his blessed Lord and Savior. The mediation of the Son has to do with the believer's relationship with and his approach to *"the Father."*

6. *Doctrinal truth must be held in proper balance.*

The truth of God concerning any subject revealed in Scripture, must be held in balance, and in the light of the *full* revelation of God concerning it. We are all naturally creatures of extremes, and are therefore prone to emphasize one aspect of a scriptural truth to the entire exclusion of the other. This can easily be demonstrated in the twin truths of the sovereignty of God and the free will of man. Both these truths are clearly revealed in the Bible, yet Christians are sharply divided into two opposing schools of thought regarding the matter, each holding one side of the truth to the entire exclusion of the other!

In regard to the subject we are now considering, we could sum up the Scripture teaching as follows: The believer should approach the Father, in worship, praise and prayer, through the mediation of His Son. The Bible also reveals that the Son of God may be approached, in worship, praise and prayer, *directly by the believer.* Thus the word of God teaches *both* aspects of this truth, and each believer is responsible to be obedient to what God has revealed in His word regarding this matter.

Regarding the true interpretation of Christ's words, as found in John 16:23, "And in that day ye shall ask me nothing. Verily, verily, I say unto you, whatsoever ye shall ask of the Father in My name, He will give it you;" I cannot do better than quote Mr. August Van Ryn's comment on this passage:

"The whole argument that, from this passage, prayer and praise should not be addressed to the Lord Jesus falls to the ground for the simple reason that the first word "ask" in that verse does not mean asking in the sense of wanting something to supply one's need, but it means to "inquire," or questioning for the sake of learning something one does not know. Both A. T. Robertson in his critical notes, and W. E. Vine in his "Expository Dictionary of New Testament Words" comment on this fact.

"One has only to look at the context of this verse to realize this fact. The Lord is telling His disciples that, in view of His going to leave them for heaven, they would no longer be asking Him questions as they had been doing all the while He was with them, as they wanted to do at that very moment. See verse 19. Now that the Holy Spirit would come, the time for asking questions from the Lord Jesus had come to an end. Thus this statement has nothing to do with praying in the normal sense of the word. It simply means that after Christ's departure, the Holy Spirit would be the "Teacher," as the Lord Jesus had been while on earth. See John 3: 2."

In this paper, however, we are particularly concerned with the matter of the scripturalness of directly addressing the Lord Jesus in worship, praise and prayer. We shall therefore concentrate on this subject.

In reply to the question: "Should the Son of God be addressed directly in worship, praise and prayer?" our answer is a most emphatic, "yes," for the following scriptural reasons:

1. God commands it.

Psalm 45:6, 11; Heb. 1:6-8

There is no doubt whatever of the Messanic character of Psalm 45. It is redolent with Christ and, to make doubly sure that there shall be no misunderstanding as to this fact, it is quoted in the New Testament. Only as we appreciate, in some measure, both the mystery and reality of the eternal Godhead can we understand these words, for here it is God addressing God, the Son: "But unto the Son He saith: Thy throne, O God, is for ever and ever!"

No wonder, therefore, that the Divine decree goes forth concerning the Son of God: "Let all the angels of God worship Him!" Nor is this worship to be confined to the angels, for the exhortation of Psalm 45 is also addressed to the "daughter," a type of the Church, and of each believer in it: "Hearken, O daughter and consider, and incline thine ear; forget also thine own people, and thy father's house; so shall the King greatly desire thy beauty: for He is thy Lord, and worship thou Him" (v. 10).

How fitting therefore, that in the epistle to the Hebrews, which sets forth the infinite superiority and absolute supremacy of the Son of God, is found this Divine command to worship the Son of God, for all He is and for all He has done. Ultimately, as we know from the Word, universal homage shall be rendered to Him, when every knee shall bow to Him, and every tongue shall confess that "Jesus Christ is Lord, to the glory of God the Father" (Phil. 2:9-11). Well may each Christian, redeemed by "the precious blood of Christ, as of a Lamb without blemish and without spot," bow low in adoration before the Son of God and render to Him what God has commanded, the worship of his redeemed spirit!

We may therefore state that since the Father has glorified His beloved Son, exalted Him to sit at His own right hand, and distinctly commanded us to worship Him, every Christian who does so is acting in obedience to the direct revelation of God Himself in Holy Scripture.

2. Scripture reveals it.

We shall notice six ways in which this is done.

(1) *In the vision of Isaiah.* Isa. 6:1-10, cp. John 12:38-41.

Who was this glorious Being, who is described as: "sitting upon a throne, high and lifted up, and His train filled the temple," before Whom the seraphims worshipped and covered their faces as they cried: "Holy, holy, holy, is the Lord of hosts: the whole earth is full of His glory"? We are not left in any doubt as to the identity of "the Lord of Hosts," for we read in John 12:41: "These things said Isaiah when he saw His glory and spake of Him." Whose glory did Isaiah see, and of whom did he speak? The context allows but one answer to this question: Isaiah saw the glory of the pre-incarnate Son of God, which glory He had "before the world was" (John 17:5). Shall redeemed Christians on earth deny, to the once crucified, but now glorified Son of God, the worship that heaven gave Him in Isaiah's day?

(2) The Theophanies of the Old Testament.

An interesting study, in this connection, are the theophanies of the Old Testament. These theophanies, or appearances of God to men were, in reality, appearances of the pre-incarnate Son of God, for He alone is the visible manifestation of God. See John 1:18. In some of these appearances He is described as "the Angel of Jehovah," and is directly addressed as Deity, worshipped as God and petitioned in prayer. See Gen. 16:1-13; 21:17-19; 22:11-16; 31:11-13; Exod. 3:2-4; Judges 2:1; 6:12-16; 13:3-22, etc. It is important to know that all that is predicated of Jehovah in the Old Testament is claimed by Christ in the New Testament. How unspeakably blessed it is for the believer to know that the "Jehovah" of the Old Testament is the "Jesus" of the New Testament!

(3) In the use of the word in the original for "worship."

There are two words that are translated "worship" in the New Testament. They are "proskuneo," and "latreuo," (also translated "serve"). Both these words appear in Matt. 4:10. Each of these words is used to describe the worship of the Father and the worship of the Son. There is "proskuneo" to the Father, in John 4:23, 24; Rev. 4:10; and there is "proskuneo" to the Son in Luke 24:52; Heb. 1:6; Rev. 5:14. There is "latreuo" to the Father in Phil. 3:3; Heb. 9:14; and there is "latreuo" to the Son in Rev. 22:3. Thus what is rendered to the Father *through* the Son is also rendered *directly* to the Son of God Himself.

(4) *In the use of the title of "The Lord."*

Mr. W. R. Lewis, of "The Echoes of Service," in his small but excellent pamphlet: "Should the Lord Jesus be addressed in praise and prayer?" points out: "Of the three hundred five occurrences of the title, 'the Lord,' found in Acts to Revelation, considerably more than half, say one hundred ninety-six, refer to the Lord Jesus. He is spoken of as 'the Lord,' more than in any other way, and the weight of evidence is in favor of taking 'the Lord' in Eph. 5:19 as referring to Christ, as it evidently does in verse 22 . . . This is not to deny that *God* is 'the Lord,' but in the New Testament, unless the context clearly indicates otherwise, the title belongs to the Lord Jesus Christ." We shall notice four things regarding this title.

(a) *This title of "The Lord" was Divinely given to Christ.*

Peter declared: "God hath made that same Jesus, whom ye crucified, both Lord and Christ" (Acts 2:36). To Cornelius he said: "The word which God sent unto the children of Israel, preaching peace by Jesus Christ, (He is Lord of all)." Acts 10:36. Paul, by the Spirit affirmed: "For to this end Christ died and rose and revived that He might be Lord, both of the dead and the living" (Rom. 14:9). We have previously seen that God has decreed that the whole universe shall ultimately be made to confess that "Jesus Christ is Lord to the glory of God the Father."

(b) *Salvation is conditioned by calling on the name of the Lord.*

Both in Romans 10:9-13 and Acts 2:21, the message is heard: "Whosoever shall call upon the name of the Lord shall be saved." Think of the countless number of souls who, in all their sin and need have cried, from the heart:

> "Just as I am, without one plea,
>   But that Thy blood was shed for me,
> And that Thou bid'st me come to Thee,
>   O, Lamb of God, I come."

All such have discovered, by joyous experience, that salvation, peace, life, light, liberty, pardon, power, righteousness and acceptance are found only in the Lord Jesus.

(c) *The New Testament assemblies were characterized by the fact that the believers, composing these assemblies, called on the name of Jesus Christ our Lord.*

Mark this carefully. Paul, in his letter to the assembly at Corinth wrote: "Unto the Church of God which is at Corinth, to them that are sanctified in Christ Jesus, called to be saints, with all that in every place call upon the name of Jesus Christ, our Lord, both theirs and ours." Here there is no doubt as to the identity of "the Lord." Each believer, in those days, called upon the Lord Jesus Christ. It was their distinguishing characteristic. The heathen called upon the name of their idols, but Christians called upon the One whose they were and whom they served. (Acts 27:23).

Notice, this was not only true of the assembly in Corinth, but it obtained in "every place" where believers met together in assembly fellowship. Thus they spoke directly to the Lord Jesus. Notice also in II Tim. 2:22. Here Paul urges believers to "follow righteousness, faith, charity, peace, with them that call on the Lord out of a pure heart." Here, again, direct address to Christ is indicated.

It is interesting to observe that Peter uses a similar phrase in his epistle and wrote: "If ye call on the Father" (I Peter 1:17). Thus the Christians of his day called on both the name of the Father and on the name of the Son.

(d) *By its use in the institution and observance of the Lord's supper.*

The institution of the Lord's supper was the subject of a special revelation to Paul from the Lord Himself. See I Cor. 11:23-34. In this revelation the purpose of its institution is plainly stated by the Lord Himself. "This is My body . . . this is My blood . . . This do for a remembrance of Me." Thus, at the Lord's supper, the Lord directs our attention to Himself in a particular way. The sole object of this ordinance is to remember the One who gave His holy body and shed His precious blood to secure our eternal salvation. How appropriate then, at such a meeting, that worship and praise be addressed directly to the blessed Son of God, as all the redeemed of all the ages shall do in a coming day (Rev. 5:9-13).

Through the years that have intervened since the institution of the Lord's Supper, many spiritually gifted and intelligent believers have composed hymns of worship and praise addressed directly to the Lord Jesus. These hymns form no small part in the worship of God's people as they gather together for the remembrance of their

Lord in the breaking of bread. We shall refer, more fully, to this later on.

From a study of reliable church history we learn that doctrinal error soon began to manifest itself in the post-apostolic church, as Paul had prophecied. See Acts 20: 28-32. Origen (born 185), one of the early "church fathers," and guilty of propogating much error concerning the Person of Christ, wrongly taught, from John 16:23, that it was improper for Christians to address prayer directly to the Lord Jesus. Thus this false interpretation had both an early and bad beginning.

(5) *Both apostles and disciples are described as directly addressing the Lord Jesus.* We shall examine seven of these instances.

(a) *Thomas,* as he saw before him the risen Son of God, with the marks of Calvary still upon Him, cried: "My Lord and My God!"

(b) *The hundred and twenty disciples,* as they met together to choose an apostle to take the place of Judas, the traitor, prayed: "Thou, Lord, which knowest the hearts of all men, show whether of these two Thou hast chosen" (Acts 1:13-26).

(c) *Stephen,* as he stood before the Council, "saw the glory of God, and Jesus standing on the right hand of God," and testified to this fact. Filled with malignant hatred they rushed upon him and stoned him. The Divine record states: "And they stoned Stephen calling upon God and saying, 'Lord Jesus, receive my spirit,' and he kneeled down and cried with a loud voice: 'Lord, lay not this sin to their charge'" (Acts 7:55-60).

(d) *Saul, of Tarsus,* arrested by the Son of God on the Damascus highway, inquired: "Who art Thou, Lord?" On being told: "I am Jesus, whom thou persecutest," he replied: "Lord, what wilt Thou have me to do?" Thus

Saul, for the first time (but certainly not the last time!) in his life addressed the Lord Jesus directly.

Paul rejoiced in the fact of the Lordship of Christ, and refers to Him many times as *"the* Lord." In I Cor. 9:1, he speaks of Him as *"our* Lord." In I Cor. 8:6, he refers to Him in these words: "To us there is but one God, the Father, of whom are all things and we in Him, and one Lord Jesus Christ, by whom are all things, and we by Him." In Phil. 3:8, he gives us his own testimony as to what the Lord Jesus meant to him personally: "I count all things but loss for the excellency of the knowledge of Christ Jesus, *my* Lord."

(e) *Ananias* now comes into the picture, as the Lord Jesus gives to him a vision in the which He commissions him to go to Saul. Note, in this account, the naturalness of Ananias' direct conversation with the Lord. (Acts 9: 10-19).

(f) *Peter* is next mentioned, and in the vision of the sheet let down from heaven, he replies to the Lord's command to "slay and eat" by saying, with typical impetuousity: "Not so, Lord." (Acts 10:10-16).

(g) *Paul,* when afflicted with "the thorn in the flesh," addressed his prayer three times to the Lord that this physical disability would be removed from him. Far from removing the thorn, the Lord replied to His servant by saying: "My grace is sufficient for thee, for My strength is made perfect in weakness" (II Cor. 12:7-9).

Here, then, are seven instances where the Lord Jesus is directly addressed by His people. It is also most significant that the last prayer of the Bible is addressed to the Savior. In reply to His promise: "Surely, I come quickly," comes the prayer: "Amen. Even so, come, Lord Jesus." (Rev. 22:20). Surely each believer can re-echo this prayer!

(6) *The doxologies of the New Testament indicate
the direct addressing of praise to the Lord Jesus.*

There are sixteen of these doxologies, or ascriptions
of praise found in the New Testament. Of these, nine
are addressed to the Father, or to God. See Gal. 1:5;
Rom. 11:36; 16:27; Phil. 4:20; Eph. 3:21; I Tim. 1:17;
I Peter 5:11; Jude 25; Rev. 7:12. Two are addressed to
the Father and the Son. See Rev. 5:13; 7:10. The re-
maining five are rendered to the Son of God Himself. See
I Tim. 6:16; II Tim. 4:18; Heb. 13:21; II Peter 3:18; Rev.
1:6. While it is true these are couched in the third person, yet so also are the doxologies addressed to the Father.

My good friend and brother in Christ, Mr. August
Van Ryn, the well known Bible teacher, believes strongly
that both Jude 25 and I Tim. 1:17 should also be included
in the doxologies addressed to the Son of God. If this be
correct, then it is not without the deepest spiritual significance that there are *seven* doxologies addressed to
the Father, and *seven* addressed to the Son. Thus the
Father and the Son share *equal honors* in these ascriptions of praise.

Thus we have abundant authority, from the word of
God, for addressing songs of praise directly to the Lord
Jesus. Realizing this, spiritual and gifted men and wom-
en, led of the Spirit, have written hymns of worship and
praise to both the Father and the Son, and these, set to
appropriate music, have provided the people of God with
the opportunity to sing and make melody in their hearts
unto the Lord (Eph. 5:19).

Let us ever keep in mind the fact that the Lord Jesus
is "God," just as much as the Father is God. In fact,
Christ is described as being, "God over all, blessed for
ever" (Rom. 9:5). John, by the Spirit, testified of the
Lord Jesus: "This is the true God and eternal life" (I

John 5:20). The Father delights to hear worship and praise directed to His Son, even as His Son delights to hear worship and praise directed to the Father; and the Holy Spirit delights to lead the people of God in such worship and praise to both the Father and the Son.

3. The Father Wills It.

In Christ's own revelation of the Father, as recorded in John 5, He makes the tremendous statement that the Father desires "that all men should honor the Son, even as they honor the Father. He that honoreth not the Son, honoreth not the Father which hath sent Him" (John 5: 23). If words mean anything, then the obvious interpretation of our Lord's statement is that it is His Father's will that equal honor is to be accorded to both Father and Son. Whatever honor it may be that is given to the Father, then that honor is equally due to the Son. It therefore follows that, since in our worship we honor the Father by directly addressing to Him our praise, we should also likewise honor the Son by directly addressing to Him our worship and praise and prayer. This, as we have seen elsewhere, is what the Bible clearly teaches.

4. The Son of God accepts it.

We shall think of four things in this connection.

(1) *He accepted it before His incarnation.*

We have already touched on the Theophanies of the Bible, and learned that, as "the Angel of Jehovah," He received worship and was petitioned directly in prayer. See Exod. 3:2-6; Jud. 6:12-24; 13:3-21; II Sam. 24:16; Isa. 6:1-10.

(2) *He accepted it in "the days of His flesh"* (Heb. 5:7).

This fact can be easily verified by a reading of the four Gospels. We will refer to eight of these instances:

(a) *At His birth.* Matt. 2:11.

(b) *By a leper.* Matt. 8:2.

(c) *By a certain ruler.* Matt. 9:18.

(d) *By the disciples at the calming of the lake.* Matt. 14:33.

(e) *By the Syrophonecian woman.* Matt. 15:25.

(f) *By the mother of James and John.* Matt. 20:20.

(g) *By the demoniac.* Mark 5:6.

(h) *By the man born blind.* John 9:38.

It will be recalled that when Cornelius attempted to worship Peter he was rebuked (Acts 10:25-26). John was similarly rebuked when he sought to worship an angel (Rev. 19:10; 22:8). Our Lord, however, accepted the worship offered Him as His rightful due as the incarnate Son of God. He quoted to Satan: "Thou shalt worship the Lord thy God, and Him only shalt thou serve (Matt. 4:10). He then proceeded to receive the worship from men which, as God, was his rightful due. If it be argued that only "God" should be worshipped, we agree, and point out that the Lord Jesus Christ is "God," and therefore should be worshipped.

(3) *He accepted it after His resurrection and ascension.*

(a) *By the women at the sepulchure.* Matt. 28:9.

(b) *By the disciples in Galilee.* Matt. 28:16-17.

(c) *By the disciples after the ascension.* Luke 24:50-53.

(d) *By the decree of God.* Heb. 1:9.

(4) *He accepts it in heaven.* Rev. 1:5-6; 5:1-14.

Remember, this was the revelation which John received from the Lord Himself, and which he was commanded to describe in writing (Rev. 1:19).

What a day that shall be when the once crucified, but now glorified Lamb of God, shall be surrounded by His redeemed people and receive their united worship! With undimmed vision and unsinning hearts they shall exultantly sing: "Thou art worthy to take the book, and to open the seals thereof: for Thou wast slain, and hast redeemed us to God by Thy blood out of every kindred, and tongue, and people, and nation; and hast made us unto our God kings and priests, and we shall reign upon the earth!"

Then, as John beheld this wondrous sight, he heard the voice of many angels around the throne, together with the living creatures and the elders, and tells us their number was "ten thousand times ten thousand, and thousands of thousands. These now all joined with glad accord, and with one heart and voice to sing, with glorious harmony and exquisite melody: "Worthy is the Lamb that was slain to receive power, and riches, and honor and blessing!"

Then comes the grand consummation of this glorious scene which John desbribes in verse 13: "And every creature which is in heaven, and on earth and under the earth and such as are in the sea, and all that are in them, heard I saying: Blessing and honor and glory and power be unto Him that sitteth upon the throne, and unto the Lamb for ever and ever!"

There will be no one in that day to raise his voice in objection to this ascription of praise and worship offered directly to the Son of God! Thus, as it was in the eternal past, is now in the present, and shall be in the eternal future, the Son of God is the Recipient of the direct worship of His people, to the glory of God, the Father.

James G. Deck has well expressed it:

"If here on earth the thoughts of Jesus' love
  Lift our poor hearts this weary world above,
If even here the taste of heavenly springs
  So cheers the spirit that the pilgrim sings,
What will the sunshine of His glory prove?
  What the unmingled fulness of His love?
What hallelujahs shall His presence raise?
What but one loud eternal burst of praise!"

5. The Holy Spirit leads it.

(1) *The Savior's revelation concerning His Person.*

Mark well the words of the Lord Jesus in this connection. He said, of the Holy Spirit: "When He, the Spirit of truth is come, He will guide you into all truth: for He shall not speak of (from) Himself; but whatsoever He shall hear, that shall He speak: and He will show you things to come. He shall glorify Me: for He shall receive of Mine, and shall show it unto you. All things that the Father hath are Mine: therefore said I, that He shall take of Mine, and shall show it unto you" (John 16:13-15).

Thus our Lord Jesus designates the Holy Spirit as His Vicar or Representative on earth. It is now the Spirit's delight to occupy the believer's heart with the beauties of the Savior, to guide each Christian into all truth, and to glorify the Son of God as He takes of the things of Christ and shows them unto him. He it is who directs our worship, both to the Father and to the Son.

(2) *The Holy Spirit's work with the believer.*

He it was that inspired holy men of old, so that what they wrote, under His control, were the very words of God. (II Peter 1:20; II Tim. 3:16-17). He it is who enables the believer to confess the Lordship of Christ, for "No man can say that Jesus is the Lord, but by the Holy Ghost" (I Cor. 12:3). He it is who convicts the sinner of his sin, leads him, as a repentant sinner, to put his faith in the Lord Jesus, seals him unto the day of redemption, indwells him and imparts to him a Divine nature, so that the Christian is empowered to live a life to the glory of Christ. See John 16: 8-11; Eph. 1: 13; I Cor. 6: 19-20.

Each time a believer's heart is led out in worship, either to the Father or the Son, it is because of the indwelling of this holy and heavenly Guest. Well may our hearts and voices be raised in praise to God for this rich provision for our needs in the gift of the Holy Spirit!

(3) *We are not instructed to directly address the Holy Spirit in worship, praise, or prayer.*

There is no precept or example in the Scriptures for addressing the Holy Spirit, *directly,* in worship or prayer. We are urged to pray *in* the Spirit, that is, as guided by the Spirit, but we are not told to pray *to* the Holy Spirit. Our worship is to be *in* the Spirit, but we are not instructed to offer it *to* the Holy Spirit. See Eph. 6: 18; Phil. 3: 3; John 4: 23. Apart from the indwelling Holy Spirit we can neither pray as we ought, or worship as we should. He alone makes this possible to the believer (Rom. 8: 26-27).

This does not, for one moment, imply that the Holy Spirit is less important, or that He holds a subordinate position to the Father and the Son, for the Bible makes clear that He is equal and eternal with Both. Let us summarize the teaching of the New Testament as to this. The Son of God, for the purpose of obtaining our redemption, became incarnate and voluntarily submitted Himself to a life of absolute dependence upon His Father, obedience to the Scriptures, and the empowerment and guidance of the Holy Spirit. So now, likewise, the blessed Holy Spirit, in this dispensation, delights to glorify the Son of God, and to draw forth, from each believer's heart, true worship and praise to both the Father and the Son.

Let us reemphasize what was stated previously: *There is no jealousy in the eternal Godhead.* Therefore when we worship "God," we include in our thought each Person of the Godhead, and bow low in adoration before such a glorious Being, and at love, "so amazing and Divine."

Having seen, from the Scriptures themselves, the fact that the Lord Jesus may be directly addressed in worship, praise and prayer, it will not be surprising to know that:

6. The writings of godly, able and sound teachers and poets endorse it.

The present day believer has a goodly heritage in the many excellent expositions written by Spirit-filled, Spirit-taught and Spirit-led teachers, writers and poets, particularly during the past one hundred and fifty years. Their writings are available to all believers. May each believer both appreciate, desire and take full advantage of these gifts of the risen Head to the members of His body, the Church, for their edification and comfort (Eph. 4: 7-16). (1) *The writers.*

While we do not, for one moment, base our beliefs upon the writings of men, however godly, gifted and sincere for, as human beings, they are liable to error; yet, insofar as their writings are in accord with the general teachings of the word of God, they are of great profit for the edification of the Lord's people. How good it is, therefore, to find that this truth of direct address to the Lord Jesus is confirmed in their writings.

We think of such writers as J. N. Darby, C. H. Macintosh, W. E. Vine, George Goodman, R. C. Chapman, W. Kelly, F. W. Grant, C. A. Coates, J. R. Caldwell, F. B.

Meyer, Griffith Thomas, Campbell Morgan, C. F. Hogg, H. P. Barker, C. H. Spurgeon, Harold St. John, J. G. Bellett, George Muller, F. R. Havergal, J. B. Watson, S. Ridout, George Soltau, H. A. Ironside, Erich Sauer, A. T. Pierson, Sir Robert Anderson, etc. Space will not permit quotations from their writings, but their books are available to all believers.

(2) *The poets.*

We can certainly praise God for the men and women whom He has raised up, through the years of the Church's history, to express, in choice poetry and fitting music, the appreciation of the hearts of the people of God, both to the Father and to the Son.

As one looks through such hymnbooks as "Hymns of Worship and Remembrance," "The Believer's Hymnbook," "Hymns for the Little Flock," "Spiritual Songs," "Hymns of Light and Love," etc., he will be impressed with the fact that practically a third of the worship hymns are addressed, wholly or in part, directly to the Lord Jesus, both in worship, praise and prayer. In some cases, both Father and Son are directly addressed in the same hymn.

It will be obvious, to all sensible Christians, that *singing* directly to the Lord Jesus is exactly the same as *speaking* to Him. Some of the most used hymns at the meeting for the remembrance of the Lord Jesus in the breaking of the bread are addressed to Christ directly.

Take, for instance, a few of the following well known hymns and notice to Whom they are addressed: "Thou art the everlasting Word," "Lord Jesus Christ, we seek Thy face;" "Gazing on the Lord in glory;" "How sweet the name of Jesus sounds;" "Lamb of God, our souls adore Thee;" "Lord Jesus Christ, our Savior Thou;" "Lord of glory, we adore Thee;" "O, blessed Lord, what hast Thou

done;" "O blessed Savior, is Thy Love;" "O, Lord, Thy
love's unbounded;" "O, my Savior, crucified;" "Thou life
of my life, blessed Jesus;" "Through Thy precious body
broken;" "Thy name we love, Lord Jesus;" "What grace,
O Lord, and beauty shone;" "Worthy, worthy, is the
Lamb;" "According to Thy gracious word;" "Around Thy
table, holy Lord;" "For the bread and for the wine;"
"Savior, we remember Thee;" "Jesus, Lord, we know
Thee present;" "O Christ, what burdens bowed Thy
head;" "Lord, we would ne'er forget Thy love;" "On that
same night, Lord Jesus;" "To Calv'ry, Lord, in spirit
now;" "When I survey the wondrous cross;" "With Jesus
in the midst, we gather;" "And shall we see Thy face;"
"Here, O our Lord, we see Thee face to face;" "Jesus,
Thou joy of loving hearts;" " 'Tis past, the dark and dreary
night;" "Lord Jesus, Thou, who only art," etc., etc.

Were the writers of these beautiful hymns mistaken
when they addressed the Lord Jesus directly in their
songs of worship and praise? Would the reader like to
see these hymns eliminated from his hymn book? The
answer, of course, is an emphatic negative to both questions. These men and women of God were led by the
Spirit of God, through the word of God, to write these
magnificent ascriptions of worship and praise to the One
who they loved, served and worshipped.

Sometime ago, at the conclusion of a meeting for the
remembrance of the Lord in the breaking of bread, a
young believer approached a visiting preacher and said:
"You did something this morning I have never seen done
before. You directly addressed your worship to the
Lord Jesus." The preacher inquired: "Have *you* never
addressed the Lord Jesus directly?" On his replying in
the negative, the preacher asked: "Did you not sing, a
few minutes ago: 'O Christ, what burdens bowed Thy
head,' and also: 'Savior, we remember Thee?'" "Yes,"

replied the young Christian. "Then who were you addressing in that hymn?" inquired the preacher. The
young man thought a moment and, as the light dawned,
he remarked thoughtfully: "Yes, I realize now that I was
addressing the Lord Jesus. It never occurred to be
before." The preacher, with a smile, continued: "Of
course, there is a difference between *singing* to the Lord
Jesus and *speaking* to Him." "What is the difference?"
inquired the young brother. The preacher replied: "The
difference is the same as that which exists between six
and a half dozen!"

7. All Christians should do it.

From what we have seen in the holy Scriptures, there
can surely be only one logical conclusion, and that is for
each believer to take advantage of his God-given privilege
and address his worship, praise and prayer directly to the
Son of God, as he is led of the Holy Spirit.

In so doing, the believer will bring pleasure to the
Father, Who delights to hear His Son thus honored; to
the Holy Spirit, Whose joy it is to glorify the Son of God;
and to the Lord Jesus Himself, Who is "worthy to receive power, and riches, and wisdom, and strength, and
honor, and glory and blessing!" (Rev. 5: 12).

How good it is, at a meeting convened particularly
for worship, to hear spiritually intelligent ascriptions of
worship and praise addressed to the Father through His
beloved Son; and also to hear the Son of God directly
addressed in worship and praise by those who know, love
and adore Him!

II. The Importance Of Maintaining Spiritual Balance.

In view of what we have been considering, it behooves
each Christian to obtain and maintain a spiritually in-

telligent balance in regard to these scriptural truths re-
lating to the worship of both Father and Son.

1. In relation to the Father.

He should ever remember that, by the regenerating
power of the Holy Spirit, he has been made a member of
the family of God. Being such, God is now his Father.
How wonderful is this thought! He has been brought
from slavery to sonship, from poverty to plenitude, from
filthy rags to royal raiment! No wonder the believer is
directed to give "thanks unto the Father, which hath
made us meet to be partakers of the inheritance of the
saints in light" (Col. 1:12). We read, in the Scriptures,
that as the Father:

(1) *He chose us* in His Son before the foundation of
the world. Eph. 1:4; I Peter 1:2.

(2) *He gave His Son* to be our Savior.   John 3:16.

(3) *He has begotten us* as His children.   James 1:18;
I Peter 1:3; I John 3:1-2.

(4) *He has blessed us* with all spiritual blessings in
Christ. Eph. 1:3-6.

(5) *He loves us.* John 16:27.

(6) *He cares for us,* and supplies all our needs. Matt.
.6:25-34; I Peter 5:7; Phil. 4:19.

(7) *He desires us to worship Him* through His Son,
and also to worship and praise His Son directly. John
4:23; Heb. 1:9.

As the believer meditates upon his privilege of thus
being in family relationship with this glorious Being who
is revealed as "The God and Father of our Lord Jesus
Christ," he will approach the Father, with becoming
reverence and godly fear, through the mediation of the
Son of His love, by whom He has been pleased to reveal

Himself in all His infinite holiness and wondrous grace.
(II Cor. 4:6).

2. In relation to the Son.

The Christian should never allow himself to forget
the fact that all his blessedness has come to him through
God's beloved Son, whom he now knows as his own personal Savior, and owns as the supreme Lord of his life.
The Bible bears witness to these facts regarding the Son
of God:

(1) *In infinite grace, He became incarnate* in order to
become our Redeemer. (II Cor. 8:9; Heb. 2:14-15).

(2) *As the eternal Son of God,* Christ has given a full
revelation of the Father, John 1:18; 14:9.

(3) *In love to guilty sinners, He* willingly offered Himself as a substitutionary sacrifice for our sins. On the
cross of Calvary He bore our sins in His own body and,
by the shedding of His most precious blood, satisfied all
the claims of a holy God against sin and the sinner. By
His death and resurrection, He has provided a free, full
and eternal salvation for every sinner who will own his
need as a lost and guilty sinner, receive Him by faith to
be his own personal Savior, and confess Him as the Lord
of his life. Heb. 9:11-28; 10:5-14; Rom. 10:9-10.

(4) *Now ascended and glorified at God's* right hand,
He is the believer's great high Priest, ceaseless Intercessor, and Advocate with the Father. By His present
ministry in the presence of God He maintains the work
which He began in every Christian's life. Heb. 4:14-16;
10:19-25; 7:17-27; I John 2:1.

(5) *As the supreme Lord and Master of His servants,*
He commissions each Christian to be a witness for Him,
both by the words he says and the life he lives. Matt. 23:

8; 28:19-20; Mark 16:15; Acts 1:8; John 15:27; Mark 5:
19-20.

(6) *At His second coming,* He shall raise the bodies
of those who died believing on Him, and rapture those
Christians who are alive at His coming. Then, with glorified bodies, like unto their Lord's, the redeemed shall be
with and like their Lord for ever. I Thess. 4:13-18; I
Cor. 15:51-58; John 14:1-3; Rev. 22:20-21.

(7) *He may now be approached directly,* by His
people, in worship, praise and prayer. Luke 24:52; Rev.
5:9-14. Let no believer fail in taking advantage of this
privilege.

3. In relation to the Holy Spirit.

While the believer is not instructed in the Scriptures,
either by precept or example, to directly address or worship the Holy Spirit; yet he must ever have before him
the fact that it is the Holy Spirit who alone can make
spiritual things vital to him in his Christian experience.
Only as the spirit is allowed to energize, lead and control,
can the believer live a life well pleasing to the Father and
the Son.

Concerning the Holy Spirit we are taught from the
Word:

(1) *He is equal and eternal with the Father and the
Son.* This is seen in the linking of the names of the Trinity, and the prerogatives of each Person.

(2) *By His divine inspiration,* He has made possible
the existence of the holy Scriptures. II Peter 1:21; II
Timothy 3:16; John 14:25-26; 16:13.

(3) *Christ's incarnation, life on* earth, and His sacrifice was accomplished through His presence and power.
Luke 1:25; 3:22; 4:1; Heb. 9:14; Rom. 1:4.

(4) *He applies the word of God to the sinner,* producing conviction of sin and leading the repentance and faith in the Lord Jesus Christ. John 16:8-11.

(5) *He seals the believer unto the day of redemption,* indwells him and makes him a partaker of the Divine nature. Eph. 1:13; I Cor. 6:19-20; II Peter 1:6.

(6) *He is the Christian's supreme Teacher,* and seeks to guide all believers into the truth of the word of God. He delights to take of the things of Christ and to glorify the Son of God in each believer's life. He also empowers the Christian for a life of service to his Lord and Master. John 14:26; 16:13-15; Acts 1:8; 4-8.

(7) *He guides the people of God in their worship,* praise and prayer to both the Father and the Son. John 4:23-24. How needful, therefore, that each Christian should be susceptible to His leading in this important matter. (Rom. 8:26-27). It is possible for a believer to grieve the Spirit by his misconduct, to quench Him by disobedience to His leading, and to limit Him by an attitude of unbelief. Eph. 4:25-30; I Thess. 5:19-20; Psalm 78:41.

It truly becomes every child of God to lift up his heart and voice in praise to God for this holy Vicar of Christ, and to seek to live his life under His control and empowerment. Only in this way can the believer glorify the Father and the Son.

4. The value of this spiritual balance.

There are two extremes to be avoided. The first consists of concentrating our thoughts on the Person of the Father to the entire exclusion of the Son; the other of concentrating our thoughts on the Son of God to the entire exclusion of the Father. Both Persons are to be worshipped: the Son directly, and the Father through the mediation of the Son as these two hymns, which follow, indicate.

When these twin truths are held in their proper balance, and exercised in the power of the Spirit of God, both the Father and the Son shall be glorified as true, proportionate, spiritual and intelligent worship shall be given to Each.   May it be so in the lives of both writer and reader, for His name's sake!

1. Father, we worship Thee,
        Through Thy beloved Son;
    And, by the Spirit, now draw near
        Before Thy holy throne.

2. We bless Thee Thou art Light,
        Righteous and true art Thou;
    Holy and Reverend Thy name,
        Our hearts before Thee bow.

3. We bless Thee Thou art Love,
        How vast that matchless grace,
    Whose breadth and length and height and depth
        No finite mind can trace!

4. We bless Thee most of all
        For Him who Thee unveiled;
    Whose precious blood redemption wrought,
        And thus Thy heart revealed.

5. For what Thou art, we praise
        And worship and adore;
    To Father, Son and Spirit be
        The glory evermore!

1. "Worthy, incarnate Word, to be adored!
   All things were made by Thee and for Thee, O Lord!
   Yet Thou didst leave Thy bright throne for earth's shame,
   And, clothed with humanity, our Savior became!

2. Worthy, O Lamb of God, worthy art Thou!
   Low at Thy blessed feet, Lord Jesus, we bow!
   For Thou was slain for our sins, blessed Lord;
   And Thou hast redeemed us to God by Thy blood!

3. Worthy, Thou risen Lord, with glory crowned!
   Now, as our great high Priest, exalted, enthroned;
   Gladly we hail Thee and praise Thy great name,
   Who art, yesterday, today and ever the same!

4. Worthy, Thou King of kings, worthy to reign!;
   When, for Thy blood-bought bride, Thou comest again!
   Then, 'neath Thy sway, shall the earth be restored,
   Creation, below, above, shall own Thee as Lord!"